# THE ARTHUR YOUNG
# MANAGEMENT GUIDE TO
# MERGERS AND ACQUISITIONS

# THE ARTHUR YOUNG MANAGEMENT GUIDE TO MERGERS AND ACQUISITIONS

**RICHARD S. BIBLER, Editor**

WILEY

**JOHN WILEY & SONS**
New York • Chichester • Brisbane • Toronto • Singapore

ISBN 0-471-63104-3

Printed in the United States of America

10 9 8 7 6 5 4 3 2 1

# PREFACE

Mergers and acquisitions are too important to leave to the experts. As with other major corporate programs, senior managers need to be in charge of the critical decisions surrounding both overall strategy and individual acquisition transactions. After all, a company's CEO will gain the credit for success or bear the blame for an ill-considered or poorly executed transaction.

On the other hand, mergers and acquisitions are too important to undertake without the advice of qualified experts. A team effort will produce the best results. Technical issues should be addressed by team members qualified in a particular field, but senior managers must assure that the strategic and operational advantages of the proposed business combination are captured in the final transaction.

Numerous publications deal with the different aspects of corporate acquisitions, ranging from oversimplified "how-to" manuals to highly sophisticated discussions of technical areas such as legal matters, tax considerations, and finance. However, the role of top corporate executives has not been well defined in these publications, and no concise resource is currently available to equip CEOs to take charge of this important activity.

This book addresses each of the components of a successful acquisition program from the vantage point of senior managers as the organization's principal conceptual thinkers, planners, organizers, and coordinators. The book attempts to strip away much of the mystique surrounding acquisitions, to identify the business issues, and to equip CEOs to make or approve judgments and decisions throughout the process.

The authors all are recognized experts in their respective fields, and each has participated in a number of acquisition transactions. Equally important, they have identified the issues in their particular areas about which senior managers should have a working knowledge, and have presented those issues in nontechnical language familiar to business generalists.

In a recent survey by Booz, Allen & Hamilton, over 80 percent of a group of CEOs interviewed in the United States, Europe, and Japan expected their companies to be participants in one or more acquisition transactions before the year 2000. A similarly high percentage of the remaining CEOs interviewed—except for the Japanese, whose business ethic historically has not included growth through acquisition—expect their companies to participate in an acquisition transaction before 1990.

Although acquisition activity decreased in the United States in the early 1980s following the merger mania of the conglomerate years, 2,500 to 3,500 acquisition transactions have been announced each year during the second half of the 1980s, according to W. T. Grimm, a Chicago-based merger and acquisition research company. The aggregate dollar value of those transactions has been $150 to $200 billion a year, and the number of individual transactions above $1 billion has increased steadily since the first one in 1981. Twenty such large transactions took place in 1987.

Acquisition prices have recently returned to the levels of the conglomerate years of the late 1970s. For the full year of 1987, the average price/earnings ratio for announced transactions was 23 times, but prices averaged 27 times during the first six months of that year before being dampened by the dramatic October fall in stock prices. The cost of making an acquisition mistake can be very high.

And a lot of mistakes have been made. Some of them have been colossal errors, such as the combination of the two troubled Texas bank holding companies into First Republic, resulting in a total loss of shareholder equity. Most ill-fated transactions, however, have eroded shareholder value in a less spectacular way and over a longer period of time, a little like being nibbled to death by a duck. The acquisition and subsequent divestiture of unrelated "entertainment" companies by CBS is a prime example of an ill-considered growth-through-acquisition strategy.

Cover articles in *Business Week* in 1985 and 1988 concluded that as many as two-thirds of the acquisitions and mergers it studied had failed (to increase shareholder value). Michael Porter, in an article in the May–June 1987 *Harvard Business Review*, observed that "the track record of corporate [acquisition] strategies has been dismal," and "only the lawyers, investment bankers and original sellers have prospered in most of these acquisitions, not the shareholders."

Why do so many acquisitions fail? Should acquisition be a part of a corporation's growth strategy? Is there a way to reduce risk and to enhance the chances for success in an acquisition program? Finally, and most germane to this book, what is the role of the CEO and other senior managers in a successful acquisition program?

Acquisitions can and should be part of a corporation's growth strategy, and many companies do make acquisitions that contribute to shareholder value on an ongoing basis. As in their other successful endeavors, those companies "do the right things and do things right." This book discusses the strategic, evaluation, and structuring issues that must be addressed in a successful acquisition program, and offers expert advice to CEOs and their senior managers on how to choose between alternative courses of action.

Successful acquisitions usually are the result of a disciplined process—a process that can be managed by a CEO like any other major undertaking. Certainly it is essential to use the advice of experienced and knowledgeable specialists such as our contributing authors, but a CEO should understand the business issues and be able to assess the impact on the corporation of alternative courses of action.

RICHARD S. BIBLER

*Milwaukee, Wisconsin*
*March 1989*

# ABOUT THE EDITOR

Richard S. Bibler is the managing director of the Corporate Development Group of Arthur Young and is a frequent lecturer on growing successfully through acquisition. He and his associates assist clients in executing acquisition programs and corporate financial restructuring. Previously, he was responsible for the commercial banking activities of a $6-billion bank and also has been president of a $100-million community bank. He was chairman of the commercial lending division and a director of the American Bankers Association.

Mr. Bibler has participated in over 200 acquisition transactions as an investor, advisor, or lender. He helped to structure and finance his first leveraged buyout transaction in 1964.

# CONTRIBUTING AUTHORS

**John M. McDonagh**  is a principal in the Corporate Development Group of Arthur Young. He has published articles on venturing and acquisition planning, and has been vice-president of strategic planning and corporate development for two Fortune 100 companies.

**Robert J. Klug**  is a principal in the Corporate Development Group of Arthur Young. A CPA, he has assisted a number of public and private companies to identify and evaluate acquisition opportunities, and to develop proposals for acquisition financing.

**Socrates H. Choumbakos**  is president of Venture Development Group, Inc., and vice-president and principal of Creative Business Strategies, Inc. A CPA, he assists large and small companies in new business development, and is a frequent speaker on strategic partnering.

**Dewey B. Crawford**  is a partner in the law firm of Gardner, Carton & Douglas, Chicago. He specializes in mergers and acquisitions and corporate finance, and has written and spoken extensively on negotiating acquisitions.

**W. Peter Slusser**  is founder and president of Slusser Associates, New York. He began PaineWebber's mergers and acquisitions department in 1975 and built it into a forty-person organization that completed eighty deals in 1987.

**Rory B. Riggs**  is a senior managing director in the mergers and acquisitions department of PaineWebber. Mr. Riggs has specialized principally in representing buyers in leveraged acquisitions of private and public companies. He has represented acquirers of companies in such fields as the media, transportation, finance, and general industry.

**Stephen M. Banker**  is a partner in the law firm of Skadden, Arps, Slate, Meagher & Flom, New York, concentrating in corporate and securities law, mergers, and acquisitions. He is a member of the New York Bar Association Committee on Corporation Law.

**C. Robert Barker**  is an associate in the law firm of Skadden, Arps, Slate, Meagher & Flom, New York. He is a graduate of the University of Virginia School of Law and Stanford University and has studied at the Fletcher School of Law and Diplomacy.

**Michael N. Sohn**  is a senior partner in the law firm of Arnold & Porter and served as general counsel of the Federal Trade Commission from 1977 to 1980. Mr. Sohn specializes in antitrust and trade regulation and regularly appears before the Department of Justice and the Federal Trade Commission in connection with the antitrust aspects of mergers, acquisitions, and joint ventures.

**Lawrence E. Fox**  manages the acquisition financing area at First National Bank of Chicago. Earlier in his career, he was the senior credit officer for much of the domestic business of the bank and had responsibility for its problem loan area, including selling nonperforming loans.

**Edward P. Collins**  is a division executive in the Corporate Banking Group of Bank of Boston. He is responsible for the regional lending offices located in Chicago, Illinois; Stamford, Connecticut; and Montreal and Toronto, Canada.

**Eric A. Simonson**  is managing director of the Corporate Finance Group of Prudential Insurance Company of America, Newark. In this position he is responsible for large private-placement investments made primarily through major New York investment banks.

**Dean D. Proper**  joined Prudential in 1964 and spent the early part of his career in Prudential's regional direct private-placement activities in Minneapolis, Milwaukee, and Chicago. He has been part of the senior management of Prudential Capital Corporation, a merchant banking arm of Prudential, since 1980.

**Joseph D. Downing** is an associate in the Capital Markets Group of Prudential, where he has focused on leveraged transactions and private placements.

**Robert H. Niehaus** is a principal in the merchant banking department of Morgan Stanley & Co. Mr. Niehaus joined Morgan Stanley in 1982 upon graduation from the Harvard Business School. He is a director of Silgan Packaging Corporation.

**Stephen L. Key** is office managing partner for Arthur Young's New York office and director of its Financial Services Group, which provides accounting and tax advice, and due diligence services. He is a frequent speaker on corporate restructuring and other acquisition-related topics.

**Jeffrey J. Marcketta** is a principal in the New York Mergers & Acquisitions Group of Arthur Young. Mr. Marcketta specializes in due diligence reviews and M&A accounting for LBO investors. He has advised numerous major investment banks and other financial institutions on M&A accounting and due diligence.

**John S. Karls** is a partner in Arthur Young's New York office, specializing in international mergers and acquisitions, and is the international tax consulting partner for Mobil and Amerada Hess. Before joining Arthur Young, Mr. Karls was a tax attorney and tax planner for Texaco.

**J. Tracy O'Rourke** is a corporate vice-president of Rockwell International Corporation, and president and CEO of its $1.2-billion industrial automation subsidiary, Allen-Bradley Co., Milwaukee, Wisconsin. He gained much of his entrepreneurial experience growing Liquid Nitrogen Processing Corporation, and also has headed major operating groups of two other large, diversified corporations.

**Larry Senn, Ph.D.,** has had over twenty-five years of experience in consulting, primarily running his own firm. Twenty years ago Dr. Senn started Senn-Delaney Management Consultants to assist organizations in improving productivity. Ten years ago he formed the Senn-Delaney Leadership Consulting Group, specializing in corporate culture change.

**James E. Nelson** is a consultant with Hewitt Associates, an international management consulting firm specializing in employee benefit and compensation programs. Mr. Nelson specializes in the design and financial aspects of employee benefit programs. He is a fellow of the Society of Actuaries, a member of the Academy of Actuaries, and an Enrolled Actuary.

**A. Lee Westervelt** is a consultant with Hewitt Associates specializing in executive compensation and wage and salary administration programs. Before joining the firm, his experience included nearly twenty years in the human resources field, most recently as director of compensation and benefits for a large automotive supply company.

**Gary A. Marsack** is president of Lindner & Marsack, S.C. He is a frequent speaker on contract negotiations, strikes, NLRB and court developments, compensation, benefit issues, and equal employment matters. He is a contributor to the book *Developing Labor Law* and has authored law review articles on the labor relations aspects of mergers, acquisitions, and successorship law.

**Laurance R. Newman** is vice-president of corporate planning, development and acquisitions for Johnson Wax. He previously was vice-president of U.S. consumer business and vice-president, regional director of commercial business for the Pacific, Far East, Mexico and Canada. Before joining Johnson Wax, he was a vice-president of Morgan Guaranty.

**R. Fraser Mason** is the national director of merger and acquisition services for Clarkson Gordon/Woods Gordon in Toronto. He was initially responsible for the business valuation practice of Clarkson Gordon/Woods Gordon and was instrumental in 1980 in establishing it as a national merger and acquisition practice. He is currently chairman of the Arthur Young International M&A Network.

**David I. Climie** is a manager in the Merger and Acquisition Services Group of Woods Gordon. He joined the group in Toronto in 1986. Before that, Mr. Climie was the assistant investment editor of a leading financial journal in Canada.

**Stephen B. Schlossstein** has lived, studied, or worked in Japan for more than twenty years and was formerly a vice-president of Morgan Guaranty. Now president of his own strategic consulting firm, SBS Associates, he is author of two novels, the best-selling *Trade War,* and a fourth book, *The End of the American Century,* to be released September 1989.

# ACKNOWLEDGEMENTS

First and foremost, I want to express my sincere thanks to all of the authors who have given so much time to this book over the last two years. They have exercised a great deal of patience through numerous iterations as we worked together to eliminate technical jargon and make the material more usable by senior managers. Thanks also to Jon H. Zonderman who also contributed much to that editorial process.

From Arthur Young, Mort Meyerson, director of communications, was most helpful in our discussions with the publisher and in guiding me through the whole process of bringing out a book. His editorial suggestions were also most helpful. Maggie Ley, my administrative assistant, deserves a great deal of credit and thanks for coordinating all of the frenzied activity of the final months. She was the principal liaison between the authors, me and the publisher's representatives.

Finally, we want to acknowledge the early contribution of Robert M. Feerick, a former managing director of the Corporate Development Group of Arthur Young. He recognized that senior corporate managers need a better understanding of the successful acquisition process, and the concept of the book was his. He recruited many of the authors and reviewed their early drafts.

# CONTENTS

# THE ARTHUR YOUNG
# MANAGEMENT GUIDE TO
# MERGERS AND ACQUISITIONS

# SECTION I

# Strategic and Valuation Issues

## INTRODUCTION

An acquisition based on an underlying strategy is much more likely to succeed than one that results from an impulsive reaction to an "attractive" opportunity. Developing a strategy and implementing a proactive acquisition program is the subject of the opening chapter in this section. In the same chapter, Richard S. Bibler also discusses strategic fit. An acquisition is unlikely to increase shareholder value unless opportunities exist for significant sharing of benefits that improve the competitive position of the participants.

In the second chapter of this section, John M. McDonagh provides a guide to evaluating the overall attractiveness of an acquisition candidate. Products, market position, management, and other characteristics must be assessed in a comprehensive evaluation. These nonfinancial factors largely determine strategic fit. In addition, thoroughly understanding the candidate's present financial situation is a prerequisite to projecting its future performance.

Value, like beauty, is in the eye of the beholder. In an acquisition, the question is not so much What is it worth? as What is it worth to us? Robert J. Klug offers three valuation methodologies in the third chapter. By using these external and internal methodologies, a buyer can construct a range of values within which to negotiate. Most important, the acquirer can determine the walk-away price, the highest price at which the transaction is likely to increase shareholder value.

Acquisition is not the only form of business combination to share benefits. Socrates H. Choumbakos discusses two other forms of strategic partnering in the final chapter in this section. Both joint ventures and corporate venturing may well be considered as preferable to outright acquisition in many instances. Each has unique characteristics, applications, advantages, and pitfalls.

# CHAPTER 1

# THE ACQUISITION PROCESS: A PROGRAM FOR SUCCESS

## Richard S. Bibler
**ARTHUR YOUNG/CDG**

Why do so many mergers and acquisitions fail to increase share-holder value?

A long list of reasons for the sorry record of business combinations could be given, and a specific reason could be assigned to each such transaction as the principal cause of its failure. In each case, however, the acquirer probably either failed to establish a strategic basis for making acquisitions, failed to create a comprehensive acquisition program, or both.

Acquisitions frequently make a significant impact on the overall profitability and financial health of a corporation, either positive or negative. Surely such transactions deserve the same thoughtful planning and execution as the introduction of a new product, the building of a new plant, or the purchase of a major piece of equipment. Unfortunately, many otherwise well-managed companies fail to assign time and resources commensurate with the importance of acquisitions to the organization.

The posture of many companies toward acquisitions is reactive. Rather than describing in advance the characteristics of a desirable candidate, CEOs often rely on their instincts: "I'll know one when I see one." Those chief executives are fair game for the investment banker's siren song: "Boy, do I have a deal for you," offering a selection from a choice of one.

In a proactive program, the acquirer is the initiator. Rather than reacting to random opportunities as they are presented, the proactive acquirer defines acquisition objectives first, then moves aggressively to achieve those objectives.

Incidentally, corporations executing a proactive acquisition program based on established objectives are much better able to respond to auctions and other time-urgent, opportunistic situations than are other potential buyers who must wrestle with the strategic questions anew each time an investment banker calls. The process need not be rigid.

With a proactive acquisition program a company is much more likely to make business combinations that contribute to shareholder value, or at least to avoid costly mistakes. Such a program also gives management considerably greater control over the corporation's destiny.

An acquisition program is a dynamic process. Both objectives and tactics can be modified in response to events and the availability of relevant data, but actions are not dependent on those events. A successful program is always proactive yet under control.

A comprehensive acquisition program should encompass all of the following tasks:

- Establishing responsibility at the policy level
- Developing an acquisition plan
- Defining acquisition criteria
- Identifying all potential acquisition candidates
- Making effective contact with candidates
- Performing thorough due diligence
- Negotiating terms that preserve the benefits identified
- Harvesting the benefits through effective postacquisition integration

## ESTABLISHING RESPONSIBILITY

The first axiom for success is to position the development and implementation of an acquisition program at the strategic level within the company—the same level as other major functions such as finance, marketing, and manufacturing. When corporate development is the part-time responsibility of an assistant treasurer, the unfavorable results or lack of substantive activity is predictable. Given the potential impact on the corporation, the planning and execution of an acquisition program deserves the attention of a company's highest-ranking policymakers.

The tasks involved are varied and ultimately draw on different areas of expertise within the company. Calling on a multidisciplinary team of policy-level officers to act as a steering committee assures that the views and concerns of each of the functional areas will be addressed. Also, the involvement and commitment of these high-ranking officers assures access to their staffs.

In larger organizations one or more task forces frequently are organized. These groups investigate and analyze in depth to formulate recommendations to the steering committee. They generally are available on short-term notice to consider time-urgent opportunities.

## DEVELOPING AN ACQUISITION PLAN

Every acquisition should contribute to a company's overall business strategy. Such a statement would seem obvious and condescending in a book directed at senior managers were it not for the number of U.S. corporations that violate this principle. In many instances, acquiring companies seemingly fail to assess the strategic fit of a company being acquired or substantially misgauge the level of contribution that an acquisition will make to achieving strategic objectives. (Admittedly, some acquisitions also fail because the execution of individual transactions is flawed, but the authors of the succeeding chapters will discuss those issues.) Some acquisitions clearly are made more to advance the self-interest of managers than to enhance shareholder value.

The mere existence of the financial capability seems to inspire pursuit of Parkinson's law: "It is the duty of every organization to grow." Utilizing excess cash flow, accumulated liquidity, and unused borrowing power to finance acquisitions simply because that financial position makes acquisitions possible is circuitous reasoning at best. The same unused liquidity and borrowing power may also present an unwanted attraction to hostile corporate raiders, giving managers another nonstrategic incentive to acquire.

Increasing market share frequently is given as a rationale for acquiring a competitor at a price that otherwise would be difficult to justify. If such an acquisition makes the acquirer the dominant participant in its market or otherwise creates a change in market dynamics that is reflected in future profit margins, that rationale may be supportable. Too often, however, increasing market share or simply increasing revenues in absolute terms becomes a justifiable acquisition objective for its own sake in the minds of CEOs.

Rather than being overly judgmental regarding the normal instincts of corporate managers for self-preservation and their motivation to achieve the personal rewards that come with absolute growth, I would suggest that pursuing an acquisition program that clearly is driven by strategic objectives is not necessarily in conflict with less altruistic motives. For example, it is prudent for a company's managers always to have under consideration a number of potential acquisition candidates and "white knight" merger partners with which a combination would be strategically sound as well as less threatening. Usually, it's too late to indulge in a strategic analysis of alternatives once an attack by a professional corporate raider begins.

How, then, can one judge whether a proposed acquisition will help a corporation achieve its primary objective of increasing shareholder value?

First, an acquisition should offer clear advantages over achieving the same objectives through internal growth. These advantages may be lower perceived risk, time savings, reduced competition, lower costs, or other similar factors, but the reasons should provide definable and measurable benefits of one course of action over the other. Choosing between internal and external growth alternatives becomes a continuous series of "make or buy" decisions.

Second, an acquisition should meet the shared-benefits test. One of the two companies must offer cost-sharing, skill-sharing, technological, marketing, or other similar benefits to the other. In the best matches, these benefits flow continuously. This happens, for example, when incremental volume is added in an acquisition and thus reduces unit costs, or when new products are added to an existing distribution system. Benefits may also be very short-lived, even one-time improvements, but the opportunity to gain the advantages or share benefits provides a strategic purpose for the acquisition.

Unfortunately, potential acquisition benefits may also be illusory or extremely difficult to capture. Too often, vaguely defined synergies are offered as a rationale for making an unrewarding acquisition—or for paying too much. "I'll bet we can make their product cheaper" somehow lacks the precision one should achieve in making an important investment decision.

We should note also that two strategies similar to each other that do meet the shared-benefits test nevertheless have only limited attractiveness or application for most acquirers.

The conglomerates of the 1970s, such as ITT, Gulf & Western, and LTV, made popular a strategy based on building a portfolio of sound, well-managed companies that are only loosely related to each other, if at all. The success of this strategy rests on management's ability to identify and acquire undervalued companies, to allocate capital between the "cash cows" and the "stars" at favorable rates, and to encourage disciplined, pragmatic, professional management on the part of the relatively autonomous managers of its constituent companies.

A centralized corporate staff, mostly financial executives, closely monitors performance through a detailed budgeting and report system at least quarterly. The first real shock of being acquired by such a company comes when the corporate reports system is introduced. The second one is when the six-month-long planning cycle is begun.

This strategy has failed to produce added shareholder value on a lasting basis in all but a minority of instances, yet the strategy continues to be practiced by a number of acquirers. Identifying and acquiring a good but undervalued company in competition with leveraged buyout funds, other takeover artists, and similar purely financial players is difficult, to say the least. Even if the acquisition is successful, the market's reward is most often a "conglomerate discount" in the price of the acquirer's stock, rather than an increase in shareholder value.

A similar strategy is to acquire companies selling at substantial discounts due to low earnings or actual losses. Ideal turnaround candidates are not those suffering from serious fundamental problems, but those whose performance can generally be improved by disposing of less-profitable operations or by simply providing capital at more favorable rates and exercising more pragmatic management. Again, such companies are difficult to identify and may be even more difficult to acquire in competition with professional acquirers who are also attracted to the breakup potential of the target.

Note that both the portfolio and the turnaround strategies are based on the acquirer's providing benefits to the acquired company and, therefore, pass the shared-benefits test. Since these benefits are relatively short-lived, however, pursuing either of these strategies with any degree of success also requires great skill in market timing, knowing when to sell a company to which the acquirer no longer is adding value. Success also depends on the ability to continue finding and acquiring attractive companies to replace those being divested. Since most companies are not skilled market timers, they are best served by viewing acquisitions as an integrated component of their overall strategic plans.

The same process that determines a corporation's overall strategic plan can be used to design an acquisition program to support that plan. This is an inappropriate place to launch into a lengthy discourse on strategic planning. Suffice it to say that an acquisition plan should be based on an evaluation of both internal and external factors, identifying competitive strengths on which to build, competitive disadvantages to correct, technological needs, volume-sensitive costs, and other strategic issues.

By a large measure, acquisitions within the same industry as the acquiring company offer the greatest chance of success. Acquisitions that extend the geographic reach of distribution, increase market share (and eliminate a competitor), allow access to new technology, or add products to an existing system all are likely to offer cost-sharing or other benefits.

Vertical integration may be the safest departure from existing activities. That strategy should not be adopted too hastily, however. Captive suppliers have a tendency to become less efficient once the rigors of competition cease, and other customers of the acquired company may be reluctant to place as much dependence on a supplier after it becomes a subsidiary of a competitor.

Diversification through acquisition, although frequently a desirable strategy, carries with it a considerably higher risk of failure. Successful diversification requires a much more sophisticated analysis of existing strengths on which to build, corporate culture, and a host of external factors.

Critical skills, those areas of expertise on which the success of the existing business rests, present the most likely opportunity for shared benefits in a diversification. But identified areas of excellence are only transferable to the acquisition if they represent opportunities for competitive advantage in the industry being entered. Being a low-cost manufacturer, for example, is of little consequence when considering the acquisition of a company in an industry where marketing excellence is the key to success.

A regulated utility seeking to diversify probably should avoid industries in which sophisticated marketing and quick reaction time are the hallmarks of successful participants. Instead, it should identify business segments where long planning horizons, large infrastructures, a high level of customer service, and/or sophisticated electronic systems are keys to success.

A common diversification error is acquiring a company with a weak competitive position (usually because the acquisition price appears attractive in comparison to an industry leader). A much more promising diversification strategy would be to build a strong position in a highly fragmented industry or, even better, to acquire an industry leader.

Concentrated diversification, building strong competitive positions in one or two new fields, is preferable to scattered purchases in several areas. If the acquirer is a public company, a rational, understandable strategy—one that can be interpreted credibly to investment analysts—will help avoid a "conglomerate discount" in the price of the acquirer's stock.

Finally, a diversifying acquirer must have an understanding of the dynamics of the industry it is entering. Industry growth and profitability are obviously important. The demand for capital investment, the importance of technology, and other factors relating to ease of entry must be considered. In sum, the acquirer must measure the overall attractiveness of an industry in a way that allows comparison with alternative possibilities. Being the best performer in an unattractive industry segment may be un-rewarding.

## DEFINING CRITERIA

A major product of the acquisition planning process is the definition of detailed acquisition criteria for each area where acquisition appears to be a viable alternative to internal growth. A list of criteria should resemble a purchase order, describing the most desirable candidate imaginable. A typical list would include such factors as the following:

- Industry or industry segment
- Method of distribution
- Size
- Geographic constraints
- Particular strengths .
- Importance of management continuation
- Preferred consideration (cash or stock)
- Maximum price

Admittedly, it is unlikely that a willing and available dream candidate will be identified, but it is important to create a benchmark against which to evaluate candidates. Weighting the importance of each characteristic, either formally or informally, also aids in the candidate-screening process and in ranking candidates in order of attractiveness.

## IDENTIFYING ACQUISITION CANDIDATES

The process of identifying prospective acquisition candidates begins with building a universe, a list of all companies that appear to meet the criteria. Multiple sources should be consulted. Easily accessible electronic databases generally can provide 80 percent to 90 percent of the names with some amount of additional information. Other sources of candidate information include the following:

- Trade association membership lists
- Trade publications
- Industry experts
- Government publications
- Acquirer's employees—purchasing, sales, and so on
- Public library

Naturally, the law of diminishing returns applies to the last few names, but more than 95 percent of the qualified candidates that exist can be identified easily.

Screening a universe of several hundred companies to identify the most attractive candidates sounds like a difficult and time-consuming task. Actually, applying unequivocal knockout criteria such as size or location quickly reduces the universe to a manageable number. Comparing the remainder against the other criteria should produce ten or fifteen priority candidates. The task of gathering comprehensive information regarding that smaller number of candidates is not nearly as formidable.

The prospect identification process also gives the acquirer a feel for the dynamics of the targeted industry. Competitive conditions, industry growth trends, profit margins, and other important data can easily be gathered at the same time. Analyzing the characteristics that distinguish high-performing industry participants is also a useful exercise.

Once the internal universe-building process is complete, it is important to turn to external sources of prospective candidates—financial intermediaries. The research company W. T. Grimm estimates that an investment banker or broker is present in about two-thirds of all merger transactions. Contact with intermediaries should be established to get an early look at as many opportunities as possible—to be plugged into the "deal flow."

Attracting and maintaining the attention of a large number of the most active intermediaries is not easy. Many would-be acquirers have the same objective, and most intermediaries have short attention spans. All major investment banks should be cultivated; regional investment banks and large brokers—a much better source of smaller opportunities, companies with sales under $50 million—should also be cultivated.

A very brief brochure (four sides, preferably two-color) is a good idea. The brochure should:

- describe the acquiring company and its products and give at least a general idea of its size (public companies should enclose their latest statement);
- list the company's acquisition criteria;
- indicate a willingness to assume the intermediary's fee; and
- give the name, address, and phone number of the person to contact with opportunities.

This part of the program should be regarded as a marketing effort with a goal to reach as many active intermediaries as possible. Contact should be made repeatedly and in person whenever possible. If the acquirer is a public company, intermediaries should be added to the shareholder mailing list.

Brokers and investment bankers are aggressive people. They may stretch the stated criteria to include their deals, even if the fit is tangential at best. This is not all bad. Frankly, nothing tends to move a candidate up the priority scale faster than knowing it is really for sale. More important, intermediaries frequently do have creative ideas regarding strategic fit, and a modest enlargement of the original criteria may accommodate attractive opportunities that are presented.

## MAKING EFFECTIVE CONTACT

How should a contact be made with an attractive candidate that is not known to be for sale? Very much like approaching a prospective customer for a very large sale.

The task is particularly challenging when the approach is to the founder. His or her attachment to the company exceeds pure financial considerations. Founders often love their companies as much as—or more than—they love their children. Convincing a founder to accept in trade whatever the acquirer is offering for her or his creation requires considerable selling skill.

The first decision is whom to approach. Unless the candidate's CEO is also a principal owner, he or she might not be the best initial contact. An introduction through a mutual friend on the board, the banker, the lawyer, or the accounting firm is frequently a good approach.

Most businesses, particularly those with annual revenues between $10 and $100 million, receive unsolicited inquiries nearly every week indicating an interest in buying the company. A successful contact must differentiate itself from those approaches, most of which are from brokers who really do not have an interested client at all, but are merely fishing.

Except in highly unusual situations, a straightforward approach works best. Typically, a letter followed by a phone call should do the following:

- Introduce the potential acquirer with financial data, descriptions of its history and major business lines, product literature, and other information.

- Explain how the candidate was identified, how it fits the acquirer's criteria, what operating advantages are perceived, and so on. (This is the time to indulge in unabashed flattery.)

- Request a meeting to discuss "a business combination" that will be advantageous to both parties. Suggest dates that would be convenient rather than simply asking if the candidate would be interested in discussing the proposition.

- Obtain an appointment to continue the discussion, even in the face of "We're not for sale." Be persistent.

- Maintain contact, even when rebuffed. Put the candidate on the shareholder mailing list. Send periodic newsy letters reaffirming continued interest. Call and visit from time to time. In acquisitions, patience really is a virtue.

## PERFORMING DUE DILIGENCE

Once a tentative but sincere indication of interest has been confirmed, it's time for due diligence to begin. Much of the remainder of this book addresses different aspects of that process.

Due diligence means different things to different people. For example, since the pursuit of an attractive candidate is much like a sales campaign, many acquirers treat the candidate like a new customer and are reluctant to ask penetrating "impolite" questions of their new friends.

The due-diligence period is a time of intensive searching for facts, thorough analysis, and constant reevaluation. A number of questions need to be asked and answered. Does the company really fit? Is it really as attractive as it appeared to be? Can we manage the company successfully and achieve the benefits we identified? Will the company's managers support our objectives?

As additional facts become available and are analyzed, a candidate may lose its attractiveness, or be unattractive at the lowest price acceptable to the seller.

If the opportunity really does not fit, walk away!

The investment of time and effort leading to those final stages too often induces buyers to complete transactions that do not measure up to their preestablished standards. It's embarrassing to discontinue negotiations, particularly after a CEO has boasted to the company's board and other confidants about the conquest. But failing to disengage can result in an even bigger embarrassment later. Do it!

## NEGOTIATING TERMS

Price considerations generally dominate negotiations between a buyer and a seller. Terms and conditions that provide an economic advantage for one party usually impose an economic disadvantage on the other. The give and take of such negotiations is pretty straightforward and familiar to most business executives.

A second, sometimes equally important, consideration in negotiating acquisition agreements is preserving attractive nonfinancial characteristics of the company being acquired. These might include patents, trademarks, processes, and other proprietary assets. Most often, however, an acquirer should focus on the best way to assure the continuing services of key employees of the company being acquired.

Successful acquirers identify the key success factors of acquisition candidates well in advance of negotiations. A manager's goal in negotiations should be to preserve and enhance those attributes after the transaction has been consummated. The lawyers will take care of the rest.

## INTEGRATING THE ACQUISITION

A whole section of this book is devoted to integrating the newly acquired company into existing operations.

The only point that should be added here is that harvesting the synergies identified in the preacquisition analysis requires considerable planning and effort. The fact that at least part of the value of those synergies probably was included in the purchase price should be a powerful inducement.

The appropriate tool should be a familiar one to good managers. A clear assignment of responsibility for achieving measurable goals, over a defined time period, within a prescribed budget, within the company's normal planning process is the most appropriate implementation methodology.

What typically happens, instead, is that the members of the multidisciplinary team that identified and quantified all of the synergies go back to their normal, previous duties. Nobody is given the responsibility for harvesting the benefits.

## SUMMARY

Whether a company expects to make a single acquisition or multiple acquisitions over time, a proactive program to manage the process carries a much higher probability of success and avoids costly mistakes. Making acquisitions need not and should not be an intuitive exercise. The time required to put together and execute a well-considered program is definitely worth it.

# CHAPTER 2

# EVALUATING THE ACQUISITION CANDIDATE

## John M. McDonagh
**ARTHUR YOUNG/CDG**

Evaluating an acquisition candidate is not very different from planning and executing a sound marketing or product program. The key to the evaluation is having reliable information, a disciplined process to evaluate the information, and a well-prepared, experienced evaluation team. Sounds simple, but in practice it requires intense effort and teamwork compressed into a short amount of time.

Think of an acquisition in this way. As part of senior management you have overall responsibility for a major new product line (the acquisition) to do market research, prepare to launch, and move forward within thirty to sixty days. The program will represent 25 percent of your total sales and 20 percent of your total assets in the first year. Do you organize this effort with an inexperienced team that doesn't have a background in this product and market area? Should you have a well-thought-out plan with timetables? The answers are obvious.

The acquisition evaluation process outlined here has proven successful because it is disciplined and focuses the energies of the acquisition team. The myriad of items that could be checked or evaluated must be prioritized and you must concentrate on the most important, especially in light of the short amount of time usually available to complete most acquisitions.

The three basic steps in the process are the following:

**1.** Acquisition team selection

**2.** Information gathering and screening

**3.** Business (company) evaluation, competitive analysis, and strategy development

## ACQUISITION TEAM SELECTION

It is important to have an acquisition team with a balance of operations and staff personnel. The two key people on the team are (1) a senior operations executive (corporate officer), who is in control of the acquisition process and who must recommend the acquisition to the chief operating officer and chairman; and (2) a senior corporate staff officer who is responsible for managing the strategic acquisition process and preparing the acquisition report.

Both of these people must recommend the acquisition and be thoroughly knowledgeable concerning the strategic reasoning for making the acquisition. This coendorsement helps minimize possible conflicts. If the operating management is strongly opposed to the acquisition, chances for its ultimate success are not high.

Other members of the team will vary according to the industry, but at a minimum we recommend that a number of specialists such as the following be involved:

- *Finance*  A financial analyst/controller who is able to analyze historic and current financials, compare them to those of competitors, and build accurate pro forma income statements, balance sheets, and cash flow statements. The basic rule of all acquisitions is that financial projections are worthless unless the initial combined financials are well prepared, accurate, and understood by the acquirer.

- *Products/technologies*  A person who can determine if both the products and technologies are current and, more important, what is required for the future.

- *Marketing/distribution*  Someone who understands exactly how the two companies will integrate marketing and distribution operations, the market dynamics, and the interactions of product lines.
- *Operations/manufacturing*  A team member to analyze manufacturing and know if capabilities and capacity are sufficient to meet worldwide competition, how much capital is needed to integrate the acquisition, and how much capital is needed for the next few years to meet growth projections. This is often an area of weakness in evaluations.

This team cannot be assembled two days before the acquisition. The team should be part of the acquisition process from the initial strategy development stage. Also, if a suitable person in each discipline is not available within the organization, an experienced and knowledgeable consultant in that discipline should be found.

## INFORMATION GATHERING AND SCREENING

Due to the short time available to evaluate acquisitions—especially those represented by major investment banks—fast, reliable information is critical. Even before the team is chosen, the information gathering should begin.

Today, with the computerization of information, facsimile, and express mail, one can obtain a wealth of information on products, markets, and competition within a week. The following table summarizes the types of information available, and likely sources.

| Information | Source |
| --- | --- |
| Industry trends and dynamics | Stock analyst and consultant reports. Computer databases, using key word techniques. |
| Products and markets | Above sources, plus trade journals, trade conferences, or shows. |
| Competition | Public information on each competitor including current annual report, prospectus, 10K, proxy, Dun & Bradstreet reports, product literature, and price lists. |

*Continued*

| *Information* | *Source* |
| --- | --- |
| Technology | Key patents of the potential acquisition and key competitors. |
| Networking | Contacting and visiting end users of the product or service to be acquired. Obtaining customer viewpoints on the acquisition and the competitive environment. This can be the most important step in the process. |

As information is gathered, the team must screen, review, and condense it in a logical manner. This takes a lot of work and most of team members' time during this period of only a few weeks. Team members cannot be devoting most of their time to other tasks. An experienced acquisition consultant can be invaluable at this stage in obtaining, screening, and analyzing the market information, especially due to the short time frame.

## THE OVERALL BUSINESS AND STRATEGIC EVALUATION

It is essential in an acquisition that all important aspects of the business be reviewed. Companies often ask for a general checklist to use in evaluating potential acquisitions. In reality, a specific checklist must be developed for each acquisition. This list usually expands during the analysis, especially after one starts learning about the competition and does some networking.

Checklists that are generally available usually concentrate on tax, legal, and accounting (rather than financial) matters, and are not very helpful in evaluating the business. The acquisition team can be of great value here in developing and continually modifying a checklist—but only if members work together, if there is a good leader, and if everyone understands that rarely is one individual a paragon of wisdom. The business should be evaluated in parallel with learning about the competitive environment.

Following the business and competitive evaluation, a team member or members should be able to construct a sound strategic analysis. Included in this analysis should be a discussion of the importance of the particular acquisition in fulfilling the long-term strategic plan for your company.

Figure 2-1 shows the elements of this final stage of the acquisition evaluation process. The evaluation is not complete until all areas of the candidate company have been analyzed in depth. When the internal company evaluation has been completed, the candidate must then be measured against the competition—not only current competitors, but also possible future entrants into the market, especially foreign competition. Although this is the most important step in the evaluation, it is often the part acquiring companies have the most difficulty performing. But only after the acquisition candidate has been realistically measured against competition can an effective, practical acquisition strategy be developed.

Most acquisition programs skim over or sometimes even neglect certain steps in the process. One key to avoiding this problem is to have an acquisition report written that details all important aspects of the evaluation. Due to the pace of the acquisition process, one shouldn't expect a novel but rather a tightly written summary. Backup data should be available to support this summary information.

**FIGURE 2-1  Elements of the business evaluation**

### The Company Evaluation (Internal)

The main elements of the business (company) review should be presented to the CEO in writing, or if orally, they should be explained concisely and well. The following text discusses each topic that should be addressed, with questions that should be answered. Because the evaluation process is intertwined—products cannot be separated from markets or technology—a number of the same questions could well be posed and answered in more than one area. Keep in mind that your company should not be rushed into an acquisition if members of the acquisition team don't understand all important points.

**History and Background.**   This part of the evaluation report should generally describe the evolution of the potential acquisition, major changes in strategic direction (product or market), and the company's environment today. The following questions should be answered:

- *Strategy*  Has the company followed a defined strategy? Summarize it.
- *Products*  What has been the evolution of major products?
- *Markets*  When have new markets been entered? How successfully? How has distribution been organized?
- *Acquisitions or other external ventures*  Has the company entered into new businesses through external means?
- *Technology*  Has the company successfully developed technology? Do any key patents exist?
- *International trade*  What efforts has the company made to diversify internationally?

**Products and/or Services.**   The general principle in any evaluation is to understand what, how, why, and when—the old newspaper story basics. The "what" is the company's products and services. Key issues and questions to be understood include the following:

- *Product description*  Has all product literature been received and reviewed? Is it understood?

- *Strength/advantages* Why do products sell over the competition? Obtain specific examples, especially economic examples.

- *Sales and earnings to date* Obtain the sales and earnings by product line for the last five years. Downturns or upswings need to be explained. Check and explain gross and operating margin variations. Focus on this year's figures on a monthly basis. Are there reasons for any trends occurring during the year? Have these trends appeared in the past? Are product sales cyclical, or are sales heading up/down for other reasons?

- *Sales and earnings projections* Do projections follow past trends and patterns? If margins increase, why? One of the great nebulous answers given by potential sellers to why margins are increasing is certain "efficiencies." Are these asserted efficiencies real? What are the economic bases for these projections?

- *New products* How do new products evolve? Is a system used? What new-product programs exist? Have the products been commercially evaluated? What has been the success rate for new-product introductions? Are new products developed internally, acquired, or licensed? Why?

**Markets.** An explanation of markets and distribution should answer the "what" question completely. For each major market segment, the following information should be reviewed:

- *Market environment* What trends could seriously affect the market or particular business?
  — Government regulations
  — Economic cycles
  — Monetary policy
  — Tax law changes
  — Currency valuation changes

- *Market growth* What were the last five years' growth and what are the projections for the next two to three years' growth? Explain specifically why and where (by major account) the growth has occurred in the past and is expected to occur in the future. What implications do growth projections have for profitability and competitive actions?

- *Breadth and depth of products offered* How important is breadth and depth to success? Explain briefly.

- *Competitive advantages with proprietary positions* To what degree is competitive advantage gained with proprietary positions? When are important patents scheduled to expire?

- *Pricing leadership (history and trends)* Have market participants been able to get price increases? How much? How frequently? Who leads? Who follows? Have rollbacks been necessary? When?

- *Importance of service* How is service defined in the market? To what extent is it possible to differentiate by extent of service offered?

- *Quality requirements* Does this industry have a defined quality system? How is it defined? To what extent is it possible to differentiate by the quality of the product and/or service?

- *Cyclical trends* What are the cyclical characteristics of this business/product line?

- *Captively supplied customers* What portion of the market is captively supplied? Is this increasing or decreasing? Cite examples.

- *Industry profitability* What has been the profitability trend in the past three to five years?

- *Barriers to entry/integration* Do strong barriers to entry exist? Will these barriers continue?

- *Foreign competitive constraints* To what extent do market constraints such as quotas and domestic content provisions inhibit foreign competition in the United States, and conversely, competition by U.S. companies in foreign markets?

- *Resources to compete* What special resources, such as R&D facilities, sales force, or capital does it take to remain a viable participant in the industry?

**Distribution.**   One often overlooked but important factor is distribution, viewed differently from markets or marketing. Some businesses (primarily consumer-related) are successful because they use a more effective distribution system than competitors. Factors to understand are the following:

- *Types of distribution* What distribution systems are used in the industry? What are the advantages and disadvantages of each?

- *Main competitors' distribution* What distribution systems do the primary competitors use? Why?
- *Changes* Has the company being evaluated changed distribution systems? Does it plan to change? Why?

**Technology.** Technology drives some businesses, and must be evaluated thoroughly. It is often forgotten that technology is driven by people, and that a loss of key technical personnel can be a disaster.

- *Patent situation* What are the key patents in the industry? What company holds them? Have they been thoroughly evaluated? How important are patents or any other proprietary position to success?
- *Complexity and maturity* Does complexity of the technology provide protection from new entry? If yes, for how long? How old is existing product technology?
- *Volatility and change* Is the technology involved in a state of rapid change? Is it better not to patent in this industry if technology changes rapidly? To what extent does technological innovation come from companies in the industry? From sources outside the industry?
- *Proliferation* What, if any, new applications are potential candidates for using the existing technology?
- *Technological changes in production processes* What is the rate of change in production processes? What drives the change? Can innovation and R&D have a major effect on improving the cost of production processes? How?
- *Technical leaders* Who are the technical leaders worldwide? How do they maintain their technical edge?
- *R&D projects* Have all major R&D projects been evaluated for commercial potential?

**Manufacturing.** Someone inside your organization, or a manufacturing consultant, must visit and assess all major manufacturing locations of a potential acquisition. This person must be knowledgeable about worldwide manufacturing techniques for the industry in question, as well as the latest quality control techniques and systems.

One primary purpose of the manufacturing investigation is to assess the capital investment required to (1) integrate manufacturing operations, if possible, resulting in production cost savings; (2) bring production to current worldwide competitive standards, including quality; and (3) expand in the future.

The following issues should be investigated:

- *Physical facilities* Describe the physical facilities, including manufacturing advantages and disadvantages. Provide a table of facilities by location, function, number and type of employees, square footage, ownership or lease status, and year constructed.

- *Planned facilities* Are any new plants planned or under construction? Include expenditures required and timetables for completion.

- *Capacity* How much capacity is available in the industry? How much is being utilized? How much is being added and deleted during the next few years?

- *Raw material availability* What is the current and projected raw material availability? Do any major shortages exist? Are any key raw materials limited to a few suppliers? How stable and solvent are these suppliers?

- *Quality standards* Are quality standards in place? How does the system used compare to those used by the best competitors?

**Organization.**    The cardinal rule to complete and integrate a sound acquisition is: Keep the good people and provide incentives for them. It is a shame to plan and implement a sound acquisition, then have the business erode because key employees leave.

It is important not only to have key personnel remain, but also to maintain the environment that made the company successful. Care should be taken to learn what that environment is before an acquisition is made.

For instance, an entrepreneurial high technology organization is unlikely to mesh well with a large, highly organized capital goods manufacturer. These acquisitions can work if, and only if, separate cultures are maintained. Each organization has its own sense of business discipline, but they are rarely compatible. (See Chapter 16 for a detailed discussion of integrating corporate cultures.)

In evaluating the organization, the following should be checked:

- *Key personnel* Have all key personnel been identified? What are their individual attitudes toward acquisition and remaining with the company? Have financial incentives been arranged to retain all key personnel?

- *Leadership* Who are the true leaders in the company? Is there depth beyond the first layer of management? Who will run the company if those who become wealthy from the acquisition leave soon? It is dangerous to assume that a manager brought in from the outside can successfully run an acquired company, unless she or he is a strong team builder.

- *Integration* Will a sound, well-thought-out integration plan be developed before the acquisition? This will be a great asset in making the acquisition successful. The entire team should be responsible for providing input for this plan.

**Financial.** As mentioned earlier, financial projections are worthless unless the base on which they are built is sound. It is important to have a good financial analyst/controller on the team. His or her job is to obtain input from all other areas to build a good financial model. For example, the marketing and manufacturing plans for the integration and growth of the business must be documented—not just in people's minds—before reliable projections can be developed.

A summary follows of information that should be developed in analyzing a candidate's current financial status and projecting future results. The information does not have to be developed in the order listed, but following this order will help in developing the financial analysis.

- *Current pro formas* Construct a current (monthly or quarterly) income statement, balance sheet, and cash flow statement portraying the potential acquisition's financials immediately after being integrated into the acquirer. All financial efficiencies and cost savings should be well documented. Pro formas should include input from all other operating disciplines, such as marketing, technical, and manufacturing, and should be reviewed and approved by the team members.

To develop these pro formas, a careful review of the company over the last few years will have to be made. Creating a quadrant chart similar to that shown in Figure 2-2 helps in the analysis since it takes into account the primary income statement, balance sheet, and cash flow items. Changes in the values over time should be well understood to construct the current financial model.

- *Break-even analysis* A break-even analysis should be done for the company as a whole. Fixed versus variable costs should be well understood.

- *Sensitivity analysis* The sensitivity of the income statement to changes in components such as sales volume, margin, exchange rate variations, and inflation should be calculated for at least worst-case and best-case scenarios. Detailed assumptions for the cases should be described.

- *Major risks and opportunities* Major financial risks and opportunities for the forthcoming year should be defined, along with

**FIGURE 2-2  Key data for the base financial analysis**

(Include data for the last two years on a quarterly basis; the current year's budget; and year-to-date financials.)

| *Sales/Income* | *Asset Management* |
|---|---|
| Net sales | Average assets employed |
| Income before tax | Asset turnover |
| Income after tax | Average gross inventory |
| Return on sales | Inventory turns |
| Return on assets employed | Days of receivables |
| Cash flow | Days of payables |
| Capital expenditures | Net fixed assets |
| Depreciation | Working capital turnover |
| | |
| *Cost Recovery* (as a % of sales) | *Statistics* |
| Material | Head count: |
| Hourly employment cost | – Salary – exempt |
| Total employment cost | – nonexempt |
| Manufacturing overhead | – Hourly |
| Actual gross margin | Sales per employee |
| Operating cost | Cost of quality (understand how this is measured) |

their probability of occurrence (low-medium-high). The effect (in dollar amounts) on pretax income should also be estimated.

- *Financial projections* All financial projections should be made only after the base case is finalized. Growth projections should be based on the acquisition team's input, relying heavily on the marketing function.

## Competitive Analysis (External)

Understanding the competition's styles and strategies is one of the most important determinants of a successful business. Being able to anticipate how a competitor will act and operate provides great advantage in planning your strategy.

In evaluating an acquisition, knowing the competition is at least as important as understanding the company being acquired. While the company being evaluated is the internal world, the competition is the external world.

From another perspective, one cannot assume that the company being evaluated will provide all—or always correct—information regarding its competition.

Recently, we interviewed all the corporate officers of a $300 million (in sales) company, as is our practice before accepting an engagement to plan an acquisition program. We were astounded at their lack of information regarding potential products and markets, and their total lack of understanding regarding competition. The fact was that foreign competitors had entered the United States in the last few years and were rapidly taking market share while this company did almost nothing. We advised the company that it was not ready to acquire, but definitely required a sound product, market, and competitive analysis.

Numerous books on competitive analysis exist. A good overall perspective can be gained by reading Harvard Business School professor Michael Porter's recent books on competition and strategy. His thoughts regarding competitive advantage are particularly germane in an acquisition analysis.

Most competitive information is sitting on shelves or in people's minds. By reviewing product information and by networking, you can develop competitive evaluations accurately and quickly. With a well-structured list of questions, you can usually obtain and cross-check information from various competitors.

This chapter is not intended to build a competitive analysis system, but to provide a framework to evaluate an acquisition candidate. We suggest that you proceed as follows with a competitive analysis:

**1.** Identify the primary competitors. Include strong foreign companies even if they are not yet marketing in the United States.

**2.** Obtain all competitive product and pricing literature. Review published information concerning competitors; read magazines, trade journals, and newspapers. Most of this information is also summarized in computer databases. Determine what products, technologies or services threaten functional substitution. How serious is any threat and in what time frame?

**3.** After reviewing public information on competitors, prepare a detailed questionnaire. Then survey all major competitors regarding each other's strengths and weaknesses in products, service, technology, and other areas. Call customers and have them evaluate the competitors. This may be the best information obtained in the entire company analysis.

**4.** Make a written evaluation of each competitor. Figure 2-3 is a fairly simple form that can be used. Each competitor should be rated in areas of strengths and weaknesses, according to a rating system applicable to your industry that you define. For instance, you might rate competitors as follows: A—industry leaders, B—major competitors, C—secondary competitors, D—marginal competitors. In the heading of the form, Estimated Competitive Annual Sales are directly competing sales; Estimated Competitive Market Share is based on these sales figures; and Estimated Total Annual Sales are total corporate (parent) sales.

The world moves very fast these days. "Old" competitive information—sometimes only a few months old in a technology-oriented business—can be valueless. The competitive information needs to be current and relative.

## FIGURE 2-3  Analysis of major competitors

Company:                                   Number of major competitors: _____

Product Line:

---

Include all competitors who, in total, account for at least 70 percent of the annual competitive volume in this product line or market; list in descending market share order. (Dollar values should be in *millions*.) *Use a new form for each competitor.*

Competitor's Name: _____   Est. Competitive Annual Sales: $____
Head Office Location: _____   Est. Competitive Market Share: ____%
Parent Co. Name: _____   Est. Total Annual Sales: $_____

Briefly describe, for each competitor, the company's approach to the business, overall marketing strategy, reputation, and competitive tactics.

---

Describe areas of major strength and weakness relative to the following aspects of each company. Define a rating system applicable to your industry.

1. Product line (Rating: _____ )

2. Pricing (Rating: _____)

3. Manufacturing capabilities (describe major plants by location, capability, quality ratings) (Rating: _____ )

4. Technical capabilities (Rating: _____ )

5. Marketing/distribution system (Rating: _____ )

6. Quality (Rating: _____ )

7. Major business added or lost during the last year (customer, sales $)

8. Cost position/extent of integration (Rating: _____ )

9. Financial position (last 3 years):

|  | | *(In Percentages\*\*)* | | | |
| --- | --- | --- | --- | --- | --- |
| *Sales* | *Income\** | *Income\*/Sales* | *ROE\** | *Debt/Equity* | *Asset Turnover* |

19__

19__

19__

(Check if ☐ divisional or ☐ parent company information.)

**FIGURE 2-3 (continued)**

Answer the following questions:

1. How can this competitor's strengths (threats) be overcome?

2. How can this competitor's weaknesses be taken advantage of?

3. How can this acquisition lead in innovations and other initiatives?

---

*Use income before interest, corporate charges, and taxes. Footnote if another basis is used. ROE is return on equity.

**Use business unit information, if available. If not, use parent company information.

## Strategic Considerations

In developing an overall strategic focus for a company, the CEO must do the following:

1. Diagnose how the company got where it is today.

2. Inventory the company's resources and capabilities versus the competition's.

3. Identify where the company is going over the long term. Find gaps in products, marketing, technology, or management that need to be filled to accomplish this vision, and determine the time needed to fill them.

This approach, although not guaranteeing success, certainly is better than running a company without a vision of where it is going. Acquisitions can greatly assist in filling the gaps to accomplish the long-term vision. They also can be used to effectively extend a company's strengths, whether these strengths are related to product, distribution, or technology. To phrase it another way, an acquisition should fit the corporate strategy. If the CEO cannot clearly see the fit, the acquisition logic should be thoroughly questioned.

Any acquisition evaluation should consider the acquisition in light of a strategic objective statement. The strategic considerations should include the following:

• The overall strategic rationale for the acquisition. How does it fit in the long-term vision?

- A defined list of strategic reasons for the acquisition. Specifically, where will the acquisition provide competitive leverage for the acquiring company?
- Quantitative and qualitative measurements of what will be accomplished by acquiring this company. What specific competitive advantages will be gained?
- A description of how the acquisition will be integrated into the acquiring company to accomplish strategic objectives and over what period of time.
- The major risks associated with the acquisition and the major issues that need further delineation or study.

A well-planned and implemented acquisition program is a great asset to a long-term strategy. There should not be a great rush to make acquisitions. Most acquisitions fail because the acquiring company uses an undisciplined, helter-skelter approach to evaluating and implementing the acquisition. If the acquisition does not fulfill part of a company's long-term strategic plan, corporate leaders must think very carefully before making the acquisition. Conversely, if an acquisition greatly enhances, or obviously complements, a company's strategy, leaders should not let it elude them by procrastinating until the company has been sold to another party.

# CHAPTER 3

# VALUING THE POTENTIAL ACQUISITION

## Robert J. Klug
### ARTHUR YOUNG/CDG

A June 3, 1985, *Business Week* article, "Do Mergers Really Work?," listed a number of "deadly sins" in conducting mergers and acquisitions. At the top of the list was "paying too much." The article proceeded to discuss a number of examples where the valuation process was given short shrift. Among these examples:

- In 1981 the Fluor Corporation acquired St. Joe Minerals Corporation, agreeing in less than a week to a $2.2 billion deal. St. Joe's chairman, on reflection, called the time spent to reach the agreement "so brief it was embarrassing."

  The deal reflected the perils of rushing into an acquisition of an unfamiliar business and, among other things, paying top dollar during a business-cycle peak. St. Joe had projected that its earnings would soar from $117 million in 1980 to more than $300 million in 1985. But it did not consider a deep recession, a cooling of inflation, or a crash in metals prices. For 1985, the company did not break even.

- In 1983, CPC International acquired C. F. Mueller & Co., an East Coast pasta maker, for approximately $124 million. CPC made its bid for Mueller on September 9, 1983, three weeks after it received a prospectus from Morgan Stanley. On September 22, CPC began due diligence investigations. The deal closed December 1.

CPC's timing was not good. The soaring dollar created a golden opportunity for foreign brands to enter the U.S. market and price aggressively. As a result, most domestic companies just held their own in unit sales for two years, even though the pasta market continued to grow.

Market share for Mueller has eroded, some experts believe, because CPC did not move aggressively to combat the foreigners either by pricing or promoting hard enough. CPC has since brought suit against both the seller and the investment banker, alleging that those parties deliberately overstated Mueller's value by more than 100 percent during the selling process.

As shown by these examples and as highlighted in the previous chapter, understanding the business of a potential acquisition is critical. Evaluating the potential acquisition—which includes determining a fair price for it—is an integral part of a well-run corporate development activity. The purpose of this chapter is not to provide an exhaustive "how-to" manual regarding performing a valuation, but rather to highlight approaches and key issues, and to help readers understand the output of the process as it relates to a chief executive's decision to acquire a company. The chapter will:

- define *value*;
- discuss integration of the due diligence effort with the valuation process; and
- describe and compare valuation techniques.

### VALUE—WHAT IS IT?

Publius defined value in the first century B.C.: "Everything is worth what its purchaser will pay for it." The IRS, in Regulation 10.1031(b), states that fair market value is "the price at which the property would change hands between a willing buyer and willing seller, neither being under any compulsion to buy or to sell, and both having reasonable knowledge of the relevant facts." Both of these definitions imply that what a purchaser will pay is often a function of who he is, what information he possesses, and the process by which value is determined.

For instance, value can change dramatically depending on the assumptions made by the potential purchaser about the expected future earnings performance and cash flow from an acquisition. Different potential purchasers can have very different ideas about appropriate value. For example, a management group whose projections and calculations support one price for a business may find themselves outbid by a corporate buyer relying on very similar projections, who is already in the acquisition target's industry. The latter is able to pay a higher price as a result of an ability to eliminate overhead or to benefit in some other way from combining the two businesses.

## INTEGRATION WITH THE DUE DILIGENCE PROCESS

As highlighted in the previous chapter, the acquiring company's senior management needs to be comfortable with the results of the due diligence process. These results are critical to developing ranges of value and establishing negotiation parameters. In particular, the following data should be gathered during the due diligence process to provide a basis for effective valuation:

*Products/Markets*
- Breakdowns of volumes/margins by product lines as a basis for determining future sales growth (existing and new products)
- Requirements/costs for future sales and marketing
- Trends for pricing/margins; future constraints/opportunities

*Operations/Organization*
- Cost structure components, current and expected
- Key people requirements/costs
- Labor costs/expected requirements/relationships

*Financial*
- Capital expenditure requirements
- Working capital relationships and the impact of growth

- Costs that stay/grow/decline after the acquisition
- Synergies that may reduce costs

*Industry/Competition*
- Competitor actions as they may affect pricing or unit demand
- General industry trends as they may affect revenues or costs

While specific questions should be answered in each segment of the due diligence process, they all have one common theme: the potential acquisition should be understood well enough so that a judgment can be made as to whether reported historical earnings are the right basis upon which to value the business or whether adjustments are needed to that number to fairly reflect value.

This due diligence process also should result in understanding the target's markets and industry accurately enough to model several alternative future performance scenarios. The various components of costs should be understood sufficiently well to model selling and administrative costs under different revenue assumptions. Changing cost relationships could significantly increase or decrease the cash flows generated by the business. The working capital and fixed capital requirements projected for the future are also critical, since these will have an impact on the cash flows generated or those required to achieve sales and earnings targets.

## VALUATION TECHNIQUES

Techniques for valuing a potential acquisition include the following:

- Discounted cash flow analysis
- Comparable transactions analysis
- Comparable companies analysis
- Other methods

Each technique will be described in turn.

### Discounted Cash Flow Analysis

Discounted cash flow analysis, diagrammed in Figure 3-1, is a very common approach. Alfred Rappaport, the Leonard Spacek Profes-

**FIGURE 3-1   The discounted cash flow technique**

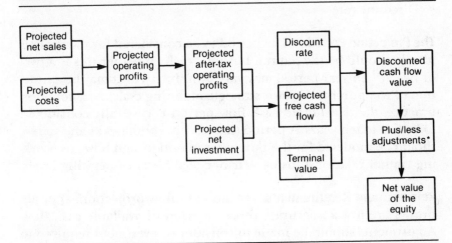

*The discounted cash flow value (or, what the total capital employed in the business is worth) has been calculated based on operating profits that do not consider financing costs (for example, interest expense) or income from nonoperating assets. As a result, the net value of the equity is derived by subtracting the market value of debt or adding the market value of nonoperating assets.

sor of Accounting and Information Systems at Northwestern University's Kellogg Graduate School of Management, has suggested that as many as half of the major acquisition-minded companies rely extensively on the discounted cash flow technique to analyze acquisitions. The same methodology used to make internal development decisions about plant or equipment additions can often be applied to an acquisition decision.

The discounted cash flow technique takes into account that a dollar received today is worth more than a dollar received a year from now because today's dollar can be invested to earn a return during the intervening time.

Obviously, the usefulness of this technique depends on the extent to which the underlying assumptions are appropriate. In addition to the income statement, four other components of this modeling technique can affect the result:

- The projection period
- Reinvestment requirements

- Terminal value
- Discount rate

**The Projection Period.**   The period to be considered for the analysis ideally should be the natural business cycle. Whether this is a two- or five- or ten-year period may vary by industry, or it may be a function of the purchaser's own strategic planning cycle. As a common practice, the discounted cash flow period is generally considered to be five to ten years. A period that portrays both peaks and valleys should be modeled for the purchaser to understand how cost/working capital relationships can change at different operating levels.

**Reinvestment Requirements.**   In any cash flow projection, after-tax profits are not an accurate representation of available cash flow. Adjustments should be made to consider reinvestment required to make the business grow. Specifically, this reinvestment can take the form of working capital or fixed capital investment or both. The determination of projected working capital requirements should consider the historic relationship to sales of receivables, inventory, and payables.

With regard to fixed asset expenditures, the relationship between past depreciation and past capital expenditures gives an understanding of how business growth (or lack of growth) has been related to investment.

Based on past trends, as well as management's input regarding likely future capital expenditure levels, a realistic forecast should be developed. The analysis must be sensitive to the strategic timing of capital expenditures. For instance, significant capital expenditures in the early years may provide substantial benefit to the company's overall value in later years.

**Terminal Value.**   At the end of the projection period, the acquired business will have remaining value. In current literature, various suggestions have been made as to what this terminal value may be. The Kellogg School's Rappaport has addressed this concept as being connected to a company's strategy.

In his essay "Coming to Grips with Residual Value" (*ALCA Review,* Fall 1986), Philip J. Enyon, executive vice president of Alcar and an associate of Rappaport's, writes: "Residual value and the method you choose to estimate it are strongly affected by two factors, the strategy being pursued during the forecast period and the competitive position of the firm.

"For a company pursuing growth, which is therefore investing heavily during the forecast period in order to achieve superior returns in the future, the residual value often represents 60–90 percent of its total value. Conversely, this percentage can be much smaller for a business that is pursuing a harvest strategy designed to maximize short-term returns at the expense of future competitiveness. Thus, while residual value reflects the value beyond the forecast period, its size is directly related to the strategy pursued during the forecast period."

Mechanically, terminal value can be calculated several ways. Two of the most common are the perpetuity method and the multiplier approach. The perpetuity method capitalizes the final year's projected cash flow/income by the discount rate, as if it were an annuity. While this approach has theoretical support, operating executives believe it can often understate the potential acquisition's value. From a theoretical perspective, this method assumes that any company able to generate returns greater than its cost of capital will eventually attract competitors, which will drive the returns of all companies in the industry down to the minimum acceptable cost-of-capital rate.

The multiplier approach applies a price/earnings ratio to the final year's net income. The higher the discount rate, the lower the effective P/E ratio. From an operating executive's perspective, this approach may give a truer sense of value, especially for businesses that command a higher P/E in the marketplace.

Since the terminal value can be a large part of the potential acquisition's overall value, the underlying assumptions and approach must be adopted on a situation-by-situation basis and the sensitivities understood.

**Discount Rate.** The discount rate (alternatively called the cost of capital) used in calculating the present value of each year's cash flow can be derived from several places, including a company's own strategic plan—which may identify required hurdle rates for any investment—or an analysis of rates of return for the industry. We will not go into the calculation process for cost of capital. However,

one of the most critical issues a chief executive officer must understand is how the discount rate used was derived and whether this
rate of return can reasonably be expected for an acquisition in the
target industry.

As Judson P. Reis and Charles R. Cory of Morgan Stanley point
out in their article "The Fine Art of Valuation" (in *The Mergers and
Acquisitions Handbook,* McGraw-Hill, 1986), the proper cost of capital
is that of the potential acquisition, not the potential acquirer. Their
reasoning is that the potential acquisition's cost of capital is the price
it must pay to the suppliers of capital to motivate them to invest
in that company. Use of the acquirer's cost of capital focuses on the
wrong bundle of risks in constructing a discount rate.

Figure 3-2 shows how the discounted cash flow method was used
to analyze a potential acquisition candidate with $28 million in sales
in 1986, net earnings of $538,000, and a net worth at the end of the
fiscal year equal to $4.7 million. The company is a custom job shop
that machines a wide range of castings to close tolerances for a variety of end markets including the automotive, agricultural imple-

**FIGURE 3-2   Discounted cash flow valuation of a company ($ thousands)**

|  | 1987 | 1988 | 1989 | 1990 | 1991 | Terminal Value |
|---|---|---|---|---|---|---|
| Sales | 34,800 | 45,000 | 50,850 | 57,461 | 64,930 | |
| Gross margin | 6,720 | 7,875 | 8,899 | 10,056 | 11,362 | |
| SG&A | 3,456 | 4,050 | 4,577 | 5,172 | 5,843 | |
| Operating income | 3,264 | 3,825 | 4,322 | 4,884 | 5,519 | |
| Taxes | 1,306 | 1,301 | 1,469 | 1,661 | 1,876 | |
| Net operating income | 1,958 | 2,524 | 2,853 | 3,223 | 3,643 | 9x |
|  |  |  |  |  |  | 32,787 |
| Capital requirements: | | | | | | |
| Wkg. capital | (505) | (831) | (268) | (304) | (344) | |
| Fixed assets, net of dep. | 134 | (1,775) | (2,027) | (2,000) | (2,000) | |
| Free cash flow | 1,587 | (82) | 558 | 919 | 1,299 | |
| Net present value at 12% | 1,417 | (65) | 397 | 584 | 737 | 18,604 |
|  |  |  | Sum of the present values | | | 21,674 |
|  |  |  | Less: market value of debt | | | 13,348 |
|  |  |  | Estimated value | | | 8,326 |

ment, and electronic component industries. The figure illustrates the projection process that models each line of the company's income statement, as well as a determination of capital requirements in future periods.

Once the initial model has been developed, second and third iterations are also appropriate to test the sensitivity of each of the assumptions used in the first projection. Figure 3-3 illustrates how the value changes based on variations in the assumptions for the discount rate and terminal value. Tests of sensitivity to changes in sales growth, expense relationships, and capital requirements are not shown, but these are also valuable in the analysis of potential value.

This analysis of sensitivities is particularly relevant in a negotiation, since it gives the buyer a sense of price ranges within which any negotiation can occur. It further helps establish a "walk-away" price above which any transaction would not achieve a satisfactory return under any of the buyer's assumptions.

Finally, the discounted cash flow approach provides a vehicle whereby operating management can make a number of "what-if" assumptions to take into account planned changes to the potential acquisition's operations and can determine the impact of these changes on the value. However, increased value the buyer will contribute should not necessarily translate into a proportionate increase in the purchase price.

**FIGURE 3-3  Testing the sensitivity of assumptions used in the discounted cash flow analysis ($ thousands)**

| | | Terminal Value Multiple of Net Operating Earnings | | |
| --- | --- | --- | --- | --- |
| | | 7x | 9x | 11x |
| | 10% | 5,715 | 10,239 | 14,760 |
| Discount rate | 12% | 4,192 | 8,326 | 12,460 |
| | 14% | 2,821 | 6,605 | 10,389 |

## Comparable Transactions Analysis

Often, the marketplace provides examples of transactions consummated within the same industry as the potential acquisition. While numerous private transactions are never recorded in the press, a variety of published sources now available can give the buyer some sense of how the real world may be valuing companies that are similar to the potential acquisition.

The overall objective of the comparable transactions approach is to identify some pricing relationships: ideally, price/earnings ratios and/or market/book value premiums for transactions consummated. Extensive research is important to identify those situations that are most similar. A number of data sources can be used, including the following:

- W. T. Grimm, a Chicago-based merger and acquisition research company
- The *National Review of Corporate Acquisitions*
- J. A. Morgan, Oak Brook, Illinois, a researcher specifically geared to manufacturing companies
- Annual reports of companies within the potential acquisition's industry (on the chance that some of these companies have made acquisitions and have also disclosed sufficient information regarding pricing)

In the example of the custom metalworking company, consider the data reported for 1986 transactions by W. T. Grimm regarding the fabricated metal products industry, as shown in Figure 3-4. Based on this data, the value of the potential acquisition can be calculated as follows (two transactions with price/earnings multiples in excess of 50X earnings were excluded as not representative):

| | | |
|---|---|---|
| 1986 reported earnings | $ 538,000 | |
| 1986 reported net worth | | $4,700,000 |
| Average P/E ratio | 17.2x | |
| Average market/book value premium | | 1.5x |
| Estimated value | $9,254,000 | $7,050,000 |

# FIGURE 3-4 Data reported for 1986 transactions by W. T. Grimm

| DATES | BUYER / SELLER (business) | ANNUAL SALES (millions) | PRICE PAID (millions) | METHOD OF PAYMENT | P/E PAID | BUYER'S P/E | PREMIUM PAID | MULTIPLE TO BOOK |
|---|---|---|---|---|---|---|---|---|
| | **AMAX INC.** | | | | | | | |
| 7/16 12/16 | ALUMAX INC. (aluminum & structural aluminum products) | $1,900.0 | $ 435.0 | Cash Stock | 12.7X | DEF | | |
| | AMAX bought back its remaining 50% interest in Alumax held by Mitsui & Co. Ltd. | | | | | | | |
| | **19 - FABRICATED METAL PRODUCTS** | | | | | | | |
| | **NORTEK INC.** | | | | | | | |
| 4/1 8/14 | UNIVERSAL-RUNDLE CORP. (makes sinks & faucets) | 138.0 | 42.8 | Cash Notes | 56.3 | 12.1X | 11.9% | 1.2X |
| | **LINGBERGER KIDD KAMM & CO.** | | | | | | | |
| 4/9 6/19 | PEERLESS CHAIN CO. (steel alloy chain, wire-rope) | 26.8 | 38.8 | Cash | 14.9 | PRV | 11.9 | 1.4 |
| | **PRIVATE GROUP - led by Berger Family** | | | | | | | |
| 5/30 5/30 | BERGER INDUSTRIES INC. (welded steel tubing, tubing products) | 64.7 | 1.9 | Cash | 16.8 | PRV | 64.0 | 0.8 |
| | Berger Family bought 23% it didn't already own. | | | | | | | |
| | **HARVARD INDUSTRIES INC.** | | | | | | | |
| 10/30 10/31 | HAYES-ALBION CORP. (metal products used in automotive industry) | 218.0 | 49.7 | Cash Tender | DEF | 13.4 | 30.0 | 0.9 |
| | **PRIVATE GROUP - led by John Castellvi** | | | | | | | |
| 11/12 | FRIEDMAN INDUSTRIES INC. (steel cabinets, plate, sheet & tubing) | 48.0 | 33.2 | Cash | 17.5 | PRV | 21.2 | 1.1 |
| | Board approves (2/2/87) subject to stockholder approval. 50% holder says he will vote yes. | | | | | | | |
| | **ALUMINUM CO. OF AMERICA** | | | | | | | |
| 11/17 | TRE CORP. (lightweight metals, high temperature alloy products) | 166.5 | 315.9 | Cash Tender | 19.6 | DEF | 11.4 | 3.3 |
| | Transaction completed 2/3/87. | | | | | | | |
| | **PRIVATE GROUP - led by Bennet LeBow** | | | | | | | |
| 12/26 | NORTHWESTERN STEEL & WIRE (fabricated steel bars & shapes) | $ 356.2 | $ 165.0 | Cash Stock | 55.0X | PRV | 39.7% | 1.0X |
| | Transaction terminated by Northwestern 2/20/87. | | | | | | | |

W. T. Grimm & Associates, Chicago, Illinois, 1987.

Thus, an approach that focuses on earnings results in a higher value than one that focuses on book value. Why is this relevant? Most likely, the potential acquisition's dividend policy or past earnings performance will suggest that an earnings-based approach gives a truer sense of current value.

In general, in using the comparable transactions methodology, the buyer needs to be aware of the following key issues:

- The research used to develop the multiples must be understood. Multiples may distort the noncash elements of any transaction. Company-specific factors such as market share, intangible assets, and technical competence may have an impact on multiples yet not be reflected in summary statistics.
- Companies that comprise the sample from which multiples are derived may not match the potential acquisition exactly.
- The buyer must be comfortable with the earnings and book value assumed for the potential acquisition. While the due diligence process will most likely reveal whether reported earnings or book value are meaningful, any valuation should likewise use the most meaningful numbers. For example, if a privately held company has significant salary expenses that would not exist under a buyer, an add-back would be reasonable and should be made to assess this potential acquisition's truer earning power.

### Comparable Companies Analysis

An additional point of reference for the buyer is provided by making some assessment of how the value of the potential acquisition compares with market prices of publicly traded companies subject to similar economic trends and risks. This approach is similar to the comparable transactions method in that it identifies some pricing relationship and then applies it to the potential acquisition's earnings or book value. While details of the process will not be elaborated here, sources of company-specific statistics include Value-Line, Standard & Poor's, and Moody's.

In the example of the custom metalworking company, the following is a summary of data about public companies that appear most comparable:

| Company | Market | Description | May 31, 1986, P/E Ratio |
|---------|--------|-------------|-------------------------|
| Blasius Industries | NASDAQ | A custom designer and manufacturer of precision metal workings (52 percent of sales) and rubber components. Customers include manufacturers in numerous industries: automotive, leisure, home appliances, office equipment, industrial equipment, radio, and TV. 1985 sales approximated $42 million. | 15 |
| Simpson Industries | NASDAQ | A manufacturer of machined components, assemblies, and cutting tools, selling its product to OEMs of automobiles, trucks, diesel engines, and heavy equipment. 1985 sales approximated $139 million. | 13 |
| Washington Scientific | NASDAQ | A manufacturer of close tolerance metal components, hydraulic motors, gear boxes, and power transmission products. IBM is a major customer. Other markets served include aerospace and agricultural. 1985 sales approximated $35 million. | 14 |
| | | Average: | 14 |

Based on this data, the value of the potential acquisition can be calculated as follows:

| | |
|---|---|
| 1986 reported earnings: | $538,000 |
| Average P/E ratio | 14x |
| Control premium | 21% |
| Estimated value | $9,114,000 |

The control premium used in this calculation is the amount an investor would be willing to pay in order to exercise control over the corporation. Theories as to why such a premium is required include the following:

- To induce present owners to sell their stock in the face of unfamiliar investment alternatives
- To compensate owner/managers for the threat to their security (particularly in unfriendly takeovers)
- To offset tax consequences to the seller if the acquisition is a taxable transaction
- To discourage other potential suitors
- In recognition of the difficulty and expense of obtaining sufficient shares to consolidate operations and tax reporting with the acquirer on a timely basis

For our valuation purposes, W. T. Grimm's research includes control premiums and shows that they vary by industry and have changed through time. For our example, data previously shown in Figure 3-4 were used to develop the control premium by averaging the premiums paid on the transactions Grimm analyzed. The 64 percent premium was excluded in developing a meaningful value because it was so far outside the range of the others.

Points to remember when using comparable companies analysis include the following:

- For purposes of comparison, pure-play companies are better than conglomerates. To the extent that a conglomerate is a potential acquisition, each business unit may need to be valued separately.
- Outlying P/E multiples (given a poor earnings history) may not be meaningful in developing comparable data.
- Always determine where current multiples stand in relation to history. P/E multiples fluctuate, and using this method requires understanding whether the averages used are at the high end or the low end of the historical range.
- Determine who is the best and worst performer in the list of comparables, and compare the potential acquisition to either extreme.

## Other Methods

Two other approaches can provide some reference points in approaching valuation, but are appropriate only under certain specific circumstances. These methods are (1) book value or adjusted book value, and (2) liquidation analysis.

**Book Value or Adjusted Book Value.**   This method can provide a starting point for the valuation discussion. However, this is an accounting-based concept that does not necessarily reflect earning power. Generally Accepted Accounting Principles (GAAP) may permit use of accelerated depreciation or alternative inventory methods that may not reflect the true value of those assets. Similarly, the value of intangible assets such as customer lists, patents, and an embedded sales force may not be reflected on the balance sheet, but may contribute to a superior earnings performance for a business.

**Liquidation Analysis.**   If the business has relatively little value as a going concern, an appropriate analysis may be to consider what individual assets would be worth if sold at auction or in a sixty-to-ninety-day liquidation. At a minimum, this establishes a floor for valuation.

## Summary of Valuation Techniques

The advantages and disadvantages of each valuation technique can be summarized as follows:

| Method | Advantages | Disadvantages |
|--------|-----------|---------------|
| Discounted cash flow | Provides a method to model expected performance and understand sensitivities | May not reflect the reality of pricing trends in the market |
|  | Aids understanding of performance, cash flow, and balance sheet relationships | Methodology may be cumbersome and may involve "soft" numbers relative to terminal values |

*Continued*

| Method | Advantages | Disadvantages |
|--------|------------|---------------|
| Comparable transactions | Provides a comparison to actual acquisitions—what other people are paying | Transaction data may be incomplete: the most similar deals are not published; the published deals may not be similar; every deal is unique |
| | Reveals who other buyers are and may offer insight into potential competitive bidders | |
| Comparable companies | Provides a benchmark of how the public markets view particular industries | May ignore the reality of expected future performance |
| | Permits comparison of performance of public companies relative to target | May not provide a truly comparable picture: the target company may not be similar to your sample |
| Adjusted book value/liquidation analysis | May be most relevant if a business is being acquired for its underlying assets as opposed to going-concern value | May not reflect economic value of the business, especially if the target generates strong earnings |

In the example of the metalworking company, the three most often used valuation techniques yield the following estimated values:

Discounted cash flow:        $8,326,000

Comparable transactions:     $7,050,000 to $9,254,000

Comparable companies:        $9,114,000

In this particular example, the discounted cash flow method results in a figure lower than the market-based approaches. Of all the methods, I believe discounted cash flow is the most useful because it can be tailored to fit the facts of each specific situation. Business judgment must be applied to determine the willingness of a buyer to pay a higher price (and potentially accept a lower return) in order to make the purchase. It is in this process that alternative discounted cash flow scenarios may suggest to a potential buyer a means of justifying a higher price while at the same time achieving desired return targets. However, the buyer should guard against including illusory synergies in the analysis to justify bidding more.

It cannot be stressed enough that valuation must include research, understanding, and judgment. Doing one's homework is often the best way to avoid the problem of paying too much.

Once completed, the valuation result must be folded into the buyer's own planning process and compared with the indicated price to determine if the desired return on equity, return on assets, earnings per share, or threshold can be met. These valuation processes are a tool to set ceilings and floors for the pricing decision and also to assess the key levers that may change the valuation. A valuation should never be done in a vacuum, but should evolve from a thorough due diligence process and should be an integral part of negotiation strategy.

# CHAPTER 4

# STRATEGIC PARTNERSHIPS AND CORPORATE VENTURE INVESTMENTS

## Socrates H. Choumbakos
**PRESIDENT, VENTURE DEVELOPMENT GROUP, INC.**

If a company does not believe in minority equity investments, or does not feel that value can be created in any relationship between two companies short of a complete acquisition, it might be passing up one of the most effective and efficient vehicles yet devised for acquiring technology and products and for building value in a company: the strategic partnership.

Strategic partnerships can be problematic. But the right kind of arrangement between the right partners for the right reasons can, with a measure of good fortune, help both parties achieve their strategic and financial objectives. This chapter will deal with three major aspects of these types of investments:

- The rationale behind the growing popularity of this form of alliance
- The factors that frequently determine success or failure and what a company can do to tilt the odds in favor of success
- The basic structural elements inherent in most partnering arrangements and the conditions that influence how they are used

## OF PARTNERSHIPS AND VENTURES

*Business Week* magazine, in its June 25, 1984, issue, described strategic partnerships as "acquiring the expertise but not the company, a new way for big corporations to tap innovations created at small companies." Strategic partnerships, which are also referred to as strategic alliances and corporate partnerships, generally involve at least two of the following elements in some form:

- Minority equity investment in a small company by a larger partner
- Distribution or licensing agreements for existing products or technologies
- Development agreements for new or next-generation products

Most strategic partnerships, in fact, involve the acquisition of technology or products by companies in fields characterized by rapid changes in technology. These partnerships generally involve arrangements between a large company that already has a strong technological base and major position in the target market and a smaller company that has developed or applied a technology important to that market as part or all of its business. The partners' goal often is to create and commercialize something together that neither partner could do as quickly or as effectively alone. In a true strategic partnership, the real value is created when both companies do what each does best in trying to satisfy their own needs and those of the marketplace.

Corporate venture investments differ from strategic alliances in both intent and structure. The primary goals of corporate venture investments are frequently the following:

- To spawn new businesses within or beyond the direct scope of the investor's current portfolio as part of an effort to identify sources of potential future growth
- To create windows on new technologies
- To generate an attractive return on investment

These venture investments may take the form of direct investment in an operating entity, or investment in one or more professionally managed venture capital funds focused on areas of interest to the company. While the investor corporation may be as active or passive in the investee company's business as its arrangement permits, the primary goal is usually not a collaborative effort aimed at a specific commercial endeavor, as it is in strategic partnering.

## WHY STRATEGIC PARTNERING?

Many successful licensing and distribution agreements have been and continue to be concluded in the absence of any partnership arrangements or equity investments. Why, then, spend the time and money and incur the risk required to structure a strategic partnership?

A large part of the answer has to do with the environment within which the company operates. Companies that enter into strategic partnerships are generally engaged in industries characterized by some or all of the following:

- Rapid (and expensive) technological change
- Short product life cycles
- Intense competition
- Dramatic changes in customer preferences or economics

These factors help explain the growing popularity of strategic partnerships in the computer, electronics, telecommunications, pharmaceutical, biotechnology, and medical devices industries. But the benefits of strategic partnering can often apply as well in areas not traditionally characterized as high technology.

The U.S. health care industry provides an example of both economic and technological factors that have helped popularize strategic partnering. In 1983 the federal government changed reimbursement to hospitals for treating Medicare patients from a cost-plus basis to a fixed amount based on the patient's specific diagnosis. This has caused many health care providers to focus sharply on cost containment—that is, on lowering the overall cost of delivering virtually every type of health care. At the same time, a growing concentration of purchasers into hospital and pharmacy chains and other voluntary buying groups has put increasing pressure on the profits of suppliers to these entities. The pace of technological change is increasing along with its cost and complexity, and average product life cycles are shortening.

In addition to these woes, many companies have seen increased competition from both existing competitors and new companies, frequently fueled by venture capital, new public stock offerings, or research and development limited partnerships. These pressures have helped foster a growing feeling among technology-driven companies that they cannot afford to do everything themselves. This feeling crystallizes as a need for a way to improve profitability and at the same time establish competitive advantage by increasing new-product development.

Companies frequently respond to these pressures first by implementing various internal programs for increasing efficiency and productivity while lowering operating costs. These moves in many cases lead to wholesale restructuring of corporate portfolios as well as corporate management structures. Once these cost-cutting activities are under way, the need often arises to find a way to lever the company's own strengths using products and technologies developed outside the company.

A number of techniques for achieving this can be combined under the broad heading "strategic partnering." The opportunity for partnering generally arises when a large company can match its substantial financial resources, considerable marketing position and distribution networks, and technological strengths with relevant technologies and products from outside the company. A properly structured alliance can give that company improved access to new products and technologies, accelerate its own new-product development and introduction programs, and help foster entrepreneurial spirit.

At the same time, strategic partnering can provide the smaller partner with access to the markets and distribution networks that could be critical elements in realizing the full potential of a new product or technology. Partnering can also provide financial resources, complementary technologies, and industry credibility, which can increase the long-term value of both the small company's technologies and frequently the company itself.

Potential partners may be established companies or start-up situations with solid technology. They can come from the ranks of either private or public companies. The guidelines for structuring these arrangements generally apply equally well in each situation.

The real value in a strategic partnership is created at the lab bench and in the marketplace, not in the documents that formalize the arrangement. So the key ingredients in each arrangement are people and flexibility. The best formula is the one that provides both partners with the opportunity and the incentive to do what each does best while maintaining their independence and all of their other prerogatives.

As an alternative to acquisitions, strategic partnerships can often avoid the risk of loss in value caused by the cultural changes that can result from a change in corporate control. Along with this change frequently comes a decrease in or elimination of performance incentives and, just as often, a loss of many key managers responsible for the performance that attracted the acquiring company in the first place. As the key principals cash out or leave for a more compatible culture, a dramatic loss of entrepreneurial spirit is often experienced. Properly conceived and structured, the strategic partnership can create substantial value while avoiding many of the pitfalls common to acquisitions.

## IMPROVING THE ODDS OF SUCCESS

The same basic rules apply to creating value through strategic partnerships as apply to acquisitions. As in acquisitions, only two important considerations really exist: price and fit.

To achieve the best fit in a strategic partnership, the two most critical elements are having a business strategy that clearly lays out what the business unit is trying to accomplish and how it plans to accomplish it, and then selecting the right partner. Once the best partner is found, the most important consideration is pursuing a deal structure with a properly assembled negotiating team, and establishing incentives for reaching partnership goals.

### The Business Strategy

Each partner must have its own strategic plan. Each business unit has to be sure of exactly where and what that unit is, and where it expects to go over the period of the partnership. This plan must identify each company's strengths, weaknesses, and precisely how the strengths of a potential partner will be applied in a way that enhances the probability of achieving the unit's objectives. The more precisely this can be formulated and communicated, the more clearly the criteria for selecting a partner can be drawn.

The essential element is defining independently each partner's goals, intentions, and expectations so the compatibility of what they want to accomplish together in the partnership and what they want to retain as their own prerogatives can be realistically assessed. Each partner should know precisely how the partnering opportunity fits into its overall strategy. Without a very high degree of compatibility in what the partners hope to accomplish in the partnership, how they intend to accomplish it, and the degree of freedom each has outside this area of common business interest, the partnership may be doomed from the start.

A relatively common situation finds a small company with a single product or a single technology with narrow applicability trying to attain market presence and good distribution rapidly by trading exclusive worldwide marketing rights to a well-established partner. At the same time, the small company CEO still expects his or her company to be valued in the same way as its strategic look-alikes, which are independent companies with their own marketing and distribution.

A large company partnering with such an entity incurs the double risk of having the small partner become increasingly dependent on it both for moving the product and for helping that company's stock increase in value in accordance with the small company's optimistic expectations. While this does not sound like a particularly attractive situation for creating value, it is not an uncommon one. The business strategies of both partners must demonstrate consistency between both long- and short-term objectives and must account for the costs and risks as well as benefits of the partnership.

Defining and communicating the fit of the proposed partnering in each company's overall plan, if done properly, increases the level of understanding and support throughout both companies. It also assures that levels of staffing, assignment of key responsibilities, levels of commitment of other corporate resources, and potential conflicts will be addressed and resolved long before the implementation stage begins.

### Partner Selection

The next step in successful partnering is partner selection. Six areas must be addressed when screening candidates for a partnership:

- Position in industry or market segment
- Breadth of interest
- Directness of competition
- Extent of resources
- Success of other relationships
- Culture

**Position in Industry or Market Segment.**   Potential candidates should be limited to those companies that have demonstrated clear leadership in their particular field of product development or manufacturing or whatever skills are being sought.

Candidate companies must generally be well established to have demonstrated the kind of superior performance that would warrant a significant investment of time and money. Occasionally partnerships have been formed where one company is a start-up. While start-ups may be founded by or attract extremely talented people, the partnership's chances for success will be affected by all the risks inherent in a start-up situation as well as the normal business risks inherent in the project.

**Breadth of Interest.**   The partner ought to have a sufficient breadth of business interest so that all of its future potential is not locked up in the partnership project. The management of the smaller company needs to feel that its drive to build the value of its company is neither dependent on nor impeded by the presence of the partnership agreement.

Early discussions must determine whether the partners' goals and expectations do, in fact, align in terms not only of where the relevant technologies and markets are going but also the role of each partner in taking them there. Differences on this issue can lead to major philosophical and practical disagreements a short way down the road.

**Directness of Competition.**   The partners should not be competitors for the same customers in the same market segment. Some relationships have been based on differentiating the partners with market segment distinctions like medical research versus clinical medicine, or mainframe computers versus small computers. Distinctions like these may soon be erased by customers or technology.

Partners who are or have the potential to become competitors will likely have difficulty agreeing on access to next-generation products or technologies and on their obligation to keep supporting the partnership's original products once new generations are launched.

**Extent of Resources.** The partnering candidates should be entities that have sufficient financial and human resources to conduct their ongoing business without constant support. In this way the partners can focus their collective attention on the partnership project without the threat of potentially disruptive distractions. Care must be taken to examine how realistically the partner candidate projects its cash needs and how any significant shortfall or new investment will be funded. The larger partner wants to avoid being in a position of bailing out the smaller one just because the partnership is too important and too far along to walk away from.

While the equity investment that frequently accompanies strategic partnerships can sometimes go a long way toward reducing this problem, it does not eliminate it. Gaps in planning and/or unexpected financial problems can precipitate a cash crisis in spite of a substantial equity investment.

**Success of Other Relationships.** Partnering with an entity that has successfully partnered before may in fact increase the probability of success. Such partners are more likely to assess themselves and their expectations realistically, and they may already know where many of the pitfalls are. A meeting should be arranged with key executives of the potential partner's other partner(s) to discuss their view of the partnership in general and the attitudes and approach of the partner candidate's people in dealing with them.

A refusal by a partner candidate to arrange such access could be a major signal that problems have arisen that the partners have not been able to handle satisfactorily.

Potential partners with too many other relationships may have a problem of overlapping commitments to competing partners. These could result in snarled business relationships as well as legal problems, so this kind of partner should be avoided.

**Culture.**  An overused but still valid concept is that of the corporate culture, and how those of dissimilar companies can clash. Since this is not an acquisition, no need actually exists to conform or integrate the cultures or to limit partnerships only to like-cultured companies. Still, it is important to develop an understanding as well as a mutual respect for the other company's culture and operating style.

It is also very helpful to have had a prior relationship of some sort with a potential partner. Many partnerships have been formed between former suppliers and customers. The most important contribution of a prior relationship is the trust that comes from being able to assess the character and intent of the other party at reasonably close range and to see what their reaction is when things don't go as planned.

## Negotiation and Implementation Teams

Critical to the long-term success of any arrangement is the composition of the team or teams that define the scope, working arrangements, specific projects, and basic structure of the partnership.

Top management may have had the vision that initially spawned the partnership. But product development, manufacturing, and marketing operations and their formal and informal network support systems must be represented in the planning and structuring process if anything of real value is to be created. The meeting of these people with their counterparts at the other company and the mutual respect and understanding thereby generated can provide a strong foundation on which to build.

The actual negotiating team should generally be kept small—two or three people—and should have sufficient authority to propose changes and compromises but not enough authority to commit to them. Negotiations can take a great deal of time over several months and be particularly draining for top management at the small company, so sufficient time and energy must be allocated to the process. It is important, too, to remember that the original sponsors and negotiators of the partnership may not be there when problems arise, so the working structure and important communication linkages must be able to survive on their own.

Once the details of the partnership have been negotiated and functional responsibilities assigned, the step all too often left out is establishing specific incentives for reaching the goals of the partnership. This is particularly important where any risk exists that the project has not yet captured the imagination of the large company, and where the period between completion of the documents and the time anything real starts to happen may be long.

The probability of success increases significantly when individual responsibility is clearly assigned before closing and is tied to individuals' performance standards, bonuses, and other incentives. The dollar amounts involved are generally not as important as the consistency of the message sent by the words surrounding the partnership and the actions and reward linkages that support it.

## SPECIFIC ELEMENTS OF A STRATEGIC PARTNERSHIP

A strategic partnership generally involves at least two of the following elements in some form:

- An equity purchase agreement
- A development agreement
- A distribution agreement

The following sections discuss the conditions that influence how these elements are used.

### The Equity Purchase Agreement

The decision to make a minority investment in a small company can be a very sensitive matter for management of many large companies. The smaller company might be private and have a limited commercial track record, and such minority investments might have no precedent in the large company's history. The decision becomes more difficult if the goal of the proposed partnership is perceived to coincide with the goal of an internal development program or if funding the partnership is seen as diverting resources from the company's own R&D operations.

While these issues must be addressed too, the final strategic decision on partnering and equity investment should be based on the carefully researched answers to the following questions:

- How ready for market is the smaller company's product or technology?

- How critical to a key strategy or business unit of the large company is such a product or technology?
- What alternatives are available for developing or acquiring an equivalent product/technology?
  - How critical is the time factor in assessing the strategic options?
  - How ready is the market, and does its timing fit the partner's basic mode of doing business (innovator, fast follower, or whatever)?
- Finally, do the breadth and depth of skills and technology of the potential partner extend far beyond the initial advantage of a single product or technology?

The answer to this last question will frequently indicate whether a true strategic alliance is called for or whether a simpler licensing or supply arrangement not contingent on equity investment is more appropriate.

Other factors mitigating in favor of a strategic partnership are the following:

- Potential partner's possession of high-caliber, unique technology and applications skills; strong patents help
- Evidence that a strong commercial linkage would provide a competitive advantage by creating a barrier to competition
- A large degree of exclusivity in the potential partner's defined field of commercialization
- Management's honest assessment that it cannot execute its strategies without key resources from outside the company

It is important to note that many small companies and development groups are making an equity investment the initial requirement for any meaningful access to the technology and the applications skills they possess. They are simply not satisfied with the valuation potential offered by royalty or contract manufacturing arrangements.

Outlined in the following paragraphs are other considerations that arise once the decision to invest has been made. A number of these are the same whether the transaction is a strategic partnership or a corporate venture investment, but they are discussed here in the context of strategic partnerships.

**Valuation.**   What is a fair value for the company at the time of investment? There are many methods and guidelines for establishing the market value of a company. The critical question for the large company often is not what the stock of a potential partner is worth on the open market, but what the specific product, technology, or productive development team is worth in a specific strategic context. This frequently boils down to the question of how much the larger company would have to spend on R&D to get a product or technology to the stage the potential partner has already attained.

The decision is often resolved when the large company projects where the small company would be by the time an internal development program or other option could deliver the product or the technology in its present state. In highly competitive markets, the elusive value of lead time over one's competitors can carry a substantial premium and make the decision to purchase equity at a reasonable price a much easier one to accept. This is not to say that the intrinsic value of the small company is irrelevant; it can be important for very real financial and accounting reasons discussed later.

Small companies often face the temptation of placing on themselves the highest valuation that can be inferred by comparison to companies or recent transactions in their industry. A valuation based on a company's actual accomplishments and reasonable future potential with fair regard for the noncash contributions the larger partner brings to the relationship may benefit the small company far more in the long run than trying to hit the jackpot on the first round of corporate financing. This allows for a reasonable increase in valuation as each major technological and commercial milestone is achieved.

**Equity Percentage.**   How much equity should the larger partner purchase? A number of factors need to be evaluated in answering this question, not the least of which is the relationship between the amount of money the small company requires and a reasonable valuation for the company. Cash can be supplied to the smaller partner in many other ways, such as product advances that are amortized over future purchases, advance payment of R&D contract commitments, or future royalties.

**Accounting Basis.**   The amount of equity purchased is the key deter-minant of the subsequent accounting method. Therefore, cost-basis accounting versus equity-basis accounting for the investment is an issue that needs to be addressed early in the company's delib-erations. Generally, any long-term equity investment of under 20 percent of the voting shares requires the large company to account for its investment on the cost basis, where the initial cost goes on the balance sheet and is not affected by the results of operations as they are reported by the small company or by the normal ups and downs of the stock market. The large company only reports income if and when the small company declares and pays dividends. The investment is only reduced if a real long-term reduction in the value of the small company occurs; any such loss in value is reflected in the investor's income statement in the period in which it is recognized.

Investments in 20 percent or more of the voting stock generally require accounting on the equity basis. Again, the initial cost is recorded on the balance sheet at the time of investment. Thereafter, the investor company reports on its income statement its equity in the profits or losses of the smaller company as they are reported by that company, and adjusts the balance sheet value of the invest-ment upward by the amount of its equity in profits and downward by the amount of its equity in any losses. Under equity accounting, the amount of the investment shown on the balance sheet is reduced by any dividends paid by the smaller company. These dividends, however, are not reported as income on the income statement.

If the investor expects to be sensitive to the magnitude of expected future earnings or losses reported by the smaller company, equity accounting should be approached with great care or avoided if possible.

The 20 percent equity figure is only a guideline and is affected by a number of other factors such as representation on the board of directors, dependence of the small company on the larger for a significant portion of its market access or cash flow, or other in-fluences exerted on the business. Because this can be a very com-plex area, involving accounting experts at the early stages of deal structuring can avoid a lot of misunderstanding later.

Equity percentage notwithstanding, accountants take a dim view of funding R&D in a small company and calling it equity in order to avoid expensing the payments as R&D is performed.

**Board Representation.**   Generally speaking, the last thing executives of large companies need is another operating unit to monitor and advise, and frequently the relative size of the investment in a part-ner would not warrant a great deal of top management attention. In addition, the most common investments—in the 5 to 30 percent range—do not themselves confer the ability to control operations or other major decisions facing the small company.

Nevertheless, the consensus of investors in these situations is that board representation provides an important source of information on all the issues confronting a partner and a unique perspective on the company and its industry.

**Rights of First Refusal.**   The stock purchase agreement is usually where certain rights of the partners and other similar issues are spelled out. Often included is a broad right of first refusal for the large partner to market other developments by the smaller partner that derive from the technology developed in the partnership pro-gram, in applications of the partner's technology in specific fields of use where the large partner becomes the primary marketing outlet in that area, or both. This can be an important asset for the large company and is frequently used as important justification for the equity investment and a partnership agreement in the first place.

From the small company's perspective, however, the granting of right of first refusal for other applications or future technological developments might be seen as reducing the future value of the com-pany directly or indirectly. The value of the technology it develops is frequently seen as the very basis for building the value of the com-pany, and hence should not be traded away too cheaply at the outset of a partnering agreement.

**Liquidity.**   The large partner will almost invariably request and get registration rights in order to provide for future liquidity. These rights may be subject to various conditions relating to other financ-ings the small partner may attempt or to other business or market conditions.

The large company under certain circumstances may also want the flexibility to consider other uses of the equity, such as contribu-tions of appreciated stock to its pension plans or in conjunction with new debt it might issue that is convertible into the shares it owns in the smaller company.

**Options and Warrants.** In many cases, at the time of its initial equity investment, the investing company may negotiate the right to purchase additional shares at specified prices. These rights may be tied to the attainment of specific milestones or to the passage of time alone. If used properly, such rights allow for the investing company to achieve an attractive financial return on all its investments in the partnership and can provide capital to the smaller company with relatively little cost or management effort and with little regard for general stock market conditions.

The various equity aspects of a strategic partnership invariably complicate the evaluation and approval process and increase both the time required and level of authorization needed to complete the transaction compared to a licensing or supply agreement. The temptation to complete and execute the documents piecemeal must be resisted. Simultaneous closing of all the agreements gives significantly greater assurance that all major facets of the arrangement have been thought through, agreed to, and documented in detail. The extra time this may require is well worth taking to avoid the risk of a miscommunication of some important element of the working arrangement and the ripple effect this may have on the entire partnering effort.

### The Development Agreement

The major issues in designing the development arrangement relate to defining the specific products and programs and deciding who owns the technology developed.

The definitions may use highly detailed technical product specifications, may take an "outside-in" approach and define operating characteristics from the intended users' perspective, or both. What is important is that both sides agree on the meaning of terms and on how to measure the performance and conditions defining each major milestone. This is frequently the most difficult facet of the arrangement and the one that receives the least attention.

While the close cooperation of the technical people on both sides is essential to completing the program definition, the early involvement and complete understanding of key marketing and management people is also essential.

The ownership of technology to be developed needs to be addressed early in the discussions. The ownership issue has already been discussed in this chapter under the heading "Rights of First Refusal," and while it is often determined by the partners' relative negotiating strength in specific areas, it needs to be resolved equitably.

Some options relating to exclusivity include granting an exclusive license in a limited field of use or granting a sole license in a broad area to the marketing partner. Sole licenses preserve the rights of the small company to use the technology in the future in particular applications and thus help preserve future options and identifiable elements of potential future value. Geographical limits on exclusivity may give the large company most of what it needs while preserving at least the appearance of direct marketing potential for the small company. This may become a significant element in future financings even if the small company presently lacks the desire or ability to pursue each marketing option.

Other questions that need to be addressed are the following:

- Who is going to manufacture the product?
- How much will transfer prices, royalties, or both, amount to?
- Who is responsible for filing and maintaining patents?
- Should everything be patented?
- What happens when the relationship finally terminates?

A partnership arrangement may complicate a marketing partner's ability to switch technologies in the future or hamper its ability to collaborate with others in the same general area. For this reason the marketing partner may wish to preserve its rights to acquire or develop products or technologies that compete with those of the partnership. This can be a very sensitive issue but one that can be worked out in numerous ways.

### The Distribution Agreement

The most significant question to be resolved in this agreement is, whose market is it? Clear definitions must be established for the boundaries of the various market segments within which the partnership's products and technologies will be distributed.

The smaller company almost invariably has as a significant corporate goal the establishment of its own name and reputation in at least certain segments of the market. The large partner's primary goal is usually defending and strengthening its market position by leveraging its partner's skills in new-product development.

Strategic partnerships work best when the partners' primary target markets do not overlap. The closer the two partners are to being competitors, the more difficult this issue is to resolve.

Another important issue to be resolved is whether or not minimum annual purchase requirements are appropriate in the arrangement. While the larger partner (generally the marketing partner) may have contributed substantial financial support to fund the product, the smaller partner frequently also insists on minimum annual purchase requirements to assure itself of a certain level of cash flow and of a reasonable selling effort by the marketing partner.

Frequently, negotiating a specific level of effort and financial commitment for the marketing of the products over a specific time period is preferable to trying to establish minimums where a wide difference of opinion exists. And rather than haggle over the size and nature of minimums, the partners might be far better off enhancing what natural incentives exist for the sales force to aggressively move the partnership's products into the marketplace. Clearly defined and quantified marketing support and incentive measures agreed to initially may serve the partnership far better than "horse-traded" minimums.

## SOME SPECIAL ASPECTS OF CORPORATE VENTURING

Corporate venturing exists when the equity investment itself rather than a specific collaborative business relationship becomes the primary goal of the transaction. Such efforts to spawn new businesses or to identify new growth opportunities or windows on new technologies have enjoyed a mixed track record.

One reason often cited for this mixed outcome is that few corporations have been able to attract and hold successful venture capital managers. Corporations simply lack a sufficiently flexible compensation structure to provide rewards truly tied to the success of the investments. The rewards offered by investment banking and venture capital firms provide a greater attraction for those most skilled in finding and nurturing successful ventures, while corporate management staffs generally have to labor under a variety of constraints venture managers would rather avoid.

Another reason cited for underrealization of corporate venturing potential is failure to establish an effective "gatekeeper" function. The gatekeeper is the corporate person or agent responsible for monitoring what goes on within the investee company relative to the needs, desires, and strengths of the investor corporation. Subject to strict and often complex confidentiality arrangements, the gatekeeper must bring together those people within the investor corporation and those in the investee company who can benefit from an exchange of information about opportunities and technology. To be successful, technology must be carried through and be exchanged and used by individuals or groups that respect each other's capabilities and understand what each is trying to accomplish.

To improve the returns from corporate venture investments, a growing number of corporations are investing in professionally managed venture capital funds. These funds are highly motivated to select and manage ventures that will succeed financially, and generally permit a high level of visibility to their corporate investors interested in following new trends in their industry.

In the end, the success of a corporation's venture investing depends on the clarity and consistency of its goals and expectations and how these get translated into the organization and compensation structures assembled to achieve them.

## HOW TO FIND POTENTIAL PARTNERING CANDIDATES AND VENTURE INVESTMENTS

The sources of potential candidates for partnering and investment are many and varied, but the most attractive partnering candidates can often be found within present supply arrangements, licensing arrangements, or other outside collaborative efforts. Both potential partners may even be working with researchers from the same university on related projects.

Numerous independent consultants specialize in particular industries and can assist in the process of defining goals, establishing criteria, identifying and screening potential candidates, and bringing the parties to the table.

Less obvious and frequently less effective sources can be industry and association directories. These are best used in consultation with knowledgeable leaders in the industry, since the newest and potentially most important candidates may not yet be listed or may be in another industry.

A good source for finding novel efforts in certain areas is the Small Business Administration's listing of groups receiving SBIR grants for the development of particular products or technologies. This and other government agencies routinely fund research projects in the private sector, and their rules often aid in partnering in that small companies receiving initial grants may have to demonstrate the ability to get products to market before they can receive later-stage and generally larger grants.

Regardless of the origin of the relationship or structure of the deal, the most important determinants of success have been found to be the personal chemistry and quality of communication among the operating leadership of the projects and the compatibility of the strategic goals of the partners. Even the earliest searching and screening efforts should take these dynamics into account.

# SECTION II

# Legal and Regulatory Matters

## INTRODUCTION

The legal documents that transfer the ownership of a corporation in an acquisition or merger transaction are necessarily complex in our society. Nevertheless, the success of a transaction may rest on how well the acquiring CEO understands the provisions of those agreements and their implications.

As Dewey B. Crawford explains in the lead-off chapter of this section, much of the in-depth due diligence process is dependent on the representations, warranties, and disclosures required from the seller under the purchase agreement. Granted, much of the arcane language, the legalese that attorneys routinely rely upon for communication, relates to matters that need not be of concern to the CEO. The company retains a qualified expert to represent it regarding those issues. However, numerous pure business issues must be negotiated and memorialized in the agreement. Senior management must understand those.

Special legal and regulatory concerns are added when securities of either the acquirer or the company being acquired are held by the public. Rory B. Riggs, W. Peter Slusser, and Eve D. Durra present some of the tactical alternatives in acquiring and merging public companies in the second chapter of this section. The sequence of events and choice of structure in such acquisitions largely are guided by applicable law and regulation.

In the section's third chapter, Stephen M. Banker and C. Robert Barker continue the discussion of the legal and regulatory constraints and advantages that accompany proposed business combinations between companies when at least one of them has publicly held securities.

All sizable acquisitions are subject to antitrust law and practice. In the final chapter of this section, Michael N. Sohn provides insights into how antitrust laws affect mergers and acquisitions and how the Department of Justice currently administers those laws.

# CHAPTER 5

# THE ACQUISITION AGREEMENT

## Dewey B. Crawford
**GARDNER, CARTON & DOUGLAS**

Negotiating an agreement for an acquisition can be a long and complicated task. Each step along the way, the parties involved must work together to insure that by preserving their own best interests they are preserving the best interests of both.

The acquisition agreement is the formal, legal version of the sum of all discussions business people have had about an acquisition; it is the articulation of the often oversimplified ideas of the parties as to the terms of the transaction. Business people experienced in this area recognize that an incredibly large number of points must be addressed, even after the handshake stage has been reached; and newcomers to the acquisition arena are often startled by the complexities of working out the formal acquisition agreement. The agreement is intended to answer in advance questions that might otherwise be subject to confusion, differing interpretations, dispute, and, ultimately, litigation. In its purest form, it accurately and unambiguously sets forth all of the rights and obligations of the parties.

The four most critical features of this agreement are representations and warranties, covenants, conditions precedent to closing the acquisition, and indemnification. Most of the discussion in this chapter will focus on those features. While other provisions of an agreement are also important, a failure by the parties and their counsel to fully understand and appreciate the interplay of these four provisions has, in my experience, caused more failures of transactions that could have been forthcoming and more undue acrimony between parties in an acquisition than any other factor. Not surprisingly, these are also the issues on which a CEO should focus in a proposed acquisition transaction. Together, they assure that the acquirer has sufficient information to make informed judgments and that the information is correct, and they determine which party shall suffer the adverse consequences of liabilities unknown or indeterminable at the time of closing.

## THE AGREEMENT IN PRINCIPLE

If the acquisition agreement represents the culmination of an acquisition, the start of negotiations is marked by an agreement in principle, often called a letter of intent or memorandum of understanding. Although the letter of intent sets forth little more than a brief sketch of the principal points of agreement, it can serve three useful purposes:

1. Although typically not legally binding, the letter of intent does represent a moral obligation that is normally taken very seriously by the parties.

2. The letter of intent memorializes the basic terms of the transaction, which helps avoid subsequent misunderstandings, both intentional and unintentional.

3. The letter of intent can form the basis of a filing under the Hart-Scott-Rodino Antitrust Improvement Act of 1986 (see Chapter 8 for a more complete discussion of antitrust) and begin the waiting period under that law while the parties negotiate the definitive acquisition agreement.

Good reasons exist for not having a letter of intent. The parties may not wish to make the public announcement that generally is required of public companies when a meeting of the minds occurs. Or the seller may be negotiating with other parties and may not wish to announce a deal and put off other suitors. If important open points remain, a letter of intent may weaken one party's bargaining position. Finally, a great deal of energy can be wasted in negotiating an agreement in principle that might be better spent negotiating the definitive agreement.

Generally, the agreement in principle is in the form of a letter addressed to the seller, or the seller's stockholders if they are to be the parties to the transaction, signed by the purchaser, and countersigned by the seller if it is to the stockholders. It normally is not intended to be legally binding, although portions of the letter, such as an agreement not to negotiate with others or to maintain confidentiality, may be binding.

A letter of intent should cover the following points:

- A description of the form of transaction—merger, stock purchase, or asset purchase—if known at the time of signing.
- Details of consideration for the purchase. If stock is to be used, the ratio or other method of valuation should be set forth. If other securities are to be used, basic terms should be described. Essential terms of contingent or deferred payment are also included.
- Significant protective provisions, such as an escrow or pledge. An escrow is an arrangement whereby a portion of the purchase price is placed in the hands of a third party to be held for a fixed period. If breaches of representations or warranties are discovered after the closing, all or a portion of these funds are returned to the purchaser; the balance goes to the seller. If the purchaser is issuing a promissory note as part of the consideration, the seller may want all or a portion of the assets or stocks acquired by the purchaser to be pledged as security for the note's payment.
- Special arrangements, such as employment contracts with the seller's directors, officers, or employees.
- Brokers' and finders' fees.
- An outline of any registration rights if stock is to be used. Registration rights are the contractual rights of the holders of unrestricted stock (stock that has not been registered under the Securities Act of 1933) to have such stock registered under the Securities Act so that such stock may be freely sold or transferred.
- Any restrictions on the seller's business pending the closing and any permitted dividends or dispositions of assets.

- A no-shop clause that commits the seller not to solicit other offers or provide information to or negotiate with other interested
  parties.

- A bust-up fee to be paid to the purchaser in the event the seller
  is acquired by a third party.

- Finally, the major conditions to consummation of the transaction, such as (1) execution of a definitive agreement containing
  representation, warranties, covenants, conditions, and indem-
  nifications appropriate to such a transaction, and (2) any other
  particular conditions that have been discussed, such as tax rulings, earnings, off balance sheet conditions, or consents of third
  parties that need to be ironed out before serious negotiations
  on the final agreement can take place.

## STRUCTURE OF THE ACQUISITION AGREEMENT

Most acquisition agreements are similar in structure and share a
number of principal features, including the following:

- The operative terms of the transaction, which include identification of the assets or stock to be acquired, the consideration to
  be paid, and the mechanics of the transaction.

- Other ancillary or related terms of the principal transaction, such
  as earn-out or financing provisions. An earn-out provision is a
  provision calling for future payment by the purchaser of additional consideration in the event certain contingencies are met,
  such as the acquired business's attaining designated levels of earnings. A financing provision is one that makes clear that the purchaser's ability to pay for the seller's business is subject to its ability
  to obtain financing from a third party, and defining the parameters of such financing.

- The seller's representations and warranties.

- The purchaser's representations and warranties.

- The seller's covenants pending the closing.

- The purchaser's covenants pending the closing.

- Conditions to be met by the seller in order to close.

- Conditions to be met by the purchaser in order to close.
- Closing and termination provisions.
- Indemnification provisions.
- Miscellaneous matters, such as finders' fees, expenses, and particular laws governing the transaction.

The discussion of representations and warranties, covenants, conditions precedent to closing, and indemnification presented in this chapter addresses the agreement from the purchaser's point of view and assumes that there will be a deferred closing—one in which the transfer of assets or stock and payment of the consideration occur only after a lapse of time following execution of the acquisition agreement. Except in the smallest of acquisitions, a deferred closing is by far the rule. This is principally due to the need for one or both parties to take certain actions, such as making the proper filings under Hart-Scott-Rodino, or to obtain third-party consents, or to allow for the requisite passage of time under applicable laws. A simultaneous signing and closing is easier in many respects, since there is no need to address changes or events that may occur between signing and closing, the seller's consent of the business pending the closing, and similar concerns of the purchaser.

The representations and warranties and the provisions for indemnification are usually the most troublesome to the seller, and involve the heaviest negotiations. The covenants and closing conditions, although normally not the subject of extensive negotiations, interrelate with the other provisions and must be considered in any discussion of the flow of an acquisition agreement.

## REPRESENTATIONS AND WARRANTIES

The representations and warranties serve three important functions:

1. They are informational. Prior to execution of the definitive acquisition agreement, they provide the means by which the purchaser is able to learn as much as possible about the seller's business.

2. They are protective. Between signing and closing, they provide a mechanism for the purchaser to walk away from the transaction if adverse facts are discovered.

**3.** They are supportive. They provide the framework for the seller's indemnification of the purchaser following the closing.

Although some practitioners and commentators make legal distinctions between representations and warranties, the common practice is to use them interchangeably.

The seller's representations and warranties normally account for the largest part of the acquisition agreement. Their scope and number are limited only by the seller's negotiating ability and the purchaser's attorney's imagination. However, the most common and most important representations and warranties fall into a few broad categories, including financial statements, assets, contracts, employee matters, litigation, and corporate organization.

The informational aspect of representations is served by forcing the seller to formally impart important information about its business to the purchaser to a degree and in a manner it probably has never before attempted. Not only does this help educate the purchaser, but also, through the focus of the representations, it may alert the purchaser to troublesome areas requiring a more detailed investigation.

The definitive investigation by the purchaser of the seller's business normally occurs after execution of the definitive agreement, although some preliminary investigation is usually made.

A standard condition of the purchaser's obligation to consummate the acquisition is that the seller must restate its representations as true at the closing. If adverse facts are discovered in the detailed investigation, the seller will be unable to reaffirm its representations at closing and the purchaser will have an out under the agreement. This is the protective aspect of representations and warranties.

If, notwithstanding the purchaser's detailed investigation, it develops after the closing that a representation was untrue or materially inaccurate, the normal indemnification by the seller gives the purchaser an indemnifiable claim—a claim that the seller will have to compensate the purchaser for—supported by this breach of a representation.

The information about the seller and its business generated by the representations is normally provided through the use of schedules and lists, the so-called disclosure schedule. For example, the seller typically represents that it has no real property, except for the property listed on the disclosure schedule. The representation then goes on to confirm that the disclosure schedule contains a description of the buildings and other improvements on the property and a legal description of the property, and that there are no liens or defects in the seller's title except as disclosed on the disclosure schedule.

The representations are the skeleton. The disclosure schedule, which appears as an appendix to the agreement, is the flesh. This streamlines the actual agreement. Additionally, if the seller is a public company it often tries to disclose information only in the disclosure schedule so it can keep the information out of subsequent proxy statements.

Preparation of disclosure schedules can be very intimidating to the seller and often creates friction between buyer and seller. However, because of the importance of disclosure schedules in protecting the purchaser, considerable care must be exercised before the purchaser agrees to reduce or eliminate required disclosures.

The seller can be expected to raise the dual issues of materiality and knowledge in negotiating the representations and warranties—that is, the seller will want to limit disclosure to material items and then only to items of which it has knowledge. The CEO must have a clear view of how these terms may limit the company's ability to recover future damages.

In acquisitions of public companies it is fairly common to employ the term *material* in the representations and warranties, but it is much less common where a privately held company is being acquired. Public companies live with materiality concepts, while privately held companies do not, and private sellers are often uncomfortable with this potentially ambiguous term.

Where an objective standard of what is material can be established, the likelihood of misunderstandings or applications of different standards is minimized. Agreeing upon a dollar standard for materiality —for instance, contracts involving payments in excess of $25,000— may solve both sides' concerns. While the purchaser wants to learn everything it can about the seller, listing every contract and commitment may be truly burdensome to the seller and may merely bog down the purchaser. Establishing a dollar standard limits the seller's disclosure to items that are truly material and may make the purchaser's analysis easier as well. On the other hand, it may be important for the purchaser to learn about every item of litigation, not just those that are material, and thus no materiality standard should be established for these items.

A knowledge qualification involves somewhat different problems. It is easy initially to be sympathetic to the seller in wanting to disclose only those things of which it has knowledge. However, if a major claim exists but is unknown to the seller, the purchaser will not want to be stuck with the risks associated with that claim. Responsibility is the essential ingredient in determining whether a knowledge qualification is appropriate. A knowledge qualification shifts responsibility from the seller to the purchaser.

### Financial Statements

The single most important representation covers the seller's financial statements. If the purchaser were limited to one representation, this is the one its counsel would recommend holding out for. The financial statements provide the most comprehensive picture of the seller's business and, when coupled with the representation, provide an excellent framework for the three functions served by representations.

The representation typically is to the effect that the seller has provided the purchaser with financial statements as of certain dates and for particular periods, some or all of which have been prepared in accordance with GAAP, and that they fairly present the seller's financial condition as of the dates of the balance sheets, and the results of the seller's operations for the periods covered by the income statements.

To bridge the gap between the date of the balance sheet and the date of execution of the acquisition agreement, there usually is a representation either that no material adverse change has occurred in the seller's operations or financial condition or that, except as set forth in the disclosure schedule, no events of certain kinds—such as losses, dividends, and asset dispositions—have occurred since the date of the most recent financial statements.

A representation is usually made that the seller has no liabilities except those reflected or reserved against in the balance sheet or as set forth in the disclosure schedule, and that since the date of the balance sheet the seller has incurred no liabilities other than in the ordinary course and consistent with past practices.

It is normal for there to be a representation that the seller has filed all required tax returns and paid all taxes due, and that adequate tax reserves are reflected in the balance sheet.

### Assets

Representations normally cover the seller's various assets: real property, machinery and equipment, patents, trademarks, trade names, and other intangibles. These representations relate to title to the assets, their condition, and similar matters.

### Leases, Contracts, and Commitments

These representations disclose leases, contracts, and commitments, with enough descriptive material to enable the purchaser to determine how much effort to spend on examining the actual documents. There also is a representation that the leases and contracts are in full force and effect and that no party to them is in default.

### Employee Matters

These representations cover employee benefit plans, compensation, employment contracts, collective bargaining agreements, and similar matters. Representations regarding employee benefit plans and their funding and compliance with the Employee Retirement Income Security Act of 1974 (ERISA) can run several pages.

### Litigation and Compliance with Laws

Invariably, the acquisition agreement contains representations concerning the seller's existing or threatened litigation, compliance with laws, and absence of defaults under other agreements, and guaranteeing that the transactions contemplated by the acquisition agreement will not result in a breach or default under any applicable laws or regulations or under any agreements. Because of the significant dollar amounts that can be involved, compliance with environmental laws and regulations is addressed specifically and at great length.

### Corporate Organization and Capitalization

Representations are made concerning the organization of the seller and its subsidiaries; capitalization, including outstanding capital stock and ownership of subsidiaries' capital stock; the seller's corporate powers and authorization; and approval of the acquisition agreement and transactions contemplated by the acquisition agreement.

### Other Representations

In addition to these standard representations, other representations usually cover a variety of other matters dictated by the particular transaction and the special concerns of the purchaser and its counsel. These items range from the location of bank accounts to a guarantee that there are no misstatements or omissions in the seller's proxy statement.

If the seller is walking away from the transaction with cash, the seller's concerns are narrowly focused on the purchaser's ability to pay, and the purchaser's representations need only cover corporate authorization and the ability to consummate the transaction—the purchaser's financial condition. If a continuing relationship is contemplated because the purchaser will be issuing securities, or a contingent or delayed payout is involved, the seller will want representations of greater scope, covering the purchaser's financial statements, published filings with the SEC, and any items of particular concern.

Unless the purchaser and seller are of comparable size, the number and extent of the seller's representations and warranties normally far exceeds those of the purchaser. The seller should only be concerned with the purchaser's authorization of the transaction and its power and ability to perform, whereas the purchaser is concerned with all aspects of the seller and its business.

## COVENANTS

Covenants cover the period between signing and closing, and consist of (1) negative covenants, which restrict the seller from taking certain actions without the purchaser's consent, and (2) affirmative covenants, which obligate one or both parties to take certain actions prior to closing.

Negative covenants are intended to protect the purchaser against the seller's taking actions that will change the nature of what the purchaser expects to acquire at the closing. The purchaser normally does not want the seller to take cash out of its business through dividends, bonuses, or otherwise; increase its debt; increase salaries; or enter into substantial commitments.

The number and breadth of negative covenants depends in part on the purchaser's level of comfort with the seller. It may be that a simple covenant to the effect that the seller will operate its business only in the ordinary course consistent with past practice will suffice. Or the purchaser may wish to cover every conceivable act. Such provisions would include all or some of the following:

- Not to change accounting methods or practices
- Not to enter into transactions not in the ordinary course of business
- Not to amend the charter or bylaws
- Not to change the capitalization or issue, or agree to isssue any new shares of capital stock
- Not to make dividends or distributions on or to repurchase any shares of capital stock
- Not to enter into contracts or commitments in excess of a certain amount, or extending beyond a relatively short period
- Not to terminate or modify leases or contracts
- Not to make any capital expenditures
- Not to transfer property outside of the ordinary course of business
- Not to make loans to directors, officers, or employees
- Not to release claims or waive rights
- Not to discharge liens or prepay debts
- Not to do, or to refrain from doing, anything that would cause the seller's representations to be untrue

If the purchaser will be issuing securities in the acquisition, there may be similar negative covenants against it, although typically these covenants go only to changes that would materially change or affect the securities to be issued or their value.

The affirmative covenants cover those things that must be done in order for the closing to take place, and frequently obligate both the seller and the purchaser. For example, if Hart-Scott-Rodino applies, each party must prepare and make the requisite filings.

Other typical affirmative covenants obligating the seller include the following:

- To allow the purchaser full access to the seller's books, records, and properties for purposes of evaluation and inspection
- To call and hold a meeting of stockholders if required and to use the seller's best efforts to obtain approval
- To make any required filings with governmental agencies and obtain any consents required of governmental agencies or third parties

Anything required of the purchaser is similarly covered by affirmative covenants.

Covenants are normally absolute, and should be if a matter is within a party's sole control. But the seller or its counsel may be fearful of a damage claim in the event that circumstances outside its control keep it from fulfilling the promise. This fear is addressed by inserting in the covenants a best-efforts qualification—the understanding that the seller will use its best efforts to achieve the stated objective. Some covenants contain aspects of both absolute obligation and the best-efforts qualification.

## CONDITIONS OF CLOSING

Conditions of closing must be fulfilled by the obligated party or parties—or by a third party, the occurrence of an event, or the passage of time—in order to legally obligate the other party to close. Such conditions may be waived, in which case the waiving party can require the other party to close.

Closing conditions enjoy a greater symmetry than other areas of the acquisition agreement, although many conditions are designed solely for one party's benefit. With certain exceptions, most closing conditions do not generate much negotiation.

The first condition in every agreement is that the representations and warranties are true at the closing as if made at the closing and that all of the covenants and agreements required to be performed at or prior to the closing have indeed been performed. This is confirmed by each party's delivering to the other a certificate to this effect. Receipt by each party of an opinion of the other's counsel covering various matters is standard in all but the smallest of acquisitions.

Other common symmetrical conditions include expiration of the waiting period under Hart-Scott-Rodino, absence of litigation challenging or threatening the acquisition, stockholder approval, listing on a stock exchange of the shares to be issued, and securities registration statements becoming effective. The need for the obligations of both the purchaser and the seller to be conditioned upon stockholder approval, stock exchange listing, and registration statements becoming effective may not be entirely clear, but must be explored carefully.

In each instance, if the condition is not satisfied, not only does one party fail to receive a bargained-for benefit, but the other party incurs a legal detriment if it is forced to proceed. For instance, if the approval of the seller's stockholders is not obtained, the seller is violating corporate law if it proceeds with a closing. If the shares to be issued are not listed on an exchange, not only is the seller not getting the benefit of its bargain, but also the purchaser may be violating its listing agreement with the exchange if it proceeds. And if securities are issued without an effective registration statement, the seller will not simply fail to receive securities registered under the Securities Act, but also will be violating that act.

Other typical conditions are as follows:

- Approval of regulatory authorities
- Receipt of third-party consents
- Receipt of favorable tax rulings
- Receipt of certain financial statements and possibly the achievement of a certain level of earnings or net worth
- Settlement of litigation

- Signing of employment or noncompete agreements by key employees
- Resignation of various officers and directors
- Any other occurrences deemed important to one party or the other

The interplay between the covenants and conditions needs to be considered. One might ask, If an item is specified as a condition of closing, why include it as a covenant as well, or vice versa?

Consider the need for the seller's stockholders to approve the acquisition. If receipt of such approval is made a condition of the purchaser's obligation to close, is the purchaser not adequately protected? But what if a seller gets cold feet in such a situation? Without a covenant, the seller has no obligation to call a stockholders' meeting or to attempt to get such approval. The converse, using a covenant but not a condition, does not work here, since the seller could not legally proceed without stockholder approval.

But consider a situation in which the seller must obtain a third party's consent to the acquisition. The purchaser may feel that the acquisition is so good that it is prepared to proceed without the consent. Including a covenant presumably will assure that the seller will make reasonable attempts to obtain the consent. Also including a condition may make the seller feel additional pressure to obtain the consent. Moreover, if only a covenant is included, the purchaser's only remedy may be monetary damages. But if a condition is also included, the purchaser will be able to walk away from the transaction and, equally important, will have leverage to renegotiate the provision, the price, or the entire transaction.

One last closing item is the date of the closing itself. If all aspects of the acquisition were predictable, the parties could simply insert a date and leave it at that. But any number of things can cause delays. Sometimes the agreement provides that the closing will occur a certain number of days after the last condition is met. But without also specifying an absolute date, this approach provides no time frame in which the acquisition is to occur.

A good approach is to set a target date and then provide that if a condition is not met, the party unable to meet the condition may postpone the closing until it is met, but in no event may postpone it until later than a specified date. If the specified date arrives and the closing is not held, either party may elect to terminate the agreement.

## INDEMNIFICATION

To this point, the discussion has focused only on aspects of the agreement leading up to closing. After closing, a number of occurrences could cause damage or expense to the purchaser. The acquisition agreement must have provisions in it that entitle the purchaser to be indemnified by the seller or its stockholders against such damage and expenses.

Indemnification provisions are unusual in an agreement for the acquisition of publicly owned companies, except where there are one or a few major stockholders from whom it may be sought. Accordingly, this discussion assumes the acquisition of a privately held company.

### Items Covered

Indemnification provisions normally address damages incurred by the purchaser resulting from either (1) a breach of a covenant or a misrepresentation by the seller that is discovered after closing, or (2) an allocation of responsibilities between the parties in the acquisition agreement.

The indemnity provisions typically begin by providing that the representations and warranties survive the closing and any investigation by the purchaser, and that the disclosure schedule and any other documents or written statements furnished by the seller to the purchaser are deemed to be representations. Then the items covered are set forth. Losses or expenses incurred as a result of a misrepresentation or breach of a covenant or agreement are invariably included. The typical harm likely to occur is that the purchaser may not receive an asset or its value may be less than represented, or that the purchaser may incur liabilities to a third party that were not disclosed or are in amounts greater than disclosed.

The impact of the knowledge and materiality qualifications with the representations and warranties become much clearer in the context of indemnification. With a knowledge qualification, the purchaser not only must show that the factual representation was not correct but also that the seller knew or should have known that it was not correct. If there is a materiality qualification, the purchaser must also establish that the inaccuracy or misrepresentation was material. As each of these qualifications is introduced, the purchaser's burden becomes increasingly difficult.

Another category of items is often covered by an indemnity. The most common are items disclosed in the representations or disclosure schedule that remain the seller's obligation. These involve an allocation of responsibilities. One often covered is pending litigation, where the outcome may be uncertain or the amount of ultimate damages is difficult to predict. Rather than factor the outcome into the purchase price, it may be easier to simply make it the seller's responsibility. The parties rarely attempt to refine the concept of damages, leaving it to be resolved at the time a claim arises.

It is also common to cover matters arising from the transaction itself, such as transfer taxes, bulk-sales liability, and similar items.

Finally, in some instances the purchaser will want protection beyond guarantees of the fair presentation of a balance sheet or the ability of a seller to warrant. Taxes are the most frequent subject of this type of indemnity, particularly if the purchaser is aware that the seller has been very aggressive with its tax returns. In this instance, it is common for the purchaser to insist on tax indemnity covering any and all taxes assessed to the extent that they exceed the reserve allocated on the seller's balance sheet.

## Common Points of Negotiation

The indemnification provisions are usually the subject of heavy negotiations, and the seller and its attorney can be expected to challenge the scope of the indemnity.

The seller may seek a "basket provision," a clause that provides the purchaser indemnification of damages only if they exceed a certain amount. Although most indemnification provisions contain a basket, rarely does the purchaser offer it in the first instance. There is no fixed rule as to the amount, which varies depending on the size of the deal. The agreement normally provides that the seller has no liability to the purchaser for any claim until the aggregate of all claims exceeds the basket, and then the seller is liable only for the excess. Any number of variations exist.

A second avenue of relief that may be pursued by the seller is a cutoff date beyond which the purchaser cannot assert claims. Most purchasers will agree in principle with the seller's desire for this kind of certainty and peace of mind. However, tax claims are normally left open until the expiration of the statute of limitations, and contingent liabilities such as litigation must be kept open until finally adjudicated. Practically speaking, the cutoff date will apply to claims arising from misrepresentations or breaches of covenants or agreements. The cutoff date should be based on the concept of a reasonable period of time within which the purchaser, through reasonable diligence, should have discovered the misrepresentations and breaches, and within which any third party will have made its demands. Three years seems to be the outside limit for a general cutoff, with earlier cutoffs often being tied to completion of the first audit of the seller by the purchaser's accountants.

Finally, the seller will likely seek an upper limit on liability. Although many commentators have suggested that this limitation is normally inappropriate, it nonetheless is quite common. If the transaction is clean, the purchaser probably risks little in putting a limit on the seller's total liability. While this argument can be turned against the seller, as the seller's actual exposure to liability is slight in a clean deal, if the principal owner is to continue working for the purchaser and is a critical part of the acquisition, his or her peace of mind may more than offset the additional risk the purchaser incurs through accepting an upper limit.

Two other arguments are often put forward by the seller. First, any indemnity should be reduced by the amount of any hidden assets of the seller that turn up or by the amount by which liabilities prove to be less than anticipated. This is rarely agreed to by the purchaser. A more troublesome argument is that the indemnity should be applied net of its tax effect. This frequently is agreed to by the purchaser, but the complications of attempting to apply it are great.

Second, the seller's counsel can be expected to insist that the seller have control of third-party proceedings if it is to be responsible for them. This seems fair and appears fairly innocent until some situations are considered where the purchaser would have good reason to want control even though the seller is responsible. Internal

Revenue Service claims that could affect future practices are a good example. Obtaining control may be desirable enough to the purchaser to warrant its giving up a portion of the indemnity.

## Provisions to Facilitate Claims Settlement

Indemnification may result in an empty victory if the purchaser is unable to collect from the seller. Suing the seller may not be the most desirable solution. To protect itself, the purchaser may provide for a deferred payment or a nonnegotiable note against which it can offset the amount of any claim of indemnity. By allowing the purchaser to offset amounts it owes the seller under the note by amounts it feels are due it under the indemnity, the note gives the purchaser direct access to the seller. The cautious purchaser—and its attorney—will write this into both the note and the indemnification provision, although the purchaser probably has this right anyway.

To protect the seller and again level the playing field, the seller's attorney will then insist that if the amount or the validity of the purchaser's indemnification claim is disputed by the seller, the purchaser must turn the note over to a third party pending resolution of the dispute. Once the dispute has been resolved or adjudicated, the third party will turn over such sum to the party determined to be entitled to it.

The best and probably fairest solution is to place a portion of the purchase price in an escrow account with a third party, which tends to equalize the bargaining position of the purchaser and seller. Not having the funds, the seller is forced to bargain with the purchaser. Because the purchaser is denied the use of the escrow fund pending resolution, it too is forced to bargain.

The principal issues surrounding an escrow are the size and duration. No formula exists, and without specific indemnity items to which dollar amounts can be fixed, most escrows range in size between 10 and 20 percent of the purchase price. Invariably, the seller will attempt to limit the purchaser's recourse to the escrow. If the purchaser is willing to consider this, it obviously should argue for a larger escrow.

The duration of the escrow also is strictly a matter of negotiation. It never exceeds the indemnification period and is often shorter, on the theory that its principal function is to protect against misrepresentations and claims arising soon after the closing.

Typically, the escrow provides that if no claims are pending at the scheduled termination, all funds in escrow will be distributed to the seller, but if claims are pending, the amount in dispute will remain in the escrow until resolution. If the amount and duration are difficult to resolve, one compromise may be to allow portions of the escrow to be released at various times along the way.

The escrow agent needs to be independent of the purchasing and selling parties. Banks are normally the first and best choice. Fees are normally split or paid by the purchaser. It is common for the escrow funds to be invested or deposited in an interest-bearing account.

Although often very complicated in their mechanics, escrows are fairly simple in substance. The purchaser gives written notice of a claim to the escrow agent and the seller, together with details. If the seller does not object within a specified period of time, the escrow agent pays to the purchaser the amount of the claim. If the seller objects within the specified period of time, the escrow agent continues to hold the funds until resolution.

# CHAPTER 6

# ACQUIRING A PUBLIC COMPANY

**W. Peter Slusser**
SLUSSER ASSOCIATES, INC.

**Rory B. Riggs**
**Eve D. Durra**
PAINEWEBBER, INC.

Because of the publicity and disclosures associated with acquiring a public company, such an acquisition has a certain glamour, but the lack of privacy brings with it both significant advantages and disadvantages. Neither the advantages nor the disadvantages are sufficient to control such a transaction if properly understood and handled. The issues generally are not terribly complex, but if mishandled can hurt an acquirer and increase costs.

## ADVANTAGES AND DISADVANTAGES

Among the advantages to acquiring a public company are that such a company has an established value, and that because of the regulatory framework set up to protect shareholders, most purchasers with the means can buy a part or all of the equity of a public company as long as there are shareholders willing to sell their stock.

In addition, because of the multitude of required public disclosures, one can gain easy access to a wealth of information about a particular company, which makes researching the potential acquisition easy. The various reports filed with the Securities and Exchange

Commission (SEC) disclose information concerning such areas as suppliers, competitors, customers, property holdings, and financial results. In addition to SEC disclosures, there are numerous independent reviews of a public company's performance and prospects. These reports provide useful, up-to-date coverage of events surrounding a company and often reveal information not readily discernible from data released by the company.

A further advantage of acquiring a public company is the flexibility a bidder has in the mode of acquisition. Since a public company has a sufficient number of shareholders to create a public market for its stock, an acquirer can offer registered securities with liquidity as part of the purchase price. The advantage of offering noncash consideration to shareholders is that if such securities are publicly traded, they are significantly easier to value and more readily accepted by the selling shareholder.

Alongside the advantages of acquiring a public company are a number of drawbacks. The most significant is that acquiring a public company may cost more in both time and money than acquiring a privately held company, principally because of the additional legal assistance needed and the time required to fulfill regulatory obligations.

The regulatory structure developed to protect shareholders sets up significant constraints to acquisition of a public company. To complete the acquisition of a public company, an acquirer has two basic choices:

- Merge subject to shareholder approval
- Acquire controlling interest through a tender offer

Of these two possibilities, a tender offer is the fastest maneuver to gain control of a company. However, a tender offer must be left open for a minimum of twenty business days and generally takes longer to complete than a merger. It is rare for either a friendly or hostile tender offer to receive sufficient shares in the time the offer is open. In addition, it is not unusual for other complications such as litigation to force an extension. The tender process is also expensive.

In the case of a merger, regulation requires that a preliminary proxy statement be filed with the SEC at least ten days prior to distribution to the target's shareholders. Under most circumstances, the SEC will review such a statement and request certain changes before it can go to shareholders. This can take anywhere from thirty to forty-five days. It generally takes a minimum of twenty days after proxy materials are sent before a shareholder vote can take place.

Besides the problems of timing and cost, there are also issues of disclosure. An offer will become a matter of public record if accepted by the target, or if the acquirer or target discloses the offer. Because of the increased awareness of their fiduciary responsibility on the part of directors of public companies, such offers generally are publicly disclosed.

Disclosure of a bid often attracts other bidders, presenting the possibility that the initial offer might put the company "in play." If that occurs, the resulting public auction increases the cost of the acquisition and frequently results in the original acquirer losing the acquisition to a "white knight" or other buyer, making a "bargain purchase" of a public company unlikely.

In buying a private company an acquirer has corporate laws and federal antitrust considerations to take into account, but is subject to none of the disclosure requirements or fiduciary responsibilities that come with dealing with a diverse group of public shareholders. Moreover, a private company need not entertain bidders until it is prepared to sell, whereas a public company, unless it has a control shareholder, is open to almost any bidder. It is their eminent approachability that sets acquisitions of public companies apart. The issue in dealing with a private company is first and foremost: Will the owners sell? The issues with a public company are significantly more complex.

## ISSUES TO CONSIDER

The issues start with the basic question of whether the target as currently valued is attractive and, if so, whether to buy shares prior to making an offer. In a public environment an acquirer can buy shares in the market and, to the extent these shares are priced less than an acquirer is willing to pay for the entire company, the acquirer should logically buy all the shares it can at the lowest price.

Often, before attempting to gain control of a public company, a bidder will purchase a substantial equity position in the target.

The advantages of buying shares prior to making an offer are obvious. First, to the extent shares are purchased at low prices, the total cost of a transaction will be lower. Second, if the acquirer is outbid in the process, the profit made on the lower-priced shares will defray the cost of attempting the acquisition. The primary disadvantage is that the act of buying shares is often considered hostile by the target's management and directors.

One of the most important strategic decisions a potential acquirer must make is how critical gaining the support of the target's management is. Because of disclosure requirements, even management-backed acquirers must be prepared to meet unsolicited bids.

The acquisition of a public company occurs in a dynamic environment. Not only are the legal considerations complex, but the applicable laws and regulations are changing every day. In addition, the diversity of financing methods currently available makes the potential universe of both acquisitions and acquirers extremely large.

Because of the dynamic conditions in public markets, independent advisors can provide valuable advice regarding the current state of the market and regulatory considerations. Two other common roles that can be performed only by certain financial professionals are:

- being dealer/manager of a tender offer, and
- writing a fairness opinion as to the value of an offer.

To execute a tender offer requires the necessary legal filings; it also requires that a registered broker/dealer manage the offer. Because one generally needs a broker/dealer who operates in all fifty states, the major securities houses are generally used. In addition, both the buyer and the seller may wish to have an independent advisor draft a fairness opinion. This opinion is done so that shareholders can have confidence that a knowledgeable third party agrees with management that the transaction is fair to the company's shareholders from a financial point of view. If a fairness opinion is requested, the shareholders may want a major securities firm to issue it since those firms have extensive experience in this area. Major Big Eight accounting firms and other professional valuation companies also issue such opinions. It is important to have the credibility required to ensure shareholders of independent objectivity.

## METHODS OF ACQUIRING CONTROL OF A PUBLIC COMPANY

A public company can be acquired in four general ways:

- Merger
- Tender offer or exchange offer
- Tender offer followed by a merger
- Proxy contest

The first three methods involve acquiring control of a company by purchasing all or substantially all of its shares. The fourth method implies acquiring control by aligning the company's other shareholders against management. The fourth is implicitly hostile (unsolicited) while the other three may be friendly or hostile.

Whether an acquisition is hostile or friendly does not change the regulatory guidelines for acquiring a company. The SEC believes in the "level playing field" doctrine. One disadvantage of a hostile offer is that if management wishes to fight the bid, the acquirer may be forced to buy shares without having an opportunity to conduct a due diligence examination before acquiring control.

Figure 6-1 shows the frequency with which each type of acquisition has been used in recent years.

### Merger

The merger following a shareholder vote is the most common way to acquire control of a public company. Only with a shareholder vote (or implicit shareholder approval through the tendering of shares) can management sell a public company. From the acquirer's point of view a merger agreement subject to a shareholder vote is probably the least complex and cheapest method of acquisition, for several reasons.

First, it gives the target's shareholders the best view of the transaction. Second, it allows the acquirer more time to conduct due

**FIGURE 6-1  Summary of types of public acquisitions made between 1981 and 1987**

(Source: PaineWebber's Merger and Acquisition Database)

| Securities Offered | Type of Acquisition | | | |
| --- | --- | --- | --- | --- |
| | Merger | Tender Offer | Tender Offer Followed by Merger | Total |
| Cash | 35% | 14% | 10% | 59% |
| Cash and Securities | 15% | – | 5% | 20% |
| Securities | 20% | 1% | – | 21% |
| Total | 70% | 15% | 15% | 100% |

diligence. Third, the expense of drafting a merger proxy statement and mailing it to shareholders is usually less than that of drafting an offer to purchase, tendering for shares, and drafting a "back-end" merger statement. Also, the acquirer gains the benefit of getting the earnings of the company during this period and funding the acquisition at a later date.

Moreover, in industries where regulatory approval is required, a merger is almost always used because gaining approval from the appropriate government agency generally takes longer than achieving shareholder approval, making the expense of a tender offer unnecessary. The savings and loan industry is a good example of an industry where such regulatory delays occur.

The disadvantage of a merger is that it can take significantly longer than a tender offer. This may not be important if the acquirer already owns or controls enough shares to assure a favorable vote or if approval from agencies other than the SEC is necessary. However, if there is a real threat that another bidder may surface, the time required to file, receive approval, and mail a proxy statement may present a risk.

The benefits an acquirer gains from electing a merger followed by a shareholder vote exposes the acquirer to the risk of losing the target company to others because of the length of time required to complete the transaction. Assessing the trade-off is a critical strategic decision.

Following is the timetable for a merger.

| | Cash | Stock |
|---|---|---|
| Preliminary | Begin due diligence investigation | Same as for cash |
| | Make open market or negotiated purchases | |
| | Negotiate lock-up agreements with key stockholders | |
| | Arrange financing | |
| | Prepare registration statement and proxy materials | |
| Day 1 | Contact target | Same as for cash |
| Day 2 | Begin further due diligence investigation | Same as for cash |
| | Begin further negotiations with target* | |
| Day 7 | Execute merger agreement | Same as for cash, plus: |
| | Execute lock-up agreements with target and/or stockholders | Begin blue sky survey |
| | Issue press release | |
| | Engage proxy solicitors | |
| Day 12 | Target files proxy materials with SEC | Same as for cash, plus: Bidder files proxy materials with SEC |
| | File Hart-Scott-Rodino notice with FTC | File registration statement with SEC |
| | | Mail blue sky applications, exemptions, and notices |
| | | File listing application with appropriate stock exchange |
| Day 17 | File Schedule 13D with SEC (if lock-up agreements cover 5 percent of shares) | Same as for cash |
| | File Form 3 with SEC (if lock-up agreements cover 10 percent of shares) | |
| Day 42 | Hart-Scott-Rodino waiting period expires (unless second request) | Target and bidder proxy materials cleared by SEC** |
| | | Registration statement declared effective by SEC** |

*May take more time than allotted.
**May take more or less time depending on SEC review.

Continued

|  | *Cash* | *Stock* |
|---|---|---|
| Day 42, (*Cont'd*) |  | Receive all blue sky clearances |
|  |  | Receive authorization of listing on stock exchange |
| Day 54 | Target proxy materials cleared by SEC** | Target and bidder mail proxy materials |
|  |  | Final prospectus mailed with proxy materials |
| Day 55 | Target mails proxy materials |  |
| Day 75 | Target stockholder meeting to approve merger | Target and bidder stockholder meetings to approve transaction |
| Day 76 | File short-form certificate of merger with secretary of state | Same as for cash |
|  | Issue press release |  |
| Day 78 | Begin to pay for shares | Same as for cash |
| Postmerger | File Form 8-K for bidder with SEC | Same as for cash |
|  | Delist target stock |  |
|  | Deregister target with SEC |  |
|  | Postmerger filings and approvals |  |

**May take more or less time depending on SEC review.

## Tender Offer

A tender offer tends to have the most drama in the merger and acquisition business. The basic risk of being a public company is the fact that within the confines of the law, any person or company can go directly to a company's shareholders and offer to buy their shares.

Tender offers give shareholders a means to "vote" without a formal proxy. If enough shareholders are willing to sell—or tender—their shares at a certain price, a formal shareholder vote is not necessary. Avoiding a shareholder vote is important in an all-cash transaction or a transaction where the cash component is large enough to acquire a controlling interest. If an acquirer has been able to execute a merger agreement, it is important to do everything in its power to limit the potential risk of losing to another bidder.

A tender offer supported by the target is the fastest way to acquire control of a company. This technique is more expensive than a merger, but the added expense generally is not significant in relation to the total cost of an acquisition and the risk of losing the bid.

Since a tender offer does not require a formal proxy, an unsolicited offer may be made to shareholders without board approval of the target. If management will not entertain a bid, a tender offer, taking the bid directly to shareholders, can force management's attention and response.

Once a tender offer begins, management's ability to prevent or delay the acquisition is severely limited. If the bid is real, management must find some alternative means of getting shareholders comparable value. If management cannot find an alternative transaction and the hostile takeover prevails, the hostile bidder may eventually be able to negotiate the final bid with the target's management. Without the tender offer, a negotiated transaction would be much more difficult.

Once an unsolicited acquirer reaches an agreement it is unusual to request a shareholder vote. Waiting for a shareholder vote risks attracting another bidder and leaving control of the company in the old shareholder/management's control for a much longer time.

Following is the timetable for a cash tender offer.

|  | *Friendly* | *Hostile* |
|---|---|---|
| Preliminary | Begin due diligence investigation | Same as for friendly |
|  | Make open market or negotiated purchases |  |
|  | Negotiate lock-up agreements with key stockholders |  |
|  | Arrange financing |  |
|  | Prepare offer documents |  |
| Day 1 | Contact target | Same as for friendly |
| Day 2 | Begin further due diligence investigation | Commence offer |
|  | Begin negotiations with target | File Schedule 140-1 with SEC (copy to relevant stock exchanges and target) |

*Continued*

| | *Friendly* | *Hostile* |
|---|---|---|
| Day 2 (*Cont'd*) | | Request stockholder list from target* |
| | | File Hart-Scott-Rodino notice with FTC |
| | | Publish summary ad |
| Day 7 | Execute merger agreement | Target or bidder (at target's election) mails offer documents to target's stockholders |
| | Execute lock-up agreements with target and/or stockholders | |
| | Issue press release | |
| Day 12 | Commence offer | |
| | Mail offer documents to target stockholders | |
| | File Schedule 140-1/130 with SEC (copy to appropriate stock exchange and target) | |
| | File Hart-Scott-Rodino notice | |
| | Publish summary ad | |
| | Issue press release | |
| Day 17 | File Form 3 with SEC (if lock-up agreements cover 10 percent of shares) | Hart-Scott-Rodino waiting period expires (unless second request) |
| Day 27 | Hart-Scott-Rodino waiting period expires (unless second request) | |
| Day 28 | | Offer expires (unless extended)** |
| | | Accept tendered shares for payment |
| | | Issue press release |
| | | File 140-1 amendment with SEC |
| Day 29 | | Begin to pay for tendered shares |
| Day 31 | | File short-form merger certificate with secretary of state |
| | | Issue press release |

*Although the target is required by law to give the bidder its stockholder list, litigation may be necessary to obtain the list, causing delays in mailing offer documents.

**The litigation that is an inherent part of hostile bids may extend the offer. In addition, each new price will extend the offer for ten days.

*Continued*

|  | *Friendly* | *Hostile* |
|---|---|---|
| Day 38 | Offer expires (unless extended) | |
| | Accept tendered shares for payment | |
| | Issue press release | |
| | File 140-1 amendment with SEC | |
| Day 39 | Begin to pay for tendered shares | |
| Day 41 | File short-form merger certificate with secretary of state (if 90 percent of shares tendered) | |
| | Issue press release | |
| Postmerger | Mail Notice of Merger to remaining target stockholders | Same as for friendly |
| | Pay for remaining shares | |
| | File Form 8-K for bidder | |
| | Delist target stock | |
| | Deregister target with SEC | |
| | Postmerger filings and approvals | |

## Exchange Offer

An exchange offer works much like a tender offer, except that the acquirer offers securities to the selling shareholders rather than cash. Like a tender offer, an exchange offer can be taken directly to a company's shareholders. However, unlike a cash tender offer, the securities offered in an exchange offer must be registered with the SEC.

The time required to register securities for an exchange offer negates the time savings available through a tender offer. The time required for an exchange offer may, in fact, exceed the time required to complete a merger via a shareholder vote. Because the same result can be accomplished in the same time and less expensively through a direct shareholder vote, exchange offers are rarely used.

Following is the timetable for an exchange offer (common or convertible stock).

|  | *Friendly* | *Hostile* |
|---|---|---|
| Preliminary | Begin due diligence investigation | Same as for friendly |
| | Make open market or negotiated purchases | |

*Continued*

| | Friendly | Hostile |
|---|---|---|
| Preliminary (Cont'd) | Negotiate lock-up agreements with key stockholders | |
| | Arrange financing | |
| | Prepare offer documents | |
| | Prepare registration and proxy materials | |
| Day 1 | Contact target | Same as for friendly |
| Day 2 | Begin further due diligence investigation | Commence offer |
| | Begin negotiations with target | File Schedule 140-1 with SEC (copy to NYSE and target) |
| | | Request stockholder list from target* |
| | | File Hart-Scott-Rodino notice with FTC |
| | | Publish summary ad |
| | | Issue press release |
| | | Engage proxy solicitors |
| Day 7 | Execute merger agreement | Target or bidder (at target's election) mails offer documents to target's stockholders |
| | Execute lock-up agreements with target and/or stockholders | |
| | Issue press release | |
| | Engage proxy solicitors | Begin blue sky survey |
| Day 12 | Commence offer | File proxy materials with SEC |
| | Mail offer documents to target stockholders | File registration statement with SEC |
| | File Schedule 140-1/130 with SEC (copy to appropriate stock exchange and target) | File listing application with appropriate stock exchange |
| | File Hart-Scott-Rodino notice with FTC | |
| | Publish summary ad | Mail blue sky applications, exemptions and notices |
| | Issue press release | |
| | Begin blue sky survey | |

*Although the target is required by law to give the bidder its stockholder list, litigation may be necessary to obtain the list, causing delays in mailing offer documents.

*Continued*

|            | *Friendly*                                                      | *Hostile*                                             |
|------------|-----------------------------------------------------------------|-------------------------------------------------------|
| Day 17     | Hart-Scott-Rodino waiting period expires (unless second request) | Same schedule as Day 12 through Postmerger for friendly |
| Day 28     | Offer expires (unless extended)                                 |                                                       |
|            | Extend offer                                                    |                                                       |
|            | Issue press release                                             |                                                       |
|            | File Schedule 140-1 amendment with SEC                          |                                                       |
| Day 42     | Proxy materials declared effective by SEC**                     |                                                       |
|            | Registration statement declared effective by SEC**              |                                                       |
|            | Receive all blue sky clearances                                 |                                                       |
|            | Receive authorization of exchange listing                       |                                                       |
| Day 43     | Mail proxy materials to bidder's stockholders                   |                                                       |
|            | Mail final prospectus to target's stockholders                  |                                                       |
| Day 53     | Bidder stockholder meeting to approve transaction               |                                                       |
| Day 54     | Terminate offer                                                 |                                                       |
|            | Accept tendered shares for payment                              |                                                       |
|            | Issue press release                                             |                                                       |
|            | File 140-1 amendment with SEC                                   |                                                       |
| Day 55     | Begin to pay for tendered shares                                |                                                       |
| Day 57     | File short-form certificate of merger with secretary of state (if 90 percent of shares tendered)*** |         |
| Postmerger | Mail Notice of Merger to remaining target stockholders          |                                                       |
|            | Pay for remaining shares                                        |                                                       |
|            | File Form 8-K for bidder with SEC                               |                                                       |
|            | Delist target stock                                             |                                                       |
|            | Deregister target with SEC                                      |                                                       |
|            | Complete postmerger filings and approvals                       |                                                       |

**May take more or less time depending on SEC review.

***A long-form merger will take at least four weeks to complete, depending on SEC review of proxy material.

## Tender Offer Followed by a Merger

The fact that an exchange offer is an unattractive means to acquire a company on a hostile basis does not mean that an offer has to be all cash. The prevailing thought is that the cash component of an offer needs to be great enough to acquire control. The shares not purchased for cash can be acquired through an exchange of securities through a shareholder vote that the acquirer controls. In other words, the acquisition can be accomplished through a cash tender offer for a majority (over 50 percent) of the shares, followed by a merger by shareholder vote.

Typically, this structure is used either when the acquirer wants to use securities as part of the purchase consideration or when an insufficient number of shareholders tender their shares to complete the transaction through a tender offer.

The very real chance exists that not enough shares will be tendered to complete a merger. This may be due not to insufficient value, but to a lack of shareholder awareness. If enough shares are tendered the acquirer may control the company, but will be required to go to a shareholder vote to complete the acquisition.

This two-step structure enables the acquirer to use cash to acquire control and securities to complete the acquisition. As an example, assume the acquirer has agreed to purchase a target and pay shareholders cash for 51 percent of the shares, and stock in the acquirer for the balance. This transaction could be handled in two ways.

On the one hand, the target could conduct a shareholder vote, and if the transaction were approved, the target shareholders would exchange their shares for the cash and equity package being offered. On the other hand, the acquirer could make a tender offer for 51 percent of the target shareholders' shares and then call for a shareholder vote in which the remaining target shareholders would exchange their shares for the acquirer's shares.

Again, the advantage of the latter technique is timing. If the acquirer believes there is significant risk of a competing bid, this is a valid reason for structuring the acquisition as a two-step tender offer followed by a merger.

The last principal use of this structure is the hostile bid in which the acquirer wants to use securities as acquisition currency. It is possible to take an offer that includes securities directly to the shareholders. What is typically done is to make a cash bid or tender offer for a sufficient number of shares to gain control, followed by a merger vote in which securities are exchanged. Essentially, including a cash component large enough to control a company is typically the only way an unsolicited offer can display enough substance to be considered a valid and competitive bid.


## Proxy Contest

The proxy contest is a way to take control of a company without owning a majority of its voting stock. In its simplest form, a proxy contest occurs when a group of "dissident" shareholders (typically a noncontrolling group) attempts to elect a slate of directors who are not currently on the target's board of directors and are not supported by management.

The nomination and election process is carefully regulated by the SEC. The dissident shareholders must register their slate with the SEC through a proxy statement, and solicit proxies from other shareholders. At the same time, management solicits proxies for its own slate of directors.

Dissidents try to gain control of a board for several reasons.

The proxy contest can be a prelude to a change-of-control transaction. The contest in this case is used to remove an entrenched board. Given the current view of directors' liability, few directors will ignore a bona fide bid, but they can take a position that the hostile bid is "inadequate," supported by a concurring fairness opinion from an investment banker.

The proxy contest is still in use in transactions in which the management is entrenched and dissident shareholders want to effect a change in management in order to improve the value of their shares. Given the timing and expense of proxy contests, the potential increase in value for the dissident shareholders has to be significant to merit such action.

An area where proxy contests of this sort were very prevalent was the savings and loan industry in the early 1980s. At the time, many buyers were limited by regulations to owning less than 10 percent of a thrift institution. However, since these same thrifts were selling for a fraction of their book value, a common perception was that significant improvements could be achieved through a change of management.

Another area where proxy contests are beginning to emerge is in response to corporate "poison pill" bylaws or state statutes designed to inhibit unfriendly offers. By gaining control of a target's board, an acquirer can repeal such bylaws or comply with the applicable statutes to make the offer "friendly."

Recently, fueled in part by the contests involving savings and loans where management was not prepared, dissidents have been winning more frequently. However, the majority of proxy contests are still won by incumbents who have all the corporate tools at their disposal.

# CHAPTER 7

# SECURITIES LAWS AND OTHER REGULATIONS

**Stephen M. Banker**
**and C. Robert Barker**
SKADDEN, ARPS, SLATE, MEAGHER & FLOM

Legal considerations significantly affect the timing and structure of the acquisition of a publicly held corporation, and indeed whether a proposed acquisition is viable. An understanding of the fundamental legal concepts in acquisitions will assist management in determining whether to pursue any specific transaction.

The legal considerations in every acquisition are unique, primarily because of differences in jurisdiction of incorporation, whether the companies are publicly traded, the nature of the target's business and the structure and financing of the transaction. Experienced counsel should become familiar with both the acquirer and the target early in the process to identify applicable legal issues.

Most frequently, the acquirer will need to consider state corporate laws, which govern the mechanics of significant corporate transactions, and the Securities Exchange Act of 1934 (the Exchange Act), which regulates trading in the securities of public companies, tender offers, and proxy solicitations. The Securities Act of 1933 (the Securities Act) and state securities laws may also be important, especially if the consideration for the company being acquired includes securities, or will be financed with the issuance of securities. With a clear understanding of the legal framework, the acquirer and its advisors can determine the most efficient structure for the transaction.

The following discussion is necessarily limited in depth and scope. Among topics that space would not permit including are the timing and substance of public announcements and the legality of various strategies used by acquirers and targets in acquisitions, including poison pills, lock-ups, "no-shopping" agreements, greenmail, dual-stock plans, defensive restructurings, self-tender offers, and "shark repellants."

## STOCK PURCHASES

A significant or controlling interest in a public company can be obtained through a tender offer, negotiated block purchases, or an open-market purchase program. These techniques are the only unilateral means of acquiring a public company without the participation or consent of the target's board of directors. The speed with which stock purchases can be accomplished is a great tactical advantage, even in friendly transactions.

### Tender Offers

A tender offer can be described as a special form of stock purchase program characterized by a concerted effort to purchase a significant amount of stock from the public at a fixed price over a short period of time. Prior to adoption of the Williams Act in 1968, tender offers went largely unregulated. The Williams Act amended the Exchange Act to impose significant procedural requirements on all tender offers and other accumulations of stock.

**Disclosure Requirements.**   At the time the tender offer commences, the purchaser must file with the SEC and deliver to the target a Schedule 14D-1. The 14D-1 must identify the purchaser, its source of funds for the offer, and the purpose of the transaction. It must also provide a discussion of any negotiations with the target, and certain financial information relating to that company and the purchaser, if material.

Most important, the purchaser must disclose "such additional material information, if any, as may be necessary to make the required statements, in light of the circumstances under which they are made, not materially misleading." This requirement serves as the basis for including in the offering materials, material non-public information concerning the target. For instance, if in the course of negotiations the target furnishes earnings forecasts or describes a pending new business development, the purchaser may publicly disclose such information because it is, or may be deemed to be, material. Releasing such information would defuse any allegation that the offer was made on the basis of inside information.

**Procedural Requirements.**   Tender offers are subject to complex and highly technical rules, the effects of which must be taken into account in structuring a tender offer.

A tender offer commences at the time the offer is first published, sent, or given to stockholders. The target must facilitate the transmission of the offer; at its election the target must either mail the offering material to its stockholders or furnish to the offeror a list of its stockholders. If the offeror publicly announces the tender offer, within five business days the offeror must file its 14D-1 and mail the offer.

A tender offer must be open to all holders of a class of securities for which the offer is made, and must remain open for at least twenty business days. If the offer is amended to increase or decrease the percentage of stock sought or the consideration offered, the offer must remain open for at least ten days after the amendment. Where the number of shares tendered is greater than the number of shares sought, the shares must be purchased on a pro rata basis from all tendering stockholders.

Tendering stockholders may withdraw their tendered shares at any time while the offer is open. As a result, the purchaser may not purchase shares until the expiration of the offer. Since a higher competing bid could be made while the offer is pending, withdrawal rights provide a significant benefit to stockholders and a risk to the offeror.

## Unconventional Tender Offers

If an acquirer determines that open-market purchases are strategically and economically superior to a tender offer, it must structure its buying program to avoid the tender offer rules. This task is complicated, since the Exchange Act does not define "tender offer." The SEC considers the following factors to determine whether a stock purchase program constitutes a tender offer:

- Active and widespread solicitation
- Solicitation for a substantial percentage of stock
- A premium over the prevailing market price
- Terms that are not negotiable
- An offer that is contingent on a fixed number of shares or subject to a fixed maximum
- An offer that is open for a limited time
- Pressure on offerees
- Publicity

Several courts have adopted this eight-point test, and have gone so far as to find a tender offer even where fewer than all of the factors are present. Therefore, if a purchaser wishes to engage in an open-market purchase program, it must structure its purchase program to avoid as many of these eight points as possible.

## Schedule 13D: 5 Percent Ownership

Frequently an acquirer will accumulate a significant amount of the target's stock before commencing a tender offer or proposing a merger. Within ten days after acquiring "beneficial ownership" of 5 percent of any class of equity security, an acquirer must publicly disclose such purchases by filing a Schedule 13D with the SEC and delivering it to the target. Beneficial ownership includes (1) the direct or indirect right to vote or dispose of shares, and (2) the right to acquire shares, by option or otherwise, within sixty days. All shares beneficially owned by a group acting in concert must be aggregated in calculating beneficial ownership.

The purpose of a 13D is to inform the investing public of the existence of a significant block of stock that could form the basis for an acquisition or other market-sensitive transaction.

The 13D must identify the acquirer, its sources of funds for the purchase, and any contracts with respect to the target's securities. Most important, the acquirer must describe the purpose of its investment, including any plans or proposals that may result in a change in control or other significant transaction. The 13D must be amended "promptly" upon any material change.

The 13D filing often signals the commencement of hostilities—or negotiations. Other potential acquirers and market professionals such as arbitrageurs frequently react to a 13D filing, putting the target "in play." Disclosure in the 13D is often the focus of litigation between the acquirer and an unwilling target; if the 13D filing is not forthcoming as to the purchaser's intention to seek control of the target, the target may seek to enjoin the acquisition.

## Trading on Inside Information

A purchaser of publicly traded securities must be aware of the antifraud and insider trading prohibitions in the Exchange Act, primarily Rules 10b-5 and 14e-3, and Section 16(b).

The broad scope of Rule 10b-5 prohibits any scheme or device to defraud, any material misstatement or omission, or any act or practice or course of business that would operate as a fraud or deceit in connection with the purchase or sale of securities. The SEC has used Rule 10b-5 and its tender offer counterpart, Rule 14e-3, to allege illegal trading on the basis of tips and other nonpublic information. The limits of Rules 10b-5 and 14e-3 in the acquisition context are neither obvious nor simple. The changing state of the law requires constant monitoring to determine whether it would apply to any specific transaction.

Section (16)b of the Exchange Act regulates "short-swing" trading by certain "insiders" by permitting an issuer to recover any profit obtained by directors, officers, or 10-percent shareholders from the purchase and sale of securities within a six-month period. To monitor such short-swing trading, the SEC requires the filing of a Form 3 to report ownership of 10 percent of a public company's shares and a Form 4 to report changes in ownership.

The rule against short-swing profits is absolute, and applies even if inside information is not used or available. Notwithstanding the draconian intent of 16(b), courts have been flexible in applying it to so-called unorthodox transactions. For example, if the owner of 10 percent of the stock (who is not otherwise subject to 16(b)—that is, not an officer or director) of the company being acquired purchases an additional 5 percent and is then outbid for the company by a "white knight" or other offeror, the 15-percent stockholder incurs 16(b) liability—losing any profits made on the sale of the shares in excess of 10 percent—if it voluntarily sells those shares in a tender offer. The purchaser has a better chance of avoiding this liability if the shares are redeemed involuntarily, as in a merger.

### State Takeover Laws

Many state laws purport to govern or limit acquisitions of corporations based in the state or those having substantial operations or stockholders in that state. These statutes take many forms, and in some cases impose substantial burdens on the acquirer (usually applying only if the acquirer owns a threshold percentage of the target's stock). Many of these statutes have been declared unconstitutional, but in 1986 the U.S. Supreme Court upheld such a state law for the first time. Many states have since adopted new takeover laws designed to withstand constitutional scrutiny.

Because the situation is fluid, an acquirer must survey all potentially applicable state takeover laws prior to commencing an acquisition, and must develop a strategy for compliance or challenge.

## MERGERS

Despite the advantages of stock purchases, it is virtually impossible to gain 100 percent ownership of a public company by stock purchases alone. The beauty of mergers is that the acquirer can obtain 100 percent ownership without 100 percent voluntary participation by stockholders. Nearly all acquisitions of public companies therefore involve a merger, either alone or as a second step following stock purchases.

State law governs the rights of stockholders and the obligations of corporations in a merger. Although the laws vary from state to state, a merger usually requires approval by the boards of directors and stockholders of both parties to the merger. The acquirer can avoid having to obtain the approval of its stockholders by causing a subsidiary to merge with the target. Even then, the ultimate parent company may need to obtain approval of its stockholders, depending on the jurisdiction and the financing structure of the acquisition.

The percentage of stockholders of the company being acquired who must vote to approve a merger is a function of state law and the company's charter. Most states also provide for a "short-form" merger, which requires no vote of the stockholders or directors of the company being acquired if the acquirer owns 90 percent of the outstanding stock.

Since mergers generally require approval of the board of directors of the company being acquired, even a successful tender offeror cannot complete a merger without friendly management. In some cases, the owner of a majority of the target's stock may call a meeting, or act without a meeting, to vote its shares for the purpose of changing management. (Proxy contests are beyond the scope of this chapter, although the utility and risks of proxy contests as an acquisition tool should not be discounted.) In some cases, use of defensive tactics by the target leaves litigation as the only recourse.

Whenever it is necessary to solicit stockholder approval of a merger, the SEC requires the preparation of a detailed proxy statement, which includes a description of the transaction and the parties, a description of stockholder rights, financial information, and other relevant data. A proxy statement must be filed with the SEC at least ten days prior to mailing, although in practice the SEC review process takes substantially longer. Depending on the complexity of the transaction and the SEC's workload, proxy material can take from four to six weeks to "clear." Allowing an additional three to five weeks to solicit proxies is usually recommended.

Even if proxies are not required because the acquirer owns sufficient shares to approve the merger without a vote of other stockholders, an "information statement" must be prepared, cleared by the SEC, and mailed to stockholders at least twenty days before the merger is approved. The information statement must include information substantially equivalent to a proxy statement.

The surviving corporation in a merger will succeed to the rights and obligations of the merging companies. All stockholders are bound by the merger, provided that dissenting stockholders may have the right to receive cash equal to the court's appraised value of their shares. The availability of appraisal rights differs from state to state, and the procedural requirements for claiming those rights often deter stockholders from exercising them.

Certain mergers that "freeze out" the minority stockholders, such as situations where a company goes from publicly traded to privately held status, are subject to an additional layer of regulation under the Exchange Act. In such "going private" transactions, including many leveraged buyouts, Rule 13e-3 requires additional SEC filings and public dissemination of disclosures concerning the fairness of the transaction, actual and potential conflicts of interest, and alternatives considered to achieve the same goals.

## ASSET PURCHASES

Asset purchases have the advantage of permitting the parties to pick and choose the assets to be purchased and the liabilities to be assumed. Many assets, however, are not freely transferable.

Unlike a merger, where only stock is transferred and not a company's assets and liabilities, an asset sale is likely to require the consent of third parties with whom the target has contractual relationships. In addition, the target's debt is more likely to be accelerated, and the acquirer is more likely to be required to seek governmental licenses and permits relating to the business being purchased. This process inevitably creates delay and uncertainty, and frequently results in substantial additional expenses.

Stockholder approval is required for a sale of all or substantially all of a corporation's assets. The solicitation of proxies for approving the sale is subject to the SEC proxy requirements described earlier. The transfer of assets may also require compliance with the "bulk sales" laws of the states in which the target conducts business.

## FINANCING THE ACQUISITION

While some purchasers are blessed with sufficient working capital or unsecured lines of credit to make an acquisition, many require financing. Acquisition financing presents a number of unique legal issues. The use of high-yield securities, or so-called junk bonds, in acquisition financing has focused attention on these issues.

## Issuing New Securities: The Need to Register

Whenever a company offers to sell securities to the public, it must register the offering under the Securities Act. The registration process, like the process of clearing a proxy statement, is time-consuming.

Some offerings are exempt from registration. The most important exemption for acquisition purposes is the so-called private placement. Although the initial offering is exempt, the securities may not be resold unless they are registered or an exemption from registration is available. Since successive private placements could be recharacterized as public offerings, issuers take precautions (such as legends and transfer restrictions) to minimize the risk of appearing to make a public offering.

The SEC and the courts have looked primarily to three criteria to determine if an offering is a private placement:

- The number of offerees and their relation to the issuer
- The number of units offered and the size of the offering
- The manner of the offering

Any offering within the SEC's "safe harbor" guidelines in Regulation D qualifies as a valid private placement. Regulation D largely codifies existing law and clarifies that offerings to wealthy and sophisticated investors generally are permitted without registration. Regulation D contains many detailed requirements, but failure to fall within its safe harbor does not necessarily invalidate a private placement.

A corporation may exchange its own securities for the target's stock. The exchange may take place as part of a tender offer (as an exchange offer), in a merger, or as consideration in an asset purchase (which typically would be followed by a liquidating distribution to the target's stockholders). Each transaction is subject to the respective legal requirements described earlier for tender offers, mergers, and asset purchases, in addition to registration under the Securities Act.

### Blue Sky Laws

States have regulated securities offerings since 1911, when Kansas adopted a law to protect unsophisticated investors from speculative schemes that had no more basis than "so many feet of blue sky." State "blue sky" laws, like the Securities Act, require the registration of securities prior to sale in the relevant state, unless an exemption is available.

Many blue sky laws also impose substantial requirements to ensure that the offering is fair. An issuer must consider the securities laws of every state in which the securities are to be offered.

### Borrowing: The Margin Rules

The margin rules adopted by the Federal Reserve Board (the Fed) currently prohibit secured lending unless the market value of "margin stock" securing the loan exceeds 50 percent of the loan. This percentage may be amended by the Fed from time to time. Margin stock includes all listed stocks and many stocks traded over the counter. While the margin rules seldom apply to mergers, they often are an issue in highly leveraged tender offers and stock purchase programs.

The margin rules apply to loans that are secured by margin stock directly or indirectly. If the loan agreement prohibits the purchaser from selling the margin stock, the loan may be deemed to be indirectly secured by the stock.

The Fed has expanded its notions of indirect security in its "junk bond interpretation." If a highly leveraged "shell" corporation purchases margin securities with the proceeds of a financing, such financing may be deemed to be indirectly secured by those securities.

## MISCELLANEOUS ISSUES

Every acquisition is affected by a myriad of other laws.

For example, New Jersey's Environmental Cleanup Responsibility Act (ECRA) may materially increase the cost of acquiring a target with manufacturing facilities in New Jersey. ECRA requires the cleanup of the target's hazardous wastes upon any change in corporate control, whether by stock purchase, asset purchase, or merger. These requirements are in addition to environmental discharge and Superfund requirements established by New Jersey or federal law. Accordingly, cleanup may be required even if the target is in compliance with its discharge permits. Connecticut adopted a similar law in 1986, and other states may follow.

The rules of the New York and American Stock Exchanges affect acquisitions of listed targets, particularly as to matters of corporate governance (such as stockholder approval) and the issuance of securities.

Employee benefits present numerous legal issues in acquisitions. Federal and state securities laws must be considered in the cancellation of stock options, or the substitution of the acquirer's stock for target stock in option plans. The Employee Retirement Income Security Act of 1974 (ERISA) governs the disposition of pension funds and employee stock ownership plans. With the phenomenal growth of pension funds beginning in the 1970s and due to the favorable treatment afforded employee benefit plans by the tax code, pension funds and employee stock ownership plans have become a more frequent source of acquisition financing, subject to state and federal limitations on the cancellation of those plans.

Other laws may apply, depending on the nature of the business being acquired. For example, the acquisition of banks and other financial institutions, insurance companies, public utilities, airlines and other transportation companies, and communications-related companies may require prior approval of the federal or state agency regulating the industry. Prior approval may also be required for a transfer of licenses, or with respect to foreign operations. This list of regulated industries and required consents is merely exemplary. A determination of all applicable laws and regulations that will have an impact on the transaction begins with counsel's preacquisition review and generally continues through the closing.

# CHAPTER 8

# ANTITRUST CONSIDERATIONS

## Michael N. Sohn
**ARNOLD & PORTER**

An important consideration in any contemplated acquisition is the potential constraint posed by the federal antitrust laws. The principal antitrust law governing acquisitions—except in regulated industries such as railroads, airlines, and television stations, where mergers must be approved by federal agencies such as the Interstate Commerce Commission, the Department of Transportation, or the Federal Communications Commission, applying specially tailored statutes—is Section 7 of the Clayton Act. This statute prohibits acquisitions "where in any line of commerce . . . in any section of the country, the effects of such acquisition may be substantially to lessen competition or to tend to create a monopoly."

Because the statute draws no clear line between lawful acquisitions and those that are potentially anticompetitive, hence unlawful, much is left to the discretion of federal agencies and the courts.

Responsibility for enforcing federal merger laws is shared by the Department of Justice (DOJ) and the Federal Trade Commission (FTC). Representatives of the two agencies meet periodically to determine which agency will investigate which acquisitions. While one cannot predict with certainty which agency will proceed in any particular case, over the years each agency has built up expertise with respect to different industries.

The FTC and DOJ both issued statements in 1982 concerning merger enforcement policy. Since then the FTC has followed its stated intention of giving "considerable weight" to the DOJ guidelines. Accordingly, this chapter focuses primarily on the DOJ guidelines.

It also deals only with "horizontal" mergers, those where the merging companies are competing with each other at the time of the proposed merger. The DOJ guidelines also provide a framework for analyzing the legality of mergers between potential competitors or between suppliers and customers (often referred to as "vertical" mergers). Few if any such mergers have been challenged in recent years.

Merger enforcement policies have shifted dramatically over the last several years. In the 1960s, the government successfully attacked acquisitions between parties with relatively low market shares. Perhaps the most cited example of this is *United States* v. *Von's Grocery Co.*, where a merger between two Los Angeles–based supermarket chains, which together accounted for only 7.5 percent of sales in that area, was ruled unlawful by the Supreme Court. In retrospect, it is clear that the courts gave little careful consideration to how a merger of two parties with such small market shares could possibly affect price or output, or otherwise reduce the level of industry competition.

Today, a fairly broad consensus exists that this level of merger enforcement was both excessive and counterproductive. Thoughtful antitrust experts favor more careful economic analysis of whether a merger is likely to have anticompetitive consequences. The DOJ stated in 1984, when it released its Revised Merger Guidelines, that "most mergers do not threaten competition . . . many are in fact procompetitive and benefit consumers."

A statute enacted in 1976—the Hart-Scott-Rodino Act—requires parties contemplating a significant acquisition to provide advance notification and extensive internal financial and economic data so that the antitrust enforcement agencies can undertake the careful analysis required under the DOJ guidelines prior to consummation of the acquisition.

Where a merger between horizontal competitors is contemplated, careful planning and management of the antitrust defense of the acquisition is essential. It seems wise in such cases to involve counsel and a competent economic expert at an early stage. Before too much time and effort is put into planning an acquisition, these advisors should be asked to appraise the likelihood of a successful governmental or private challenge. If serious problems seem likely, attention should be devoted at an early stage to the possibility that a sale to a third party of part of the assets to be acquired might lessen anticompetitive concerns.

## ACQUISITION BETWEEN COMPETITORS: THE REVISED DOJ MERGER GUIDELINES

The best road map to current antitrust enforcement policies is the DOJ guidelines first promulgated in 1968, with a major revision in 1982 and relatively minor revisions in 1984. The main theme of the DOJ guidelines is to identify and challenge only those mergers likely to make it easier for a business to exercise "market power," defined as the ability to "maintain prices above the levels that would prevail if the market were competitive."

### Market Definition

Central to identifying such competitively harmful mergers is the definition of the market—the geographic area and the product or bundle of similar products—potentially affected by the acquisition.

The importance of product and geographic market definition to merger analysis cannot be overstated. For example, in the highly publicized effort by Coca-Cola and Pepsi-Cola to acquire Dr. Pepper and 7-Up, respectively, counsel for the companies seeking to make the acquisitions argued for an "all beverage" market, which would pit soft drinks against such other cold drinks as iced tea, fruit drinks, and juice. In such a broadly defined market, the shares of carbonated soft-drink manufacturers would appear relatively small and their ability to restrain competition correspondingly limited. But the FTC and Royal Crown, which would have been the only major carbonated soft-drink manufacturer other than Coke or Pepsi had the acquisition been approved, disagreed with that broad definition of the market. They believed that the carbonated soft-drink market was a discrete competitive arena and that the two proposed acquisitions would raise the level of concentration in that market to the point where vigorous competition might cease. The FTC prevailed in court in *FTC* v. *The Coca-Cola Co.*

Often, it is not easy to define the product market in which the acquisition should be judged. The DOJ guidelines seek to resolve such questions by attempting to predict what would happen in the event of a "significant and nontransitory" postacquisition rise in price. DOJ uses a hypothetical increase of 5 to 10 percent and time frame for consumer response of one year. (However, it recognizes that when judged by the rate of return on invested capital, a given percentage price increase might be more significant in some industries than in others.)

If good substitutes exist to which consumers readily could switch in response to such a price increase, then the definition of the product market must be expanded to include those substitutes. For example, if juice or iced tea is a substitute for carbonated soft drinks to which significant numbers of consumers would readily switch in the event the price of carbonated soft drinks rose, an "all beverages" market definition might be appropriate.

As Jeffrey Zuckerman, an official involved in drafting the DOJ guidelines, noted, one way to think about what is involved in defining a relevant market is to ask the question: Whose membership would be necessary to make a cartel work in this market?

Under the DOJ guidelines, one begins with a provisional market definition consisting of the goods or services provided by both merging companies. Next, if readily available substitutes exist, the product market definition is expanded to include them. The analytical process continues to the point where prices could hypothetically be raised profitably without loss of customers to suppliers of still other substitute goods.

Similarly, the geographic market is determined by projecting what buyers would do in response to a "small but significant and nontransitory" increase in price by sellers in the area or areas where the merging companies are located. If companies located elsewhere could easily provide the relevant product to the merging companies' customers, a postacquisition attempt to raise prices would not prove profitable, and the tentatively identified, provisional geographic market definition would be too narrow and would need to be expanded to include the more distant sellers.

## Permissible Postmerger Concentration Levels

Intense debate occurs among merger analysts today concerning what constitutes "too few" companies to insure vigorous competition. All experts agree that the fewer companies there are in a market, the easier it is for them to collude or engage in parallel pricing policies. However, disagreement exists as to the precise point at which further increases in concentration should be precluded.

Robert Pitofsky, a respected commentator viewed as a moderate on antitrust issues, has suggested that allowing mergers that result in control of up to about 20 percent of the market, as long as four or five strong competitors remain, is probably acceptable to a majority (*New York Times,* July 27, 1986). Others, generally associated with the Chicago school of economics, have suggested that mergers that result in control of up to 40 percent, or even 50 percent, of the market are acceptable, if two or three vigorous competitors remain.

The DOJ guidelines address this question by adopting a refined measure of market concentration and by characterizing specified levels of industry concentration as either "unconcentrated," "moderately concentrated," or "highly concentrated." The guidelines employ the Herfindahl-Hirschman Index (HHI) as a measure of market concentration.

The HHI for a market is computed in two steps. First, the number of HHI points contributed by each market participant is calculated by squaring the participant's market share. For example, a firm with a 20 percent market share would contribute 400 HHI points to the HHI of that market, while a firm with a 30 percent share would contribute 900 points. This gives greater weight to the market share of the larger companies, which DOJ believes is in line with their relative importance in any postacquisition effort to collusively raise prices.

The second step in the HHI calculation is to sum the HHI points of all market participants. For example, a market in which each of ten companies has 10 percent of the business has an HHI of 1,000 (each of ten companies contributes 100 points), while a market in which each of five companies has a 20 percent share of the market has an HHI of 2,000 (each of five companies contributes 200 points).

Under the DOJ guidelines, where the market is "unconcentrated"—has a postmerger HHI of below 1,000—DOJ will not challenge acquisitions, "except in extraordinary circumstances," because with so many companies remaining and none of them dominant, it would be difficult to coordinate pricing above competitive levels.

Where the market is "moderately concentrated"—has a postmerger HHI of between 1,000 and 1,800—DOJ is likely to challenge mergers that produce an increase in the HHI of more than 100 points, unless other factors indicate that the acquisition will not be anticompetitive. (The increase in the HHI occasioned by a proposed merger can be calculated by multiplying the merging companies' market shares and doubling the product. For example, a merger between a company with a 5 percent market share and one with a 10 percent market share would increase the HHI by 100 points ($5 \times 10 \times 2$).

Finally, in a market that is "highly concentrated"—that has a postmerger HHl of above 1,800—DOJ is likely to challenge mergers that increase the HHI by more than 50 points, and "only in extraordinary cases" will it not challenge mergers at this level of concentration if the merger increases the HHI by more than 100 points.

Even where a merger would not raise concentration to the stated danger points, the authorities are likely to challenge a merger between a "leading firm" (one with 35 percent or greater market share) and a small company, because of the danger that the market power of a single, dominant firm would be enhanced.

## Other Factors Relevant to an Antitrust Analysis

Unless the HHI levels are either well below or well above the parameters of the "moderately concentrated" range, a variety of other factors are considered by antitrust authorities in deciding whether to challenge a particular acquisition. All of these factors—and others that will occur to business people and their counsel in a particular industrial setting—are designed to shed light on the extent to which the increase in concentration occasioned by the proposed acquisition might reduce competition and lead to higher prices.

**Ease of Entry.** By far the most significant factor other than the postacquisition level of concentration is the ease with which new companies could enter the market in the event of an increase in prices after the acquisition. As stated in the DOJ guidelines, "If entry into a market is so easy that existing competitors could not succeed in raising prices for any significant period of time, the department is unlikely to challenge mergers in that market."

As an aid in assessing whether significant barriers exist to entry by new competitors, the DOJ guidelines proceed, once again, by hypothesizing a significant, nontransitory price increase and asking whether, under the particular conditions prevailing in the industry in which the merging companies compete, a likely response would be for others to enter that competitive arena by constructing new facilities or substantially expanding existing ones. If such a response is likely within two years of the hypothetical price increase, barriers to entry are considered to be low.

A variety of factors should be considered in assessing ease of entry. These include the following:

- Recent instances of entry and exit, including any examples of vertical integration by customers choosing to make rather than buy
- Cost advantages of existing competitors, including advantages afforded by technology, distribution systems, or natural resources acquired at a lower price than presently available
- The existence of patents that would block entry or make it more expensive
- Environmental or other governmental regulatory barriers
- Economies of scale: savings associated with relatively high levels of production that make entry on a small scale difficult

In many cases, careful economic analysis of entry barriers can make a substantial difference in the attitude of enforcement authorities toward a particular acquisition. Indeed, even where postacquisition concentration levels are in the "moderately concentrated" or "highly concentrated" ranges and the increase in those levels occasioned by the acquisition is substantial, a strong showing that new entry is easy has been known to lead to the conclusion that an acquisition is not unlawful.

The DOJ guidelines point to a number of other factors that are considered in order to determine if the acquisition will make it easier to exercise "market power." These factors can be particularly significant where mergers are in the gray area between legality and illegality, and include product characteristics, information about specific transactions, capacity of fringe sellers, conduct, market performance, and efficiencies.

**Product Characteristics.** Where the product offered by the merging companies is a homogeneous and undifferentiated commodity, such as natural gas, a postacquisition cartel would need to establish only one price. Thus, it would be relatively easy to agree on price and to detect any deviation from that agreement. The more one finds heterogeneous or differentiated goods or services within a product market (such as women's apparel), particularly when accompanied by a complex pricing system, the more difficult it is to establish or maintain a cartel. Accordingly, where a significant degree of such heterogeneity can be shown, the merger is less likely to be challenged.

**Information About Specific Transactions.** The enforcement agencies are more likely to challenge a merger where detailed information about specific transactions is readily available to competitors. Where there are public reports by the press or government sources, private exchanges of information among sellers, or other similar mechanisms, detection of deviation from collusively established prices is facilitated. Therefore, the DOJ guidelines suggest, such deviations are less likely to occur for fear of retaliatory pricing actions by competitors. In this context, a significant merger is more likely to have adverse consequences.

**Capacity of Fringe Sellers.** Where industry members who currently have a small share of the market possess the ability to increase output rapidly in response to a significant price increase by larger competitors, they have the ability to undermine a cartel. The antitrust enforcement agencies are less likely to challenge a merger where such small sellers exist.

**Conduct.** The FTC and DOJ are more likely to challenge a merger in an industry where:

- there is a history of collusive activities and the market conditions that existed when such activity took place have not materially changed,
- there are pricing practices such as mandatory delivered pricing, price or output information exchanges, or price protection clauses, which make collusion easier, or
- the company to be acquired has been a particularly aggressive price cutter whose disappearance might lead to a lessening of competition in the industry.

**Market Performance.** A merger is more likely to be challenged where the industry involved is not performing competitively. Non-competitive performance may indicate to the enforcement authorities that obstacles to collusion can be overcome and that further increases in concentration by merger could make it even easier to engage in such conduct.

The factors considered in assessing the extent to which an industry is performing competitively include the stability of relative market shares of leading companies in recent years, and profitability compared to companies in other industries where capital investment and risk are comparable.

**Efficiencies.** In deciding whether to block a merger, antitrust agencies consider whether the merger will create a more efficient, low-cost operation than is possible if the companies remain separate. The rationale here is that such gains in efficiency increase competitiveness and result in lower prices to consumers.

The enforcement authorities take into account such potential efficiencies as economies of scale, better integration and utilization of production facilities, and lower transportation and distribution costs. Reduction in duplicative selling costs or administrative and overhead expenses are also considered.

It should be borne in mind, however, that the DOJ guidelines leave it to the parties seeking to merge to demonstrate with "clear and convincing evidence" that such efficiencies will be achieved. Moreover, the parties must show that comparable efficiencies cannot be achieved by means other than a merger.

## PRIVATE SUITS TO BLOCK MERGERS

Although this chapter emphasizes the DOJ guidelines and the possibility of challenge by the FTC or DOJ, the possibility of a private-party lawsuit against the merger should not be overlooked. Such litigation might be instituted by competitors, customers, suppliers, or, in the case of a hostile takeover, the target company.

In *Cargill v. Monfort of Colorado*, the Supreme Court considered the extent to which a competitor has the right to challenge a contemplated acquisition. The Court ruled that a competitor does not have standing to file such a suit, except in the relatively rare situation where the challenged merger creates such a high level of concentration that the merged entity is likely to have the market power to drive smaller competitors from the market by below-cost, predatory pricing, the ultimate result of which would be higher prices to consumers after the competition is driven from the field.

The mere fact that a merger will create a more efficient entity, which will compete vigorously and take sales from the complaining competitor, does not give that competitor the right to sue. That kind of injury, the Court pointed out, flows from the very conduct— vigorous competition—that the antitrust laws are designed to protect. In sum, the Court restricted, but did not eliminate, the ability of companies to block acquisitions. In any event, the ability of customers or suppliers of the merging parties, or unwilling targets, to challenge an acquisition on antitrust grounds is unaffected by the *Monfort* case.

The likelihood of a potential private challenge must be considered at the acquisition planning stage, because the federal courts are not bound by the DOJ guidelines and many of them have not fully accepted the more lenient attitude reflected in those guidelines. Some courts continue to apply more expansive antimerger precedents established in the 1960s and to block acquisitions the government has decided not to challenge. Thus, where private challenge is anticipated, the likelihood of successfully completing a horizontal merger is harder to predict.

## PREMERGER NOTIFICATION

The Hart-Scott-Rodino Antitrust Improvements Act of 1976 introduced the concept of premerger notification. A basic understanding of Hart-Scott-Rodino is necessary to those involved in planning for merger, particularly where the timing of the transaction's consummation has significant business consequences.

Basically, Hart-Scott-Rodino provides that parties of a specified minimum size must report and provide information to the FTC and DOJ concerning their intention to acquire voting securities or assets having a specified minimum dollar value. After filing this report, the parties must wait a prescribed period of time before consummating the transaction.

The purpose of this premerger notification mechanism is to allow the antitrust enforcement agencies sufficient information and time, prior to consummation of an acquisition, to consider whether to seek a preliminary injunction to prevent the closing of the deal pending a full trial, at which the anticompetitive potential of the transaction could be adjudicated.

If both the purchaser and the seller meet one of several "size of person" thresholds set out in Hart-Scott-Rodino and the implementing regulations issued by the FTC, and the assets or voting securities to be acquired are valuable enough to meet applicable "size of transaction" criteria, the parties must complete and file a standard reporting form. At present, the implementing regulations exempt from filing transactions that involve the purchase of assets valued at $15 million or less and those that involve the acquisition of a controlling interest in the voting securities of a company that has annual net sales or net assets of less than $25 million.

The initial report provides enforcement authorities with various kinds of information, principally revenue data by Standard Industrial Code (SIC) category. This data provides the enforcement authorities with a general sense of the product markets, if any, in which both parties participate.

CEOs and other management officials planning an acquisition should be aware that most documents prepared by or for officers or directors of a company to assist in their analysis of the acquisition are required to be submitted as part of the initial filing. These documents often provide insights into the parties' motives for entering

into the transaction and can be suggestive of likely areas of competitive concern, if any exist.

After both companies have filed these initial documents, they must
wait thirty days before they can close the proposed acquisition. In
the case of cash tender offers, this initial waiting period expires
fifteen days after filing of the notification form by the acquiring
company.

When the enforcement agencies perceive no antitrust problem,
the companies are formally notified—usually at the end of the thirty-
day period—that the waiting period has expired and they are free
to close. Where delay could cause adverse business consequences
and no antitrust problems exist, requests for early termination of
the waiting period are usually granted.

In cases where the initial filings raise potential antitrust concerns
the FTC or DOJ wants to pursue, the agency involved serves the companies with a request for additional information. This so-called second request must be issued before the expiration of the initial
waiting period and has the effect of prolonging the period of time
before the companies can consummate the transaction. The second
waiting period does not end until twenty days after both companies
have substantially complied with the government's second request.
In a cash tender offer, the second waiting period expires ten days
after compliance with the second request.

The second request can be quite formidable. In large merger cases,
it is not unusual for the request itself to exceed twenty-five single-
spaced typewritten pages and for the responsive documents to be
tens of thousands of pages long. Typically, the request for additional
information seeks a wide variety of information designed to facilitate
an economic analysis of a merger's anticompetitive potential.

For example, extensive company data concerning shipment patterns and transportation costs might be called for to help delineate
the geographic market. The companies are often asked to provide
historical sales and capacity data for all goods or services deemed
to be within the product market. They are asked for their own data
on this subject as well as whatever information they have regarding
sales and capacity of their competitors. Such information enables
the government agency to calculate market shares and the impact
on concentration of the proposed acquisition. Customer files are
typically sought to gain insight into the level of competitive intensity

in the industry. Detailed information on the cost of building new facilities or substantially expanding existing ones is sought in order to shed light on the extent to which new entry would be likely in the event of a postacquisition price increase.

It should be noted that the government has taken the position that a request for additional information need not be limited to existing documents. Requests for the compilation of data and essay answers to questions concerning various economic issues are quite common. Moreover, the agencies have also taken the position that detailed cross-indexes to all documents and data must be submitted to facilitate expeditious review before the second Hart-Scott-Rodino waiting period expires.

In most instances, government authorities do not insist on literal compliance with the second request. Where particular requests are unduly burdensome, the opportunity exists for negotiations with agency staff to find a sensible shortcut to providing the essential information. However, in the end, an agency has considerable lever-age when it insists on production of documents. Few parties wish to litigate whether the request is unauthorized or unreasonable, since they are usually precluded from closing the transaction while such litigation is pending.

## IN SUMMARY

Where a merger between horizontal competitors is contemplated, careful planning and management of the antitrust defense of the acquisition is essential. It seems wise in such cases to involve counsel and a competent economic expert at an early stage. Before too much time and effort is put into planning an acquisition, these advisors should be asked to appraise the likelihood of a successful govern-mental or private party challenge. If serious problems seem likely, attention should be devoted at an early stage to the possibility that a sale to a third party of part of the assets to be acquired might lessen anticompetitive concerns. Careful management of the Hart-Scott-Rodino notification and document production process is also essential if needless delay and disruption of the business is to be avoided.

# SECTION **III**

# Financing Alternatives

## INTRODUCTION: A TREATISE ON LEVERAGE

The company's financial staff is generally responsible for formulating financing alternatives, working with external advisors and potential funds providers. Senior management does, however, have a vital role to play in this process.

Why should a senior manager, who is caught up in the strategic and negotiating dynamics of an acquisition while continuing to direct the existing enterprise, be burdened further by becoming involved with the dynamics of acquisition financing? It seems logical that these somewhat arcane arrangements should be left to the chief financial officer, the company's bankers, and its other financial advisors. However, second only to accurately assessing the strategic fit of the proposed acquisition, the most important decision regarding a proposed acquisition transaction may be the method of financing. Financing considerations are closely related to pricing considerations, since the impact of the acquisition on future earnings and shareholder value will be influenced by both how much is paid and how it is paid. The ultimate success of an acquisition will be judged by how the combined entity performs.

Equally important is the extent to which the acquisition financing may influence not only strategic thinking but also day-to-day

operations. In the euphoria surrounding negotiations, the announcement, and the closing, weighing the respective implications of different financing alternatives may be hard. But the issues are vital
to the business and are properly within the CEO's purview.

While the company's financial staff and advisors are likely to focus
on rates, fees, and other similar considerations, the CEO must concentrate on potential strategic and operational conflicts. The CEO
and other policymakers should use this opportunity to review and
consider internal sources of financing. Sale of an underperform-
ing division or product line, either existing or to be acquired, may
be a better overall source of funds than external alternatives. The
sale of other assets may be warranted. The CEO is probably the only
person who can make some of those decisions and trade-offs.

These decisions must be made from a postacquisition perspective. The acquisition and the acquisition financing are likely to have
a significant effect on the company's future cost of capital and to
present the higher level of risk that is associated with increased
leverage. When these factors are considered, an asset or product line
that seems like an acceptable corporate investment before the acquisition may not seem as desirable a holding afterwards. If the proposed acquisition represents a change or narrowing of corporate
strategy, the sale of businesses that do not enhance the new strategy
should be considered as a potential source of acquisition financing, even when they are highly profitable.

A postacquisition perspective should also encourage management
to identify ways to increase operating cash flow. In today's fiercely
competitive environment, most companies already have adopted
leaner staffing, reduced inventories, installed incentive-based compensation systems with fewer perquisites, and become generally more
efficient. The acquisition process, with its strong focus on future
cash flows (see Chapter 3), provides an ideal opportunity to re-
examine these areas. Providers of financing are more attracted to
cost-efficient companies and generally willing to grant more favorable terms to highly regarded management.

The CEO needs to take a hands-on approach. It is important to
become well acquainted with the principal providers of the proposed
financing and their agents. An exchange of business philosophies,
discussion of strategic plans, and a comparison of styles will help
a CEO determine how comfortable a long-term relationship will be.

Assessing the temperament of these people and their organizations and how they might act in the face of unexpected liquidity problems could be critical. The CEO must also understand the expectations of those providing financing, the degree of control they will expect to exercise, and what a loss of some control may mean to management's flexibility and the company's operations.

Perhaps the major consideration in assessing any prospective acquisition and its financing is the amount of leverage involved—both the amount the company would ideally want and the amount the financing source would provide. Leverage is the use of money owed—trade credit, other deferred payments, and borrowed debt—as a supplement to shareholder capital in financing a business. The degree of leverage is measured by the ratio of all liabilities on a company's balance sheet to its capital accounts.

After an acquisition, the combined entity likely will have higher leverage than either of the participants had prior to the transaction. A high degree of leverage can provide a greatly enhanced return on shareholder capital accounts when things go well. But nothing is more pernicious when things go wrong and cash flow is insufficient. The heavy burden of debt can literally crush overleveraged capital.

The use of higher leverage to finance acquisition transactions is entirely appropriate. In fact, many transactions would be insufficiently rewarding without it. But the use of leverage, like all powerful tools, should be carefully planned and thoughtfully executed.

The degree of justifiable leverage is directly proportionate to the perceived reliability of a company's cash-flow projections. Characteristics of the industry, company, and the specific transaction largely determine the extent to which leverage is appropriate and available:

- Companies in industries that are highly cyclical or subject to rapid technological obsolescence may experience unpredictable external forces that can have a substantial negative impact on cash flow. Such companies are poor risks for high leverage.
- Competitive position is important. Dominant market participants are likely to have control over margins, and may put pressure on smaller competitors that are loaded with acquisition debt.
- Companies making and selling end products generally can support more debt than manufacturers of nonproprietary component parts.

- Transactions that present alternative sources of repayment if operating cash flow is inadequate justify higher leverage. The existence of freestanding subsidiary businesses or other salable assets may offer such an alternative. Some acquisitions contemplate an immediate partial divestiture and, therefore, can temporarily support extremely high leverage.

- An appropriate debt structure justifies higher leverage. A layer of "mezzanine capital"—debt that is subordinate to other creditor claims—generally supports more senior debt. The existence of obligations on which principal repayments are deferred provides protection for shorter-term credit. A mix of floating-rate and fixed-rate instruments is a hedge against substantial changes in the overall level of interest rates in either direction.

- Acquisition financing sources are greatly attracted to good managers. Companies that have superior operating records and whose management is highly regarded are often provided high leverage on favorable terms. Such has been the case in almost every acquisition in the 1980s where a major company has been acquired by a much smaller acquirer using a rich mix of debt and equity financing.

Entering into an agreement that calls for high leverage and managing a company with a high degree of leverage both present special challenges for management.

Financing sources and their agents exact a higher level of accountability than many boards and expect to be treated as partners, which they are. Cultivation of these relationships, as well as frequent and comprehensive communication, is vital. Much of this effort is properly the responsibility of the company's chief financial officer, but the CEO should be a frequent participant and should seek to develop strong relationships at the highest possible policy level within each investor and creditor organization. Calling on these CEO relationships may never be necessary, but it is usually too late to develop them after problems occur.

For some senior managers, the mandatory shift in management emphasis from quarterly earnings per share to a near obsession with cash flow is a difficult one. Continued earnings are important, but only cash pays debt. The sooner leverage is reduced to industry norms, the sooner the company and its management can regain their former freedom and flexibility.

The CEO and the rest of the organization must be pragmatic in setting priorities. It would be foolish to cancel, or defer unreasonably, critical expenditures for product development, asset replacement, marketing, and other similar purposes. But a period of high leverage is a good time to review staffing levels, compensation programs, working capital levels, low-margin businesses, and other areas that might generate additional cash, even if the company does not need the cash to pay its debt.

Finally, when debt is increased substantially, senior management should develop and frequently review contingency plans to deal with potential adverse future environments. These plans should contemplate all scenarios that have a significant probability, and should be sufficiently detailed that they could be implemented without delay. If threatening problems do develop, this contingency planning should provide solutions that preserve the company's core business. Having such plans available may also help the CEO maintain control over company direction.

To a lender or investor, high leverage is high risk. A borrower with a well-considered plan during a crisis frequently can calm financial backers' fears and gain their cooperation. Having played war games with potential alternative solutions also prepares the CEO to rebut with assurance less attractive remedies presented by others.

Each possible source of acquisition financing offers advantages and disadvantages in cost, flexibility, restrictions, risk, and other considerations. To further complicate the analysis, a change in the mix may cause an alteration in the terms of each other component. The CEO should have a basic understanding of each possible source of financing and should thoroughly evaluate several alternatives to gain an accurate view of the relative attractiveness of each.

The CEO should make the final decision on the acceptability of individual trade-offs:

- Higher equity with less leverage should result in less liquidity risk and less stringent terms, but the dilution of stock reduces shareholder rewards.

- A higher proportion of equity and of subordinated debt should result in less stringent bank loan covenants and leave additional borrowing capacity for unforeseen needs. The cost is higher interest plus additional claims on equity in the form of warrants or conversion rights.

- A mix of more term debt and less revolving debt hedges against potential liquidity problems at the cost of greater payment flexibility.

- Fixed interest rates make costs predictable and are a protection against ultrahigh rate environments, but these rates could prove expensive in an extended low-rate environment. Floating rates present the opposite risk.

- Other trade-offs are possible, and some are unique to individual transactions.

Every manager has a different tolerance for risk and loss of control. The CEO is the best judge of how acceptable a proposed financing plan is in managing the company's ongoing operations.

The following four chapters present the role and characteristics of four possible types of financing for an acquisition. Each of the authors would be quick to agree that the traditional lines separating the activities of commercial banks, investment banks, and asset-based lenders have become considerably blurred as each has aspired to become a "one-stop shop" for financing acquisition transactions. Many of the somewhat subtle traditional differences remain, however, and the types of financing discussed have distinct differences.

The first chapter in this section, written by Lawrence E. Fox, presents the types of financing generally provided by commercial banks, and also reveals much of the philosophical attitude on which bankers base their lending decisions.

Asset-based lending is discussed by Edward P. Collins in the second chapter of this section. Not surprisingly, the increased use of leverage by corporations has been accompanied by a greater use of asset-based lending techniques, and those lenders have also become considerably more flexible.

The third chapter, by Eric A. Simonson, Dean D. Proper, and Joseph D. Downing, discusses the characteristics of long-term financ-

ing generally offered by institutional lenders. The authors also provide a rationale from the lender's viewpoint for why the terms of
this financing for acquisitions differ from those offered by other
lenders.

In the final chapter on financing, Robert Niehaus makes a case
for the use of high-yield subordinated debt, both public and private
issues. The rapid growth of "junk bonds," although alarming to some
observers, has made this vehicle increasingly available to corporate
acquirers.

Not included in these discussions is the use of straight equity.
The impact of additional equity on future earnings is a relatively
straightforward calculation. It is important to assess the trade-offs
between additional equity and additional debt, and to settle on a
mix of financing types and sources that is both attainable and comfortable. Equity may well be a part of that mix.

"Seller financing"—paying part of the purchase price with debt
or equity instruments held by the seller—is more a source of financing than a unique type. Lease financing does have some unique
characteristics, but is basically a secured term loan. Neither of these
is discussed.

As in other financing, the acquisition financing structure should
be tailored to meet a company's specific situation and to fit the
characteristics of the transaction.

# CHAPTER 9

# BANK FINANCING

## Lawrence E. Fox
**FIRST NATIONAL BANK OF CHICAGO**

This chapter deals primarily with acquisitions of a size or complexity that produces significant, new, and different financing needs for the acquirer, either to finance the merger or to finance the ongoing operations of the new company after the acquisition.

But even small acquisitions raise at least three issues, and therefore provide opportunities in which the CEO of all but the very largest companies should consider being personally involved.

**1.** Even a small acquisition that requires limited new financing may cause a violation of the covenants of a tightly drawn prior term-loan agreement.

**2.** Whether the banker has a say or not in determining if the company can complete an acquisition under existing agreements, an acquisition represents an ideal time to explain and reinforce the company's strategies.

When a company is planning a small acquisition, the CEO has an opportunity to test the banking relationship to find out if the banker understands what the company is trying to accomplish, if the banker will applaud plans that clearly make sense, if the bank will be willing to make waivers and amendments of current loan agreements, and if it can make fast decisions on these questions. The time to test, and to build a firm relationship, is during the small transactions. The testing and building are critical in order to have the right basis for the large transaction that may come.

**3.** With any merger may well come a need to add a new bank, usually to provide for local operating needs, even if these are as simple as a local payroll account. Whether the CEO should become involved in selecting a new bank depends on the level of financial support within the company. Adding a bank is not a decision that should be made cavalierly.

## MONEY AND MORE

The role of a commercial bank in the acquisition arena comes down to providing much or all of the money to make the purchase a reality. While both commercial bankers and their corporate clients for many years considered delivering the cash to be the critical factor, today getting enough money together is easier and structuring the way the cash is delivered has become the more important focus.

Acquisitions are exciting, traumatic times. A tremendous number of pieces have to fall into place for success. Almost every company has a horror story to tell. The minimum a company should insist upon and require from a commercial bank in financing a merger or acquisition is four elements to make the process work: money, advice, speed of response, and confidentiality.

### Element 1: Money

The bank had better say yes, or else have an excellent reason to say no. Any bank that decides to say no and can convince its corporate client that a potential acquisition is unwise, as opposed to un-financeable, is worth its weight in gold.

### Element 2: Advice

Advice is the first real differentiating element. Money plus good advice is worth more than money alone. A loan sufficient to make the deal but poorly structured will almost certainly present problems down the road—if not with the deal, then with the bank relationship.

It is critical to an acquirer that the loan agreement allow sufficient operating flexibility. The bank should negotiate in the context of an overall agreement, not point by point, and should help expressly to consider the sensitive trade-offs between operating flexibility for the company and appropriate risk controls for the bank.

Bad advice can differentiate banks as well as good advice. A friend tells the story of his banker advising him that what he really needed to do was raise his gross margins. Since the conclusion was absolutely correct, the natural question was asked: "What would you suggest?" The banker replied, "You can either raise prices or reduce costs." This bit of wisdom suggested a quick decision: get a new bank.

### Element 3: Speed of Response

Along with good advice and the willingness to say yes to sensible requests, the bank must offer a fast response. Every deal has a moment when it can fall apart or come together, and at that moment the acquirer needs the money.

How long it takes a bank to make a decision depends in part on the personality and practices of the bank and the individual banker. But the time period also depends on the quality and organization of the information presented as the basis for that decision. Working with the bank, if the acquirer has only one, or with a banker acting as agent and advisor all the way through the process, should assure a good package, whether that package is ultimately directed at a single bank or at many. Ideally—and there is every reason to attain this ideal—the package should be a self-sustaining credit analysis to which the bank needs only to add its own credit approval form.

It should not be a problem to prepare this kind of package as a by-product during the normal process of identification, structuring, negotiation, and approval. With a proper information package, a lending decision should be reached in under one week, with feedback on significant policy issues within one day. The decision will almost always be subject to documentation, to audit verification of the facts, and to other normal due-diligence requirements.

### Element 4: Confidentiality

A mixture that includes many people, plus time, plus confidential information is inherently unstable. The list of people who have to be "in the know" about an acquisition is staggering: senior management, the board of directors, accountants and lawyers (times two, one set on each side), and the bankers. The acquirer wants, and has every right to require, the bank to respond in effort and speed so as to minimize the number of organizations that need to be involved. All news leaks in time.

## BANK–LOAN STRUCTURE

While there appear to be at least thirty-one different flavors of bank loans, there are really only three basic types, each with a great many variations. They are:

- demand loans,
- short-term notes, and
- term loans.

The three basic loan structures deal with unforeseen risks differently. With a demand loan, the lender has great leverage to demand repayment or to insist on basic changes in terms. With a ninety-day time note, the bank has slightly less leverage. With a term loan, the ability of the lender to act and the ability of the borrower to deviate from the plan without having to be inordinately concerned about how the lender may respond is dependent on the covenants negotiated at the time the loan is made.

### Demand Loans

The demand loan, just as its name implies, is payable on demand by the bank. Demand loans may be couched in terms that make their essential demand nature difficult to discern; but any loan, notwithstanding its other terms, that is payable on a demand that can be made for any reason and at any time, is a demand loan. People have been buying and selling unappetizing products for many years, so it is not surprising that significant acquisitions continue to be financed with demand loans.

One could say that nothing is inherently wrong with a demand loan. One could also say nothing is wrong in a business context with signing a one-sided contract, contingent on the continued good faith of the other party not to take unfair advantage.

An acquisition, by its very nature, presents many uncertainties. Financing an acquisition on a demand-loan basis can only compound those uncertainties. The common exception to this rule is asset-based transactions with a commercial finance lender or the commercial finance affiliate of a bank or other multiline lender, where the transactions are often on a demand basis.

Most traditional acquisition loans made by banks, however, including secured loans, are not on a demand basis.

### Short-Term Notes

When a loan is not on a demand basis, it may be either a short-term note or a term loan. Commonly, a short-term note has a stated maturity of ninety days and is rolled over at maturity. Most current lines of credit extended by banks are for one year, with each note under the line being a ninety-day time note and with the continued willingness to lend at the maturity of each note left to the discretion of the bank. In an acquisition, a short-term note is only slightly preferable to a demand loan.

### Term Loans

Certainly, from the point of view of the borrower, the ideal way to finance all or at least the bank-debt portion of an acquisition is with one or more term loans.

There are two types of term loans. The first kind is a revolving-credit loan, so-called because all or any part of the total amount committed can be borrowed, repaid, and reborrowed any reasonable number of times during the commitment period. A straight, or conventional, term loan is an amount borrowed once to be repaid on the basis of an agreed-on amortization schedule.

Term loans are not unique to banks, but are also available from insurance companies, from the public markets, from asset-based lenders, and from a variety of specialized lending sources. Traditional bank loans usually have somewhat lower interest rates and tend, as a practical matter, to be the easiest to amend or prepay. In turn, bank loans typically do not have as long a maturity as insurance company loans and are typically at a variable rather than a fixed rate.

Given the almost unlimited variety of financial structures used in acquisitions, it is extremely hard to generalize about rates a bank will charge for acquisition loans. As a general rule, any term loan will carry a rate at least ½ percent higher than a short-term note, and a highly leveraged acquisition will be in the range of 1½ percent on top of that. As a rule of thumb, consider that most of the highly publicized major leveraged buyouts or takeovers are priced at the prime rate plus 1½ percent, while those companies were borrowing before the acquisition at a rate of about prime minus ¾ percent.

It is quite common for an acquisition to be financed with a conventional term loan plus revolving credit, where the revolving credit is designed to finance seasonal or other peak borrowing and the conventional loan to finance the company's permanent debt needs. Term loans can be, and generally are, secured either by specific assets or by stock of subsidiaries, or both. The distinction between a bank loan and an asset-based loan is not in the security, but in the greater frequency in monitoring and verifying of collateral values in an asset-based or commercial finance loan.

Different banks have strikingly different attitudes about the appropriate duration of term loans. Some have policies requiring repayment in five years or less, some in seven. Few banks will extend a loan past eight or ten years. Whatever the ultimate maturity, banks want the borrower to provide financial projections showing payment of the full acquisition debt. At the very least, the period the projections cover must be one during which the term-loan portion is paid in full, or paid down to such a low level that the remaining amount represents just normal working capital financing.

The bank will insist on projections and a detailed, written explanation of the logic supporting the numbers. Usually, the bank will consider both a base case, representing what can be agreed is really likely to happen, and a downside or pessimistic case, representing within the bounds of reason just how bad business could get.

The most common three failings of projections in support of an acquisition are:

- assuming that all the efficiencies to be realized will happen easily or quickly,
- ignoring the business cycle and projecting straight-line growth, and
- ignoring the possibility that interest rates will rise significantly during the loan term.

While projections can and absolutely should accommodate each of these real-world risks, all parties to a loan understand that whatever the numbers show, risk still exists.

## HOW A COMMERCIAL BANKER VIEWS THE TRANSACTION

The banker's view of a large acquisition differs from that of the company contemplating the acquisition. From the point of view of the corporate client, any acquisition before it is seriously considered must pass the test of offering an appropriate balance of risk and return. The facts the banker sees should always be the same facts the client sees. But the bank, if it is smart, looks for the risks and rewards both to the client business and to its own business. The bank operates at a gross margin of 3 percent or less, and with leverage of 12 or 15 to 1, so the bank is and ought to be reasonably conservative without being scared into inaction or second-guessing. From the bank's point of view, many large acquisitions financed primarily with debt represent an unknown and potentially large risk at what may be a less-than-commensurate return. Acknowledging this, the paradox is that the bank will usually acquiesce.

Clearly, a major corporate event like a large acquisition is a litmus test for the relationship between the client and the bank. If the bank does not step up to help make the acquisition possible, the relationship will be, at best, wounded. But the bank hates to lose a relationship. Therefore, when the banker says yes, that yes does not necessarily signal comfort. Comfort and acquiescence are very different.

## COMFORT FACTORS

In the absence of external support to help the bank feel comfortable after a major corporate financial event, the borrower can demonstrate an ability to provide three "comfort factors": interest coverage, balance sheet stabilization, and a second way out. In a well-crafted loan agreement, each of these three things will be required in the form of covenants to which the borrower agrees. A violation of these covenants will put the loan in default, and this may result in a waiver or amendment, a significant renegotiation, or even acceleration and demand for payment of the loan.

### Comfort Factor 1: Interest Coverage

The first comfort factor is strong projected interest coverage, expressed as the ratio of the sum of earnings before interest and taxes to interest alone (EBIT/Interest). If the history of the acquired company coupled with conservative projections of the performance of the combined entity is normal in terms of interest coverage for the industry and size of the new company, then the bank has one comfort factor.

The specific level of interest coverage the banker expects to see is hard to specify. A reasonable and almost absolute minimum is 1.25 to 1, but only for a company with very strong presence in an important and stable market that has very little business cycle sensitivity. The norm for an aggressive transaction is interest coverage of 1.5 to 1.

### Comfort Factor 2: Balance Sheet Stabilization

The second comfort factor is balance sheet stabilization, represented by the ratio of total liabilities to equity. If this leverage ratio stays at a normal level following a merger or returns quickly to a normal level, the bank has a second comfort factor. The outer horizon for stabilization is three to four years in most cases.

What is normal in terms of balance sheet stabilization is again hard to specify. In a typical manufacturing environment, a maximum ratio of total liabilities to equity of 2 to 1 is a common target; in a distribution company, 3 to 1 is common. An association of credit professionals, Robert Morris Associates, publishes a series of standard ratios by size of company in various industry classes.

### Comfort Factor 3: A Second Way Out

Given interest coverage and balance sheet stabilization, the third comfort factor the banker will consistently consider is a demonstrated second way out of all bank loans. Interest coverage is necessary, but it depends on projections, which are uncertain by their nature. Balance sheet stabilization is important in analyzing the potential for refinancing, but balance sheets do not repay debts. The second way out is the alternative means of repayment if projections are not met. The second way out may be provided by a guaranty, by the liquidation value of corporate assets, or by the breakup, ongoing-business value of subsidiaries or divisions.

If the company's operations degrade to the point where interest or other ongoing expenses cannot be met in a timely fashion, will the bank get all its money out? Quite often not, as evidenced by the billions of dollars in charge-offs banks take each year. So the bank will almost always design a safety net, in the form of loan covenants constructed to give the banker the opportunity to act— or at least to consider acting—long before a situation degrades to the point where bills cannot be met.

### Loan Covenants

Properly designed covenants are like a well-built corral. They provide proper room for exercise, but limit roaming. They allow for growth, but not overgrazing.

Very few elements of mergers, as opposed to other corporate financing transactions, require specialized covenants. The covenants in term-loan agreements associated with mergers or acquisitions vary from the norm largely in defining and limiting merger accounting treatment and in protecting the bank from acquiring, along with a company, a "black hole" for the senior lender. These covenants relate to existing liens, adverse contracts, ERISA claims—particularly those associated with terminating plans or with multiemployer pension plans—and contingent liabilities like suits or environmental claims.

The covenants of an acquisition loan deal with each of the comfort factors. If more than one of the factors is not addressed, it is virtually certain that the banker is not truly comfortable. At best, a transaction lacking the comfort factors is hard to finance conventionally.

How important is it for a banker to be comfortable with and truly committed to the loan decision? Advertising claims aside, in the corporate environment the range of behavior among banks when they are searching for business is not great. On the other hand, the differences in behavior among banks and bankers when the financial outlook of the corporate client is uncertain or difficult is very great. In many ways, when banks are actively seeking corporate business, there is both the possibility and the tendency to cut price, to weaken terms, or even to extend more in commitments than the bank is really comfortable with. This is what competition is all about.

## THE DECISION TO ADD A BANK

No set of projections represents certainty, and in uncertain times the borrower must be confident of a rational, reasoned, and thoughtful response from bankers. Banks with the lowest price, weakest terms, and greatest commitments are not likely to be the most rational, reasoned, and thoughtful. As with all suppliers of key products, the company should choose its banks well. This process too often breaks down when major acquisitions or mergers are consummated. Banks are often added with less than the appropriate thought.

Two questions should be asked and answered explicitly. The answers are not obvious, although all too often acquirers act as if they are.

**1.** Should a company retain banks inherited along with an acquisition?

**2.** What is the CEO's role in deciding whether to add banks?

### Inherited Banks

Quite often, an acquirer inherits line-credit banks with an acquisition. One common reason for retaining them is to maintain the morale of the financial staff of the acquired company. They had favored banks and, in the interest of demonstrating that the acquired company will continue to have a measure of autonomy, those banks are retained. A common reason among large companies for retaining inherited banks is that international operations usually have banks that provide local currency facilities.

While it is generally good advice never to say never, a corporation should never retain inherited banks. There is a long list of companies that have been put in a position of financial jeopardy by irrational actions of banks that they inherited, particularly foreign banks. This is also true of non-U.S. companies that inherit U.S. banks. The acquirer may choose to add banks when an acquisition is made; it may have to. Some of the acquired company's banks may be appropriate, but the choice should be made explicitly.

## The CEO's Role

Senior officers of both present and prospective banks like to call on the CEO. These meetings can take on the status of state visits, but they can also be used for substantive discussion of corporate style and strategy on both sides. It is neither unlikely nor inappropriate for the senior banker to ask the CEO how the company will behave if things get tough; nor should the CEO hesitate to ask the banker the same question.

Even if a pressing need to add banks after an acquisition does not exist, it may be a good idea to do so. If the present banks need to see more competition in terms of price, products, or ideas, an acquisition is an ideal time to introduce new banks without necessarily offending present banks. Often, a small number of banks are told that they are "on the bench" and will be the next into the game.

Acquisitions are near the top of the priority scale for many if not most CEOs. The big decisions are hard, and the small decisions are many. Of all the many interactions that must succeed to consummate a merger or acquisition, the interaction of the CEO and the bank(s) is one of those most often overlooked, and therefore one of those most likely to cause problems. Yet, with all the uncertainties that attend any significant corporate reorganization, one of the easiest interactions to manage well—and one that must be managed well from both sides—is the interaction between the senior management and the banks.

## RECOURSE, NONRECOURSE, AND
## LIMITED-RECOURSE FINANCING

The most common reason by far to finance a major acquisition on a nonrecourse basis—structuring the transaction so that the lenders have only the assets and business prospects of the acquired entity to look to for repayment—is the intention that the operating management of the acquired company will maintain a very high degree of autonomy. An important element of that autonomy is maintaining the competence and morale of the financial staff—keeping them in place after the acquisition rather than having them quit *en masse.*

The issue the borrower ought to face is what the banks mean when a transaction is styled as a nonrecourse transaction or a limited-recourse transaction, the latter being when the parent company gives some support but not a 100 percent guaranty or a cosignature. Often banks ask for, or corporate borrowers give, "comfort letters"—letters that express the intent of the company to see that an affiliated company makes good on its debt.

While comfort letters may be long or short, detailed or general, their specific character is that they are not a legally binding guaranty. That said, it is quite common for banks to view comfort letters as no more than a convenience to the corporation to avoid accounting consolidation, but as giving, in essence, a full guaranty. Under some circumstances, particularly outside the United States, the law may view a comfort letter as a guaranty.

Even with no written support, and even in some cases with no verbal support, the bank may view the parent company's name on the door of the acquired company as a promise of substantive direct support. While the client is clearly not responsible in any sense for what others may hope is a degree of support that was never intended, banks in an environment where financing is formally structured with only limited recourse or nonrecourse may well ask just what support the acquirer intends to provide under different circumstances. This is an appropriate inquiry, and should be welcomed. If the intent really is for the bank to have no recourse, that should be said and stressed.

# CHAPTER 10

# ASSET-BASED LENDING

## Edward P. Collins
**BANK OF BOSTON**

There is no magic to successfully completing a leveraged acquisition. Leverage does not create value where none exists. Rather, the use of financial leverage is an appropriate financing technique for the acquisition of businesses that fit certain profiles.

When arranging financing, the purchaser is usually trying to resolve four conflicting elements:

- Most important, the purchaser wants to get the deal done quickly, with the least equity and the most leverage tolerable in order to maximize return on investment.

- The purchaser normally is after the lowest rate and the longest amortization.

- The purchaser's primary objective is to accumulate wealth by retaining as much ownership as possible.

- The purchaser wants a financing source that will make an effort to understand the business, not just the numbers, and one that will not have a knee-jerk reaction or panic if problems develop.

The trade-offs among these conflicting goals vary with each deal. In most instances, however, the amount of capital required—equity and mezzanine financing—is driven by the amount of senior debt available.

A secured, or asset-based, acquisition financing, while it can be just as complex as an unsecured one, focuses on the underlying collateral value of the accounts receivable, inventory, and fixed assets of the acquired company as well as on the cash flow. The structure and amount of financing available is, therefore, closely related to the estimated liquidation value of the underlying assets, not solely the cash flow. Since the lender is able to develop a greater comfort factor when the loan is collateralized, often significantly more leverage is available, either to pay a higher purchase price or, more important, to lower the amount of capital needed in order to maximize returns to investors and managers. Loan terms are also generally more flexible.

Although collateral is taken as security to protect the lender against default, to be sold only as a last resort when no other means of payment exists, the projected cash flow is what lenders look to first as the primary source of repayment.

In their analysis of prospective acquisition financing, both secured and unsecured lenders focus on (1) the competitive and economic characteristics of a company's industry, as well as (2) its business strategy and (3) its management. In effect, these three factors combine to create the cash flow and collateral asset values that will be the primary and secondary sources of debt repayment. As was suggested earlier, the lender that takes an asset-based approach has a significantly higher tolerance for leverage and, due to its collateral position combined with the cash flow, is much more tolerant of business downswings.

## STRUCTURE AND TERMS

How, then, does the asset-based lender determine the level of debt to extend and the structure under which it is willing to make the loan?

A typical loan package consists of a revolving loan tied to the current assets, and a term loan supported by fixed assets. The revolving portion normally has no amortization schedule, but the amount outstanding at any time is limited to certain percentages of accounts receivable and inventory. Over the years, lenders have developed standard percentage norms for different industries and collateral.

Accounts receivable are the most liquid assets, and as a result, lenders are willing to lend as much as 85 percent of eligible receivables. Ineligible receivables are generally those sixty days past due, poor credit risks, and accounts subject to offset for any reason.

Inventory advance rates vary widely, coinciding with the liquidity of the goods. Advances against inventory, however, normally carry a maximum of 50 percent of manufactured costs for raw materials and finished products. Work in process is usually considered ineligible.

Since the levels of the current assets are constantly changing, the lender requires periodic reports from the borrower, usually weekly, in order to insure the loan stays within the limits established. In effect, the revolving portion of the loan serves as a substitute for the initial capital and, to a great extent, the future capital as a business grows. The borrower has substantial flexibility because the revolving loan limit actually grows as asset values increase with increased business activity.

Term loans for the most part are expected to amortize over seven years, although some lenders agree to ten years. The machinery, equipment, and real estate supporting the term loan usually warrant much lower rates of advance than the current assets, due to their illiquidity and the dependence on future cash flows to amortize the debt. The asset-based lender always requires a current appraisal prepared on a liquidation or quick-sale basis. The rates of advance vary from as low as 50 percent to 100 percent of liquidation value.

Loan covenants typically involve limitations on capital expenditures, an interest-coverage test, a net-worth test, and leverage targets. From a practical standpoint, the lender attempts to develop targets using company-prepared projections. The lender will want to trigger a default early enough so that both parties will still have maneuvering time to take corrective action.

The process of establishing rates of advance and degrees of collateral liquidity is an art rather than a science, and takes into consideration all aspects of a company's profile as well as lender comfort factors. Typically, the lender sends a field audit team to visit both the acquirer and the company to be acquired to review the books and records and the collateral as a part of setting these terms.

The greater the dependence on term debt, the more emphasis the lender places on cash flow. As a general rule, the more consistent the cash flows have been, the more aggressive the rates of advance will be. Conversely, an inconsistent or weaker cash flow will prompt a lender to use conservative rates of advance.

Pricing of asset-based loans varies greatly, but customarily involves a closing fee of ¾ percent to 1½ percent, and an interest rate of anywhere from 1 to 3 percent over the prime rate. Pricing is a function of overhead, the cost of monitoring the collateral, and risk for the lender. The closing fee is used by a lender to enhance yield in the first year of the loan, which is usually the riskiest. For the most part, the asset-based lender attempts to limit risk to zero by carefully determining rates of advance, collateral coverage, and predictability of cash flows. In effect, rent is charged for the use of the money, since the risk has been somewhat mollified. Equity, on the other hand, receives the greatest potential payoff and, therefore, should be the most at risk.

In some instances, particularly where cash flows are very strong, asset-based lenders lend more than the advance rates against the collateral would otherwise dictate. In these cases, however, due to the greater incremental risk, the lender expects to receive a significantly greater return than just the rent for the use of funds. The lender considers the "overadvance" a quasi-equity or bridge-equity loan, and expects to be compensated with additional fees and/or a percentage of future earnings or cash flow.

There are significant advantages to buyers in dealing with a lender willing to take this approach, since it generally means they have to provide less equity. On the other hand, both the lender and the buyer must balance the stark fact that too little equity or capital in a financing could turn out to be somewhat punitive if things do not go as planned.

## PURCHASER EXPECTATIONS

Up to this point we have focused on many of the things a lender expects from a purchaser, as well as some of the methods and approaches used by lenders. Of equal importance to a purchaser is what to expect from a lender. Unfortunately, most buyers experience, at least once, a situation where a potential lender does not deliver what has been promised. A lender, like any other business, establishes qualifications; the fact that a buyer fails to pass these qualifications may be as much a reflection on the lender as on the buyer.

For a purchaser, screening and finding a lender should receive the same priority as finding an acquisition candidate. When looking for a lender, the purchaser should make sure the institution has a reputation for delivering what it says it will, and, equally as important, that the individual at the institution with whom the buyer will be doing business has a similar reputation.

Purchasers should:

- deal with an institution and an individual that have "time in grade,"
- find out the size and number of financings both the institution and the individual have done, and
- determine the lender's approval process.

The individual should be able to give a date when a final decision will be made; any major deviation from that date should be treated as a danger signal that the lender may be struggling to gain internal approval. Another danger signal is an individual's stressing collateral and paying little attention to the business plan, strategy, and projections. The astute buyer regularly takes the lender's pulse.

Given the volume of leveraged acquisitions and financings completed in the past several years and the attractiveness of yields, it is not surprising that many lenders are claiming to be experts in the field. In fact, it has been so lucrative that most, if not all, independent finance companies have been purchased by major bank holding companies. The strongest and most experienced players are generally the money center banks and large regional banks that have dedicated entire groups to acquisition financing. The smart buyer seeks these groups out.

# CHAPTER 11

# INSURANCE COMPANIES

## Eric A. Simonson, Dean D. Proper, and Joseph D. Downing
PRUDENTIAL INSURANCE

Insurance companies are an attractive alternative to commercial banks as a source of acquisition financing because of their strong commitment to investing for the long term.

The insurance business is characterized by both regular—even predictable—cash flows derived from sales and premium payments on a wide range of insurance products, and by continuing yet well-defined obligations. The investment or lending opportunities most attractive to insurers are ones that enable them to match asset flows to liabilities that have already been scheduled. While some liabilities have final maturities of less than five years, the overwhelming majority have longer maturities, with many as long as twenty or thirty years. Thus, insurance companies can be committed to the long end of the market as lenders.

For the same reason, insurance companies typically lend at fixed interest rates, to normalize current cash returns as well as to establish a level of financing cost that a borrower can agree to with a measure of certainty. Though not central to this discussion, the fact should be noted that several insurance company investment operations have, over the years, developed a complementary floating-rate investment capability, financed through the issuance of commercial paper or other variable-rate notes.

Acquisitions provide a nearly ideal opportunity for matching the resources and resourcefulness of a fixed-rate term lender to the requirements of the company and its proposed acquisition. By creating an immediate need for long-term financing, acquisitions demand responsiveness, flexibility, and long-term commitment from both parties to the transaction.

Beginning in the 1970s, growth of financial markets and new forms of competition led insurance companies to expand on their distinctive strengths. Given their institutional appetite for long-term investments and their deal-structuring expertise, insurance companies sought out new ways to manage the risks and opportunities that arise over a ten- to twenty-year horizon.

As major participants in corporate lending and investment management, many insurance companies have moved further, through their own acquisition programs, to establish themselves as more broadly based financial service organizations. In part, this is to take advantage of the kinds of opportunities generated by the rapidly growing market for acquisition financing. Adding investment banking and securities trading to their existing investment activities and strengthening money management capabilities in both the institutional and retail markets have also contributed to insurance companies' understanding of markets and customers for financial services.

But the insurance companies' métier continues to be long-term, fixed-rate debt.

## THE ACQUIRER'S LONG-TERM FINANCING DECISION

Unless a company has a sizable hoard of cash on the balance sheet, it most typically considers a variety of options when financing an acquisition, including intermediate- to long-term debt, asset sales or sale/lease-backs, equity offerings, and seller financing.

The use of term debt will depend on the structure of the acquirer's balance sheet, its ability to service existing debt and any that is taken on to finance the transaction, and the extent to which incremental leverage can be optimally employed. The optimal use of leverage will in turn depend on variables such as current and expected interest rate levels, the ability to use additional interest expense deductions from a tax standpoint, and current valuations of the company's equity.

To the extent that a private transaction providing for a fixed interest rate and tailored repayment schedule fits the company's acquisition and overall financing requirements, then a long-term financing agreement with an insurance company is an appropriate alternative.

## THE INSURANCE COMPANY'S LENDING DECISIONS

It is important to reiterate that insurance companies are long-term lenders that approach their universe of lending opportunities against an in-house slate of fixed liabilities generated by the activities of its insurance operations. It is this aggregate schedule of financial obligations, fixed by amount and repayment schedule, that makes long-term, fixed-rate investments relatively more attractive than others.

A key corollary of this set of financial appetites is that by pushing the investment focus toward the long end of the market, the scene is set for an insurance company's willingness to lend on an unsecured basis—that is, to base its lending decision on the company's proven ability to generate cash from operations for the repayment of the loan. The relative attractiveness of the company as a borrower, and hence the basis for the loan commitment, is its viability as an ongoing concern, not just a list of the assets it owns.

Compared with the so-called asset-based approach to lending, whereby specific assets of established value are placed under lien for the benefit of a lender in the event of a nonrepayment, unsecured lending is more of an informed judgment, so to speak, of the company's ongoing creditworthiness. Rigorous financial analysis is obviously critical to the lender's decision-making process.

A readiness to lend unsecured does not mean that a lender is inclined to leave itself without adequate protection for its loans, any more than an acquirer would neglect to ascertain and document the assets it purchases. Insurance companies generally require a "negative pledge" from the borrower as one of several provisions, or covenants, in the loan documents. One such covenant stipulates that the borrower will not permit liens to be granted on any asset in favor of other lenders. While the intent of such a covenant is similar to the basic principle underlying a secured, or asset-based, loan agreement, it provides two attractive features:

- Negative pledges can be modified from time to time by the borrower and the lender as circumstances warrant.
- The unsecured approach does not require the often cumbersome "asset verification" procedures, which necessitate periodic on-site visits by auditors or inspectors on behalf of the lender to document the pledged asset and its condition.

Well before documentation is an issue, however, an insurance company will analyze carefully the borrower's business and financial condition and prospects. In undertaking this analysis, the lender will explore the following principal areas:

- *Industry considerations:* How essential is the company's product or service to its customers and to the economy? Do supply/demand imbalances exist? What is the pricing structure? What has been the rate of sales growth in the industry? Is it capital-intensive or people-intensive?
- *Company position within an industry:* Who are the competitors by product line, and what has been the trend in the company's market share? How do the company's operating margins and other measures of financial performance compare with those of competitors? Are competitors more fully integrated, with resultant cost or marketing advantages?
- *Stability and quality of management:* Does management have a strategic plan for beating the competition? Have the expected product cycles been identified? Are financial controls and information systems sufficient? Are contingency plans in place in case volume fails? Is management strong across all functions? What are the prospects for orderly management succession?
- *Quality of earnings:* What are the trends in operating margins? Do inventory, depreciation, tax, and other accounting methods minimize or maximize charges against earnings? How much

growth has been real versus nominal? Do any customers account
for a large percentage of sales?

- *Quality of balance sheet:* Are property, plant, and equipment worth
more than stated? If substantial intangibles exist, how are they
reflected in earnings? What is the nature of any off-balance-sheet
financings? What are the trends in asset and liability turnover?
Is depreciation cash throw-off being reinvested in plant, property,
and equipment on a regular basis? What is the funding status
of the company's pension plan?

- *Financial leverage:* Is the relationship of pro forma, long-term debt
to total capital on a par with the industry norm? Does the company employ seasonal lines of credit in amounts that permit those
lines to be fully repaid on a predictable basis? What is the maturity
structure of the company's existing debt?

- *Coverage ratios:* What are the quantitative relationships between
a borrower's earning power and cash flow generation to pro forma
total debt and to annual fixed charges? While varying from lender
to lender, coverages usually relate to some mix of net income,
interest expense, rent, taxes, and depreciation compared to pro
forma, long-term debt.

In addition to these representative elements of analysis, an insurance company will want to determine how the company's financial and business risks are likely to change with the acquisition.
Depending on whether the acquired business fits within existing
business, complements it, or represents a diversification into new
markets, the acquirer's business-risk profile will change.

A thorough understanding of the company and its markets will
enable both parties to respond to ordinary and extraordinary
changes on an ongoing basis. Two points are important here.

First, no long-term lender can predict the future with any degree
of certainty. In that context, the lender fully expects that the loan
agreement, once documented, will need to be modified to accommodate unforeseen changes in the borrower's business.

Second, and more important in view of the difficulty of forecast-
ing the future, the lender must focus its analysis sharply on the borrower's historic performance. The demonstrated ability to manage
a company through both robust and lean economic environments

is what the unsecured lender is really after in the analytical or due-diligence phase of putting a financing together.

Having achieved a better understanding of the borrower's business, an insurance company may occasionally suggest, as a condition of its loan, the refinancing or other restructuring of liabilities on the borrower's balance sheet. This process is generally referred to as rationalization, whereby the debt and equity accounts of a company's balance sheet are structured to achieve a more "rational" mix of floating and fixed-rate debt, short and long maturities, high- and low-interest-bearing obligations, and sufficient shareholder investment.

While rational or typical capital structures vary from industry to industry, a rational one for any company reflects its ability to generate cash and service its obligations on an ongoing basis after a candid assessment of its business prospects.

With a fresh grasp of the business and financial risks facing the company in the context of the proposed acquisition, an unsecured lender can better maintain an appropriate distance from the company's operating affairs once the deal has been closed. This relatively passive disposition toward operations by the lender reflects its recognition of the plain fact that its strengths are deal-oriented and not related to running the borrower's business.

## STRUCTURING THE LOAN

Once the company has determined to incorporate long-term borrowing into its plan for financing the acquisition, it needs to develop ideas regarding the most desirable deal structure. The principal elements of a debt financing can be highly tailored in a privately placed transaction to conform to the specific cash flows of either the acquired business or the corporation as a whole.

For example, it could be especially attractive to structure a loan based solely on the creditworthiness of the acquired operation if it can be set up as a discrete corporate entity. Such financing, which is designed to be nonrecourse to the parent, can preserve significant borrowing capacity for other situations.

Alternately, the use of a parent guarantee could reduce the cost and enhance the attractiveness of a loan made to the subsidiary.

Principal elements of any debt financing include amount, maturity, pricing, and call features, as well as other features.

## Amount

The amount of permanent financing required in a given situation is not always obvious. An insurance company will want to be satisfied that the borrower is being adequately capitalized, with enough long-term debt and equity to handle the business's operating cycle. Reliance on the use of seasonal or short-term credit to fund longer-lived assets places too great a risk burden on the borrower; and the long-term lender may suggest refunding some of the short-term floating-rate obligations with fixed-rate term debt over and above the amount otherwise required to fund the acquisition.

## Maturity

The loan's final maturity will naturally depend on the borrower's needs. In most instances, regardless of the final maturity, a regular repayment schedule will be negotiated to fit the borrower's expected cash flows. Insurance companies do have a strong preference for "self-liquidating" loans, in part to offset the illiquid nature of these investments, but also as a function of the insurance companies' structural needs, as dicussed earlier.

However, if it makes sense to establish the beginning of the amortization period several years downstream, that can usually be accommodated. If it makes sense to graduate the required repayments—called required prepayments in the trade—that can also be addressed. Final maturities are not often extended beyond twenty years, however.

## Pricing

The rate offered today on any particular fixed-rate debt instrument is a basis-point spread added to the yield on comparably long U.S. Treasury notes and bonds. Here, maturity is expressed in terms of the average life during which the total principal is outstanding. Overall, the size of the spread reflects the lender's assessment of the borrower's creditworthiness and market rates for comparable credits. For example, if the loan finally matures at the end of the tenth year, with equal repayments of principal required in each year, the formula for calculating its average life would be:

$$\frac{\text{number of annual principal payments} + 1}{2} = \text{average life}$$

$$or \quad \frac{10 + 1}{2} = 5.5 \text{ years}$$

If the loan has a twenty-year final maturity, with equal required repayments beginning in the eleventh year, the average life calculation would be:

$$\frac{\text{number of annual principal payments} + 1}{2} + \frac{\text{number of periods without principal payments}}{} = \text{average life}$$

$$or \quad \frac{10 + 1}{2} + 10 = 15.5 \text{ years}$$

Since Treasury securities are obligations with no required prepayments except at final maturity, the average life of a Treasury bond is, by definition, the number of years to final maturity. So a privately placed loan with an average life of, say, eight years and a final maturity of ten years would be priced at a spread over a Treasury bond maturing eight years from the time the loan is made.

Finally, spreads are set by market forces and vary by credit quality and term. The better the credit and shorter the average life, the lower the spread and the more attractive the price to the borrower.

## Call Features

Long-term loans provide the borrower various opportunities to prepay the debt. In fact, the lender agrees to give the borrower a call option on the note. Restrictions on the borrower's right to exercise the call, principally restricting when and at what price, vary with the quality of the credit and the final maturity, and should vary with both the current and expected level of interest rates.

Traditionally, a period is specified during which the loan may not be prepaid. For example, loans with final maturities of seven to ten years might have a four- to seven-year noncall period. After the noncall period, the option would provide for prepayment in whole or in part at par plus accrued interest plus some stipulated premium. The premium should bear a relationship to expected levels of interest rates at the time the loan is called. Both the length of the noncall period and the level of prepayment premium reflect market conditions and are subject to negotiation.

As insurance company portfolio managers have become increasingly sensitive to the volatility of interest rates, they have paid closer attention to the option value given the borrower. This has led to a host of new ideas on structuring call features on long-term fixed-rate loans, including the concept of permitting optional prepayments at any time, provided the lender is completely protected against reinvestment rate risk. This is accomplished through a formula that gives effect to actual market interest rates at the time the option is exercised.

## Other Features

The loan agreement nearly always includes, in addition to the money terms just described, a set of covenants designed to maintain the borrower's liquidity. These covenants relate primarily to the maintenance of adequate working capital, the use of additional financial leverage, the payment of dividends to shareholders, investments in nonmainstream operations, and merger or sale of significant assets.

The lender has no desire for a set of covenants that result in technical defaults when the company is performing at or near its business plan. Rather, the covenants are meant to provide for a discussion between borrower and lender in the event financial performance varies materially and adversely from a plan.

A close review of the business plan and projected monthly operating results is fundamental to a rationally structured set of loan terms. Recognizing that no one can write a loan agreement that perfectly predicts the future, the borrower and lender both should expect the terms to be modified during the life of the loan. Each side trusts the other and acknowledges that for the business

to be successful and grow, some terms will simply have to be adjusted. Only in instances where loan agreement modifications are
triggered by, or designed to accommodate, a substantial increase
in credit risk is an adjustment to the interest rate required.

## The Role of Equity

The popularity of the leveraged buyout in the 1980s has given equity
a prominent role in certain forms of long-term lending. This, in
turn, reflects the capacity and willingness of institutions to take on
additional investment risk for a commensurately increased rate of
return.

An equity feature, whether warrants, convertible debt, contingent
interest, or outright ownership of common shares, compensates for
some particular element of risk that would otherwise impede a
straight-debt financing. In effect, it accomplishes an adjusted allocation of potential upside return to conform with the lender's willingness to absorb a greater proportion of the investment risk.

Under such circumstances, a long-term lender will require a rate
of return in excess of the fixed-rate coupon on its note. The lender
will look at the financial leverage in the borrower's capital structure and the lender's position in that capital structure. Comparing
the borrower's financial profile to others in the same industry helps
define what is normal or above-average leverage for companies with
comparable operating characteristics.

Clearly, the more junior in terms of claim in bankruptcy is the
debt security held by the lender, the higher is the yield requirement.
More to the point, as total financial leverage begins to exceed the
norm, the lender takes on above-average risk. It may be supplying
debt capital with a fixed rate of return in a situation where the more
conventionally leveraged company is being financed more with
equity capital. An analysis of the relative risks and returns leads the
lender to the conclusion that the amount of overloan deserves incremental return features above and beyond the fixed rate of interest, generally in the form of equity.

In leveraged buyout financing, the providers of risk capital in the
form of junior debt securities generally require substantial equity
to compensate for their position in a capital structure where as much
as 90 percent of capital is in the form of debt. In less extreme cases—

those where the degree of financial leverage is still greater than the norm but has not been taken to the maximum—less equity is required or justified.

Notwithstanding the risk tolerance implicit in an insurance company's approach to leveraged acquisition financing, in no instance can an insurance company lender be induced by an equity "kicker" to make a loan that it is not otherwise confident will be repaid on time. Equity is not a substitute for satisfactory answers to fundamental credit issues.

# CHAPTER 12

# JUNK BONDS

**Robert Niehaus**
MORGAN STANLEY & CO.

The increase in acquisition, recapitalization, and leveraged buyout activity in the 1980s has produced a dramatic increase in the issuance of publicly registered noninvestment-grade subordinated debt, often referred to as junk bonds. The emergence of the junk bond market has given companies that lack investment-grade debt ratings access to a public capital pool aggregating more than $200 billion to fund acquisitions, capital spending for internal growth, and share repurchases in amounts that were previously unfinanceable. The annual rate of new high-yield debt issuance has grown from $7.4 billion in 1983 to in excess of $30 billion in 1987. The aggregate value of publicly traded noninvestment-grade debt in the United States today is approximately $200 billion. Because approximately 95 percent of all U.S. corporations would be noninvestment grade were they to issue debt, the development and continued sustainability of the junk bond market has dramatically impacted many sectors of American industry.

The public capital markets had a limited awareness of the nature or existence of high-yield subordinated debt securities until the early 1980s. The technical definition of a junk bond is a bond that has

a rating below investment grade: below BBB – as rated by Standard
& Poor's and/or below Baa as rated by Moody's.

The market for high-yield bonds was initially developed in the
late 1970s by several individuals at Drexel Burnham Lambert who
convinced a number of lending institutions that the level of losses
incurred due to default in a portfolio of noninvestment-grade debt
relative to the default losses in a portfolio of investment-grade bonds
was more than compensated for by the higher interest income that
the noninvestment-grade debt generated. Several empirical studies
have since found that the default-adjusted rate of return from a diver-
sified high-yield-bond portfolio will exceed that of an investment-
grade-bond portfolio by 100 to 300 basis points per year over the
life of the bonds.

Drexel Burnham's commitment in the late 1970s to provide liquidity in the secondary trading market for junk bonds was another
important factor in the market's development. Such liquidity enabled
investors to adjust their portfolios of debt securities through buying and selling such securities through Drexel Burnham as their
liquidity needs and risk profiles changed. In the early 1980s a number of the other leading investment banks (including First Boston,
Goldman Sachs, Merrill Lynch, Morgan Stanley, and Salomon
Brothers) made the capital and personnel commitments necessary to
become significant factors in the high-yield new-issue and secondary-
trading markets. These entrants provided additional growth and
liquidity to the high-yield market by convincing some of their traditional clients to issue high-yield bonds, often in the context of
recapitalizations and by persuading some of their institutional investors to buy and hold subordinated debt. These factors, coupled
with a decline in long-term interest rates after 1982 and the growing acceptance of leverage in the U.S. financial community, resulted
in the explosive growth of the high-yield new-issue market just
described. This increase in liquidity ultimately convinced many different types of institutions—primarily insurance companies, pension funds, mutual funds, savings and loans, and wealthy individuals
—to become purchasers of high-yield bonds.

The development of this $200-billion-plus pool of capital has
enabled growth-oriented companies to expand their business
through acquisitions at an exceptionally rapid pace. Lenders are
often willing to make this cash available as subordinated debt to

help finance acquisitions for companies that can barely cover interest expenses during the first several years on a pro forma consolidated basis. Often there are no principal repayment obligations for such subordinated debt for the first five to ten years. Many commercial banks have come to view high-yield subordinated debt as quasi-equity in a company's capital structure, due to its subordinated nature and its long average life. Banks often lend significant amounts of senior debt to companies that have a large amount of subordinated debt, further increasing the borrowing capacity of such companies.

## DETERMINING THE APPROPRIATE AMOUNT OF HIGH-YIELD SUBORDINATED DEBT

In determining the appropriate amount of leverage in the pro forma capital structure of a company about to consummate an acquisition, the potential issuer must analyze the risk/reward trade-offs of financial leverage. A greater degree of financial leverage increases equity returns if the combined companies perform well in the future. However, financial leverage also increases the acquirer's risk of financial distress and/or bankruptcy if future cash flow is not generated in the amounts required to service the resulting higher level of fixed payments. Long-term subordinated debt with no principal repayment requirements during the first five to ten years, and sometimes no cash interest requirement during the first five to seven years, significantly reduces the risks of a company's being unable to meet all of its interest and principal obligations during the first few years.

In addition to the higher burden of interest and principal obligations, financial leverage also increases the potential control of lenders over the operating decisions of a company. The restrictive covenants contained in many debt instruments may deny a company the operating flexibility needed to deal appropriately with a major business problem.

Another aspect of the financial leverage issue is that issuing too much debt may limit future financial flexibility. Future funding needs may have to be met through the issuance of equity, as debt capacity has a theoretical limit, whereas equity capacity does not. If an acquirer's debt capacity has been filled and its financial projections are not met, the availability of either additional debt or equity may be limited. Therefore, companies often retain some unused debt capacity in their capital structure to have funds available for future unforeseen circumstances.

Once the appropriate amount of leverage in the combined companies' capital structure has been established, the appropriate mix of senior and subordinated debt and the relative maturities of each must be determined. As a rule of thumb, high-yield subordinated debt furnishes the amount of desired borrowing whose principal cannot be amortized over the first seven to eight years, with the exception of a permanent working capital facility, using reasonable financial projections of the combined businesses. Many acquirers borrow high-yield subordinated debt in excess of the amount determined by the principle just described, thus reducing the amount of funded senior bank debt, because of their desire to maintain some excess senior bank borrowing capacity for capital expenditures, future acquisitions, and other capital requirements. Acquirers also may issue a greater amount of subordinated debt and borrow less senior bank debt than our rule of thumb would indicate due to the fewer restrictive covenants that characterize high-yield debt instruments as compared to bank senior loan agreements.

## CHARACTERISTICS OF HIGH-YIELD DEBT

The principal characteristics of high-yield subordinated debt reflect the fact that such securities rank somewhere between senior debt and equity with regard to security interests, financial risks, financial covenants, and return to investors.

### Maturity and Call Provisions

The maturity of a high-yield debt instrument is generally between ten and twenty years. Some industries, such as noninvestment-grade utilities, may issue bonds of longer maturities, and companies occasionally issue bonds of less than ten years, often in anticipation of a rating upgrade.

Call provisions are as important to buyers of high-yield securities as the final maturity of the issue. Since many investors have bond portfolios structured to match long-term liabilities, investors often expect to be protected from calls for at least five years, and then to receive a premium during the first several years that a call becomes available.

## Size and Ranking

Large high-yield issues are often structured with more than one "tranche," or maturity, of financing. For example, a $1 billion issue might be comprised of a $350 million issue of senior notes with a ten-year maturity, $250 million of senior subordinated debentures with a fifteen-year maturity, and $400 million of junior subordinated discount debentures, priced at a discount and not paying interest for the first five years (such securities are often referred to as "zeros"). A high-yield issue with several different tranches provides alternative maturities for investors, thereby increasing the issue's marketability and enabling the issuer to tailor maturities and interest payments to its needs.

## Interest Rate

With regard to maturity, the yield curve is generally positively sloping as maturities lengthen. A ten-year debt instrument requires a higher yield than a five-year debt instrument. With regard to ranking, yields also increase as debt tranches become increasingly subordinated in the capital structure. In the previous example, the senior subordinated debentures might have an interest rate 25 to 75 basis points higher than the senior notes, but 200 to 400 basis points less than the yield to maturity of the junior subordinated discount debentures.

Historically, senior subordinated debenture new-issue yields have been 350 to 550 basis points above U.S. Treasury bonds of comparable maturities. Junior and discount subordinated debentures have historically yielded 500 to 800 basis points above comparable U.S. Treasury bonds.

These higher rates are required by lenders because of historical patterns of default, the accrued interest aspect of zero coupon debentures, and the subordinated, unsecured position in the capital structure.

### Public vs. Private Issuance

As mentioned earlier, the development of significant liquidity in the secondary market for high-yield subordinated debt bonds was a critical element in the market's growth. For such bonds to be publicly traded, they must be registered with the Securities and Exchange Commission (SEC). If feasible from a timing and disclosure perspective, a new issue of high-yield bonds is generally registered with the SEC as soon as possible in a transaction. Sixty to ninety days are generally required from the time audited financial statements for the previous three years are available to draft a registration statement, submit such a statement to the SEC for review, comply with the SEC's comments, and market and price the bonds.

If for timing or disclosure reasons, a public registration process is not feasible—as is sometimes the case in acquisitions consummated under tight time schedules or acquisitions that cannot be disclosed in advance—the high-yield subordinated debt is placed privately. The buyers are often the same institutions that would purchase the public issue. A commitment is given by the issuer to register the bonds with the SEC within six to nine months of the private placement. Such private placements generally require yields 25 to 75 basis points higher than a comparable public issue because of the six to nine months of illiquidity that such an issue bears.

### Sinking Fund

A sinking fund is generally not required for issues that have a maturity of ten years or shorter. For maturities of fifteen years or longer, if there is to be a sinking fund it will usually begin in year 10 or 11. Substantial principal amortization prior to maturity through a sinking fund may result in interest rate savings to the issuer by shortening the average life of the issue. Such interest rate savings due to sinking funds normally don't exceed 25 basis points.

### Covenants

Covenants of high-yield securities, reflecting their quasi-equity status, are often not as restrictive as those of bank debt.

Two principal restrictions of high-yield debt are:

- significant restrictions on dividends and other restricted payments until an improved equity/debt ratio has been achieved, and
- restrictions on additional indebtedness until interest coverage and equity/debt ratios have reached specified levels.

## RATING SUBORDINATED DEBT

Two major rating agencies, Moody's and Standard & Poor's, rate public bond issues on the following scale:

| Moody's | S & P | |
|---------|-------|---|
| Aaa | AAA | |
| Aa | AA | Investment |
| A | A | grade |
| Baa | BBB | |
| Ba | BB | |
| B | B | Below |
| Caa | CCC | investment |
| Ca | CC | grade |
| C | C | |
| Defaults | Defaults | |

The two rating agencies also assign intermediate ratings, such as Bal by Moody's and BB + by S&P.

These rankings are in descending order of perceived security of payment and, therefore, ascending order of risk. Some of the factors important to the rating agencies include:

- interest and fixed-charge coverage,
- cash flow to total debt,
- reduction over time of debt/capitalization ratio,
- quality of management, and
- length of operating history.

The development of the high-yield subordinated debt market has enabled companies to acquire companies three to six times as large as themselves. For example, Pantry Pride, Inc., had $445 million in sales and a market equity capitalization of $240 million in 1985 when it acquired Revlon, Inc., a company with annual sales of $2.4 billion, for $2 billion. In this transaction, an aggressive entrepreneur —Ronald Perelman—felt that value could be created by buying a cosmetics conglomerate, selling the noncosmetics businesses, and improving the returns of the base cosmetics business. Pantry Pride was able to recoup most of its $2 billion purchase price through the sale of Revlon's noncosmetics businesses, thus acquiring the Revlon cosmetics business for less than half the price that many analysts estimated the business would have brought in an open-market auction. Pantry Pride's initial approach to Revlon's board of directors was rejected. Pantry Pride subsequently initiated and successfully completed a hostile takeover of Revlon, financing $575 million of the purchase price through the sale of high-yield subordinated debt.

In the Pantry Pride/Revlon transaction, the high-yield bond market was prepared to lend significant amounts of subordinated debt to Mr. Perelman based on his business reputation and his thesis that the aggregate value of Revlon's individual businesses was significantly greater than the value that Pantry Pride would have to pay for Revlon as a whole.

## CASE STUDY: JSC/MS HOLDINGS' LEVERAGED ACQUISITION OF CCA

The financing of the acquisition of Container Corporation of America (CCA) from Mobil Oil Corp. provides a good case study of the use of high-yield securities in a highly leveraged transaction. High-yield bonds enabled an already leveraged Jefferson Smurfit to undertake this off-balance-sheet transaction and capitalize on synergies between itself and CCA.

This acquisition was particularly attractive to Jefferson Smurfit for a number of reasons:

• Paperboard prices were beginning an upturn.
• Mobil was ready to sell the division and concentrate on its oil and gas operations.

- Significant cost savings could be achieved from combining the two companies' management and operating staffs.

In July 1986, a newly formed joint venture between Jefferson Smurfit and Morgan Stanley, called JSC/MS Holdings, signed an acquisition agreement with Mobil to purchase CCA for approximately $1.15 billion.

CCA is a major multinational integrated producer of paperboard and paperboard packaging products. The company manufactures and sells container board, corrugated shipping containers, and folding cartons, and, to a lesser extent, plastic containers. The acquisition was financed in the following manner:

*Sources of funds ($ millions)*

| | |
|---|---:|
| Bank term loan | 500 |
| Bank revolving loan | 125 |
| Senior subordinated debt | 180 |
| Subordinated discount debt | 225 |
| Preferred stock with no cash dividend | 50 |
| Common stock | 20 |
| Cash on hand | 48 |
| | 1,148 |

*Uses of funds ($ millions)*

| | |
|---|---:|
| Payment for stock | 700 |
| Refinancing of existing debt | 395 |
| Payments for tax reserves and expenses | 53 |
| | 1,148 |

The issuance of high-yield subordinated debt enabled JSC/MS Holdings to undertake this acquisition with an initial equity investment of approximately 6 percent of the purchase price.

Jefferson Smurfit was given an option to buy Morgan Stanley's 50-percent ownership position once the debt of CCA was sufficiently reduced to allow consolidation of CCA with Jefferson Smurfit.

The pro forma capitalization of JSC/MS Holdings merged with CCA was as follows:

| | $ Thousands | Percentage of Capitalization |
|---|---|---|
| Long-term debt: | | |
| Existing CCA indebtedness (excluding current portion of $10,000) | 53,800 | 4.4 |
| Bank term and revolving loans | 655,000 | 53.4 |
| Senior subordinated debentures | 180,000 | 14.7 |
| Subordinated discount debentures (net of unamortized discount of $275,000) | 225,000 | 18.4 |
| | 1,113,800 | |
| Minority interest in subsidiaries | 41,900 | 3.4 |
| Stockholder equity: | | |
| Preferred stock, par value $0.01 per share; authorized, 380,000 shares; issued and outstanding, 50,000 shares | 50,000 | 4.1 |
| Additional paid-in capital and common stock, par value $0.01 per share; authorized, issued, and outstanding, 20,000 shares | 20,000 | 1.6 |
| Total stockholder equity | 70,000 | |
| Total capitalization | 1,225,700 | 100.0 |

JSC/MS Holdings was able to finance this transaction in the senior bank and subordinated debt markets on such a highly leveraged basis because of a number of factors:

- *Jefferson Smurfit's management experience:* Jefferson Smurfit has one of the best records in the industry for acquiring assets on a highly leveraged basis and significantly improving the financial returns from such assets.
- *Identifiable cost savings:* Jefferson Smurfit had identified a significant amount of annual cost savings to be realized from managing CCA jointly with its own operations.

- *Strong cash flow and debt to be paid down quickly:* Based on JSC/MS Holdings' projections, all debt would be paid off within ten years. Domestic pretax cash flow was projected to increase significantly in 1987 due to paperboard price increases and the cost savings mentioned earlier.

- *CCA's position of being well-invested in assets:* CCA had spent over $800 million in capital expenditures during 1981 to 1986, which significantly reduced the level of capital expenditures required over the next five years.

- *No requirement of significant asset sales to repay acquisition debt:* Although the breakup analysis yielded realizable asset values in excess of the purchase price, no asset sales were assumed or required in the projected debt repayment schedule.

Three months after the consummation of the acquisition, Jefferson Smurfit's stock price had approximately doubled from the day prior to the acquisition announcement, resulting in an increase of approximately $350 million in the market value of Jefferson Smurfit's common stock.

# SECTION **IV**

# Accounting and Tax Considerations

## INTRODUCTION

Most nonfinancial executives tend to avoid reading all treatises on the subject of accounting. When it comes to acquisitions, however, senior management needs to have at least a basic understanding of the implications of the accounting treatment that will accompany different transaction structures. Both the negotiations and the way an acquisition is portrayed to shareholders may depend on the accounting method chosen by, or imposed upon, the parties at the time of the transaction.

The tax implications of alternative transaction structures must also be understood by the acquiring company's senior management. In keeping with the embedded perversity of U.S. tax law, the impact on financial reporting and tax planning of any two alternative structures may not be the same.

The financial staff of the acquiring company, working with qualified accounting and tax advisors, undoubtedly will identify the issues. But the CEO frequently becomes the final arbiter, choosing the trade-offs between conflicting accounting and tax considerations. A transaction frequently can be structured to achieve a tax treatment providing an economic benefit at the expense of future reported earnings, for example. Such a decision clearly rests with the CEO, who must live with the consequences.

Obviously, the tax implications and, to a lesser extent, financial reporting differences frequently become bargaining points. In the latter stages of the negotiations, senior management may have to make the final call on these issues.

Finally, one acceptable method of accounting for a transaction may seem to present the intent and result of the acquisition more appropriately than another, equally acceptable method. Does the acquirer want to restate historical earnings? How much goodwill is the acquirer willing to carry on its balance sheet and amortize against future earnings? These are policy-level decisions.

The first chapter in this section presents the two acceptable methods of accounting that may be adopted to reflect an acquisition: pooling of interests and purchase of assets. Stephen L. Key and Jeffrey J. Marcketta explain the rules that govern the adoption of each method and discuss the implications of each one.

John S. Karls, the author of the other chapter in this section, identifies the tax issues that pertain to an acquisition. The chapter also presents the seller's tax considerations, how those frequently are in opposition to the buyer's tax objectives, and how buyer and seller can work toward their mutual tax benefit in structuring a transaction.

# CHAPTER 13

# ACCOUNTING PRINCIPLES

**Stephen L. Key**
**Jeffrey J. Marcketta**
ARTHUR YOUNG

The principal authoritative source of generally accepted accounting principles (GAAP) governing the appropriate financial accounting for a merger or acquisition (technically a business combination) is Accounting Principles Board Opinion No. 16 (APB No. 16), "Accounting for Business Combinations," issued in 1970. APB No. 16 establishes two mutually exclusive accounting methods to account for acquisitions:

- The pooling of interests method
- The purchase accounting method

The initial step in applying APB No. 16 is to evaluate the proposed structure of the acquisition and determine the appropriate form of accounting to be used, pooling or purchase. Once the form of accounting is determined, the acquirer usually must prepare projected financial statements on a combined basis to evaluate the proposed transaction and obtain any required financing. Because these two accounting methods result in significantly different post-acquisition financial statements, achieving the acquirer's financial reporting objectives may dictate a change in the proposed structure of the transaction.

Determining whether a proposed transaction qualifies as a pooling of interests can require a significant degree of professional judgment. Many transactions that on the surface appear to be exchanges of common stock and that would therefore be accounted for as poolings in fact do not meet the pooling criteria and must be accounted for under the purchase method.

The pooling of interests method may offer certain advantages to a public company in acquisitions that involve the payment of a large premium. Since the pooling method does not adjust the historical carrying value of assets or record goodwill for the excess of its purchase price over the fair market value of assets and liabilities acquired, there are no charges against future earnings for additional depreciation or goodwill amortization. Of course, the acquirer must take into account the potential dilutive effect on earnings per share resulting from issuing additional shares.

## THE POOLING OF INTERESTS METHOD OF ACCOUNTING

An acquisition involving the issuance of common stock by an acquirer for substantially all of the shares of another company generally requires the use of the pooling of interests method if the transaction meets certain criteria. Conceptually, a pooling results in a combining of shareholders' interests, so that each group shares proportionately in the risks and rewards of ownership of the new entity. Under the accounting rules for a pooling, the accounts of the two companies are simply combined and carried forward at their previously recorded amounts. In addition, results of operations of the separate companies for the periods prior to the combination should be restated and presented on a combined basis.

The pooling criteria set forth in APB No.16 fall into three general categories:

- The combining of companies
- The combining of interests
- The absence of planned transactions

In each category are a number of specific criteria. Unless the business combination meets all of these criteria, it must be accounted for as a purchase.

## Combining of Companies

The two conditions regarding the combining of companies are as follows:

**1.** Each of the combining companies is autonomous and has not been a subsidiary or division of another corporation within two years before the plan of combination is initiated (generally announced to shareholders).

**2.** Each combining company is independent of all other combining companies. For purposes of meeting this test, intercorporate investments of less than 10 percent are allowed.

The intent of these two conditions is to require that a pooling involve the combination of two independent shareholder groups. If one of the companies is or has been a subsidiary of a third company, the transaction could be viewed as a spin-off by the parent, and thus would not qualify as a pooling.

## Combining of Interests

The criteria regarding combining of interests are intended to reinforce the concept that the separate stockholder groups of the combining companies share mutually in the risks and rights of ownership of the combining entity. Accordingly, transactions that alter the relative voting rights of the stockholder groups or involve the distribution of assets or debt for common stock do not achieve this goal.

The specific combining-of-interests criteria are as follows:

**1.** The transaction is effected in a single transaction or completed in accordance with a specific plan within one year after the plan is initiated. (Delays due to governmental authority or litigation do not affect this requirement.)

**2.** The transaction involves the issuance of only common stock with rights identical to those of the majority outstanding voting common stock in exchange for substantially all (at least 90 percent) of the voting common stock interest of another company.

Cash or other consideration may be issued to acquire fractional shares or holdings of dissident shareholders. However, the exchange offer cannot include a pro rata distribution of cash and stock to all shareholders, even if such distribution meets the 10-percent test. In addition, any cash offered to acquire a portion of shareholders' stock holdings is considered for the purpose of this test to be an offer for all of the holdings.

**3.** None of the combining companies changes the equity interests of the voting common stock in contemplation of the combination (within two years before the plan of combination is initiated). "Normal" distributions based on earnings or prior history are allowed. Such distributions can consider the normal dividend pattern of either the acquirer or the potential acquisition. Accordingly, a private company being acquired in a pooling can pay a dividend based on what the shareholders would have received had the combination been effective earlier.

**4.** Each of the combining companies reacquires treasury stock for purposes other than the combination, and only a "normal" number of such shares are reacquired.

Conditions 3 and 4 are intended to prevent large distributions to certain shareholders, which would be in substance a cash purchase of their shares and thus contradictory to the theory of pooling. Additionally, significant reacquisitions subsequent to a transaction that otherwise qualifies as a pooling may invalidate the applicability of that method.

**5.** The ratio of the interest of an individual common stockholder to the interests of other common stockholders remains exactly the same.

**6.** The stockholders retain the voting rights they are entitled to.

Conditions 5 and 6 are intended to require the continuation of ongoing shareholder relationships, again stressing the "sharing of risks" concept.

**7.** The combination is resolved at the date the plan is consummated.

This serves to preclude the ability to agree to distribute stock as additional consideration contingent on future results, such as in the form of an earn-out agreement, and still qualify as a pooling. It does not preclude the ability to revise the number of shares based on a contingency existing at the acquisition date in an amount different from the amount recorded.

## Absence of Planned Transactions

Three additional conditions relating to future transactions must be met in order to qualify for the pooling treatment:

**1.** The combined company does not agree to reacquire all or part of the common stock issued. To do so would in substance be a cash purchase from the former shareholders and would violate the pooling concept.

**2.** The combined corporation does not enter into financial arrangements on behalf of former stockholders, such as the guarantee of a loan secured by stock issued in the combination, since to do so would in effect negate the exchange of equity securities.

**3.** The combined corporation does not intend to dispose of a significant part of the assets of the combining companies within two years after the combination, other than in the ordinary course of business.

## THE PURCHASE METHOD OF ACCOUNTING

Many business combinations involve the payment of cash or other consideration in addition to or in place of issuing common stock, and therefore do not meet the pooling of interests criteria. Generally, any transaction in which more than 10 percent of the purchase price is paid in cash, notes, or other nonstock form must be accounted for as a purchase.

The purchase method is more complex than the pooling method in that it goes beyond a mere combination of accounts. Rather, it establishes a new basis of accounting for the acquired company as of the date of acquisition, and the companies are combined for financial reporting purposes from this date forward.

The purchase price is generally determined based on the cash and fair market value of other assets (including stock) issued, and liabilities assumed, plus direct acquisition costs incurred. This is allocated to the assets and liabilities of the acquired company based on a revaluation at fair market value of all assets and liabilities acquired, including any acquired assets and liabilities that may not have previously been reflected on the acquired company's historical balance sheet.

Any excess of the purchase price over the net fair market value of the assets and liabilities acquired is recorded as an intangible asset: goodwill. Goodwill should be amortized to income, generally using the straight line method, over the future period during which it is expected to be of benefit. However, in no circumstances can that period exceed forty years. Many factors must be considered when determining the appropriate amortization period of goodwill, including market conditions, product demand and obsolescence, and legal or contractual provisions. However, for tax purposes, a specific life cannot be determined for goodwill, due to its unidentifiable nature. Therefore, it is not deductible when determining taxable income.

Any part of the purchase price that is contingent on the outcome of future events, such as earnings, should not be recorded until such time as the amount of the additional consideration is determinable.

Because the determination of fair market value in many instances is subjective and requires the use of numerous estimates and assumptions, considerable professional judgment must be exercised throughout the process of allocating purchase price, since it will have a significant impact on the future reported earnings and, possibly, the acquirer's tax liabilities.

Careful analysis may be required in some situations to determine the accounting acquirer, as it may be different from the legal acquirer. A company that distributes cash or assets or incurs liabilities to acquire another company is clearly the acquirer. However, in a purchase transaction effected principally by the exchange of stock, the identity of the acquirer is not always evident. The SEC has issued a Staff Accounting Bulletin (SAB Topic 2A) giving guidance as to its views on the topic.

## CASE STUDY: CGA AND ALLEN SERVICES CORP.

*The following case study illustrates the effect of financial statement differences between the pooling and purchase methods of accounting. CGA Computer Associates, Inc., purchased Allen Services Corporation. The transaction was originally accounted for as a pooling, but the Securities and Exchange Commission disagreed with this accounting treatment. In the settlement, CGA was required to prepare financial statements in accordance with both the pooling and purchase methods. Because of this, the case provides an excellent example of some of the differences between the two accounting methods.*

On February 27, 1981, CGA acquired from the sole stockholders of Allen, computer software program packages that had been marketed by Allen. CGA issued approximately 1.4 million common shares to the Allen shareholders in exchange for the net assets and business acquired, and shortly thereafter filed a registration statement covering approximately 1 million common shares, principally including those owned by the former Allen shareholders.

CGA accounted for the acquisition of Allen as a pooling, based on the fact that the transaction involved issuing common stock. The SEC disagreed with this treatment, however, and instituted proceedings under Section 8(d) of the Securities Act of 1933 with respect to the accounting treatment.

The SEC alleged that CGA's accounting treatment as a pooling rather than a purchase was inconsistent with GAAP due to the fact that CGA and the selling shareholders entered into a financial arrangement that provided (1) that the selling shareholders would sell at least 50 percent of their stock within two years through a registration statement filed by CGA, and (2) that in the event the selling shareholders did not sell the stock, CGA was to make them a loan secured by their stock.

CGA and the SEC reached a settlement on this issue in January 1982, in which CGA agreed to report its financial statements by both a pooling of interests and purchase method of accounting in "equal prominence," meaning that neither method was designated as supplemental. This dual presentation is to continue for as long as the financial statements differ materially as a result of using the different methods.

The primary differences between the two methods of accounting are the recording of certain assets, the amortization of those assets, the tax effects of such amortization, and the time period relative to the inclusion of the results of Allen in CGA's consolidated income statements. Specifically, the differences are as follows:

1. The purchase method valued the transaction at $19.5 million, based on an independent appraisal of the value of stock issued. This amount was allocated principally to the value of software acquired ($11.8 million) and goodwill ($6.5 million).

2. Software packages and goodwill were amortized over five years under the purchase method. Amortization of the software is deductible for tax purposes, resulting in a reduced tax bill. However, under the pooling method, the software must be accounted for as an increase in capital.

3. In the year of the transaction, the results of Allen's operations were included in the purchase accounting financial statements for only two months from the date of acquisition. For the pooling of interests income statement, they were included for a full year.

It is interesting to note the differences between results produced by those two methods both at the acquisition date and thereafter. Specifically, these differences are as follows:

1. Net income under the purchase method ($815,000) was less than under the pooling method ($2,175,000) because of the effect of the amortization of the software packages and goodwill, and related tax effects, and because Allen's results were included for only two months. After the amortization period, however, reported net income was the same under either method.

**2.** At the end of the five-year amortization period, the balance sheet was the same under either accounting method, except that two components of stockholders' equity, retained earnings and capital in excess of par value, differed in offsetting amounts. Retained earnings under the pooling method were $19,349,000 greater than under the purchase method. (This is simply the difference between the amounts in the capital in excess of par value accounts under the two methods, resulting from the incorporation of Allen's income prior to the transaction into the combined financial statements.)

**3.** Cash flow was the same under the two methods of accounting.

The following information extracted from the CGA Annual Report for the year ended April 30, 1981, highlights the differences between the pooling of interests and purchase accounting methods. The difference codes in the right-hand column are explained in notes below the table.

| | Pooling-of-Interests Method ($ Thousands) | Purchase Method ($ Thousands) | Difference |
|---|---|---|---|
| *Income statement:* | | | |
| Revenues | 20,358 | 15,510 | A |
| Interest income, net | 640 | 536 | |
| | 20,998 | 16,046 | |
| Direct costs | 10,091 | 8,587 | A |
| Selling, general and administrative | 6,668 | 4,893 | A |
| Amort. of software | – | 392 | B |
| Amort. of goodwill | – | 219 | B |
| | 16,759 | 14,091 | |
| Income before taxes | 4,239 | 1,955 | |
| Income tax provision | 2,064 | 1,140 | C |
| Net income | 2,175 | 815 | |

*Continued*

*Condensed balance sheet:*

| | | | |
|---|---|---|---|
| Current assets | 11,034 | 11,034 | |
| Fixed assets, gross | 701 | 603 | |
| Accum. depreciation | (232) | (134) | |
| Fixed assets, net | 469 | 469 | |
| Software packages, net of accum. amort. | – | 11,387 | D |
| Goodwill, net of accum. amort. | – | 6,343 | E |
| Other | 75 | 75 | |
| | 11,587 | 29,299 | |
| Current liabilities | 2,711 | 2,711 | |
| Stockholders' equity common stock | 326 | 326 | |
| Capital in excess of par value | 4,024 | 23,373 | F |
| Retained earnings | 4,517 | 2,889 | G |
| | 8,867 | 26,588 | |
| | 11,578 | 29,299 | |

A. This difference results from the inclusion of the results of Allen's operations for a full year with the results of CGA's operations for a full year under the pooling method, rather than from the date of the acquisition under the purchase method.

B. This difference results from the amortization, over a five-year period, of software packages (appraised at $11,770,000) and goodwill ($6,562,000) for two months during the year ended April 30, 1981, under the purchase method.

C. This difference in the income tax provision results primarily from two offsetting components: (1) Under the purchase method, income before taxes is substantially less than under the pooling method because the results of Allen's operations for only a two-month period are included. There are also additional charges to expense for amortization of software packages and goodwill, thus resulting in a lower tax provision. (2) The tax provision under the purchase method also includes taxes related to the amortization of goodwill that is not deductible for income tax reporting purposes.

D. This difference results from allocation of acquisition costs to software packages acquired based on an independent appraisal of fair market value, under the purchase method.

E. This difference results from acquisition costs not allocable to indentifiable tangible and intangible assets (goodwill), under the purchase method.

F. These differences result from the issuance of CGA common stock with an appraised value of $19,500,000 to acquire Allen under the purchase method.

G. This difference results from different net income achieved under the purchase and pooling methods; and distribution to former Allen stockholders and the related tax effect of such distributions.

# CHAPTER 14

# FEDERAL INCOME TAX CONSIDERATIONS

**John S. Karls**
**ARTHUR YOUNG**

The value of an acquisition can be affected drastically by the structure of the deal. The same is true from the seller's viewpoint: the structure chosen can have a significant tax impact that will affect how much the seller nets. Achieving the best tax structure requires recognizing that there is a zero-sum game involving the buyer, the seller (including shareholders if the acquired company is incorporated), and the government. If the parties minimize the present value of their combined tax payments, they will increase the size of the pie over which they are negotiating. This chapter will address some of the key tax considerations for both the buyer and the seller.

As noted in the prior chapter's example of the ASC/CGA combination, the difference in the accounting treatment of an acquisition—as a pooling or as a purchase—may have no current or cumulative effect on the resulting business. Differences in tax treatment, however, have an impact both on reported earnings and cash flow.

## BUYING ASSETS OR STOCK

One of the key issues facing a purchaser of a company is whether to acquire the company's stock or its assets. While these transactions are economically similar if not identical, significantly different tax results may occur from the purchase of assets, stock, or a combination of both.

A purchaser often acquires assets in order to acquire only selected items; to avoid incurring responsibility for liabilities that are undisclosed on the balance sheet; to avoid having to continue with a perceived unfavorable accounting method; or to get a stepped-up asset basis (to turn the current fair market value of assets into its tax cost). This may lead to adverse postacquisition tax results.

A seller, on the other hand, often wishes to sell stock instead of assets to get rid of contingent liabilities; to avoid the need to value components of a purchased business; or to avoid the tax that may arise from prior depreciation or LIFO reserves.

A tax-free reorganization (as discussed on page 209) will help the seller's cash flow at the time of the initial transaction because the recognition of the seller's gain is deferred and no taxes need be paid by the seller at the time of the sale. However, this type of transaction may cost the purchaser more over time if the company acquired is later deprived of the benefit of decreased income tax payments that would have resulted from additional depreciation and amortization deductions.

For pre-1987 acquisitions, this conflict between the purchaser's desire to buy assets and the seller's desire to sell stock could be resolved simultaneously by having the acquired company sell its assets and liquidate. Under the "General Utilities" doctrine, which was eliminated by the Tax Reform Act of 1986, a corporation being liquidated could sell its assets and distribute the cash proceeds without recognizing gain or loss on those sales; the only tax on the liquidating corporation would be the "recapture" or repayment of the value of some past tax benefits (such as depreciation). Accordingly, the acquirer could reflect its acquisition cost in the depreciable basis of the assets without the selling corporation having to recognize full taxable gain. (The shareholders of the selling corporation would, of course, have to recognize taxable gain, but they would have done so anyway if they had sold their stock instead of having their corporation sell assets in liquidation.) As a result of the Tax Reform Act's elimination of "General Utilities," a liquidating corporation must recognize full taxable gain or loss on the sale of its assets. In addition, this treatment of the liquidating corporation cannot be avoided by having the corporation distribute the assets to its shareholders in liquidation; the liquidating corporation will be treated as if it had sold its assets to its shareholders at fair market value.

Such treatment of the acquired corporation does not mean that an asset sale should always be avoided. The acquired company may have tax attributes, such as past tax losses, that can be carried forward to offset the taxable gain that will be triggered by the asset sale. If the use of those tax losses would be subject to restrictions if the stock of the corporation were sold (as discussed on page 212 under *Assess Sec. 382*), it may make more sense to have the acquired company sell assets so that the restrictions can be avoided with the benefit of the losses taking the form of a higher depreciable basis in the assets for the purchaser.

Most corporate acquisitions involve tax considerations for four taxpayers or groups of taxpayers:

- The purchaser
- The purchaser's shareholders
- The seller (or target)
- The seller's shareholders

Most acquisitions fall within one of four basic formats:

- Taxable purchases
  - stock
  - asset
- "Nontaxable" or tax-deferred acquisitions
  - stock
  - asset

These four forms of acquisitions have different tax consequences for the four taxpayers/groups as summarized in Figure 14-1.

## TAXABLE TRANSACTIONS (STOCK OR ASSET PURCHASES)

Taxable purchases of another company are similar to transactions accounted for as purchases under generally accepted accounting principles (GAAP), as discussed in Chapter 13.

**FIGURE 14-1. The four basic acquisition formats**

| | Type of Transaction | | | |
| | Transfer of stock | | Transfer of assets | |
| Parties to the transaction | Nontaxable | Taxable | Nontaxable | Taxable |
|---|---|---|---|---|
| Shareholders of target | Selling shareholders of target company have no taxable gain or loss. The basis of the stock of the purchasing company received by the selling shareholders is the same as that of their target company stock. | Selling shareholders will recognize gain or loss. | Selling shareholders have no taxable gain or loss. The basis of the stock of the purchasing company received by the selling shareholders is the same as that of the target company stock. | Shareholders of target company will have gain or loss if target company liquidates. |
| Purchasing company | Purchasing company recognizes no gain or loss. The basis of the target company stock received by purchasing company carries over from the target shareholders. | Purchasing company generally recognizes no gain or loss.<br><br>The basis of the target company stock received by purchasing company will be what was paid. | Purchasing company has no gain or loss.<br><br>The basis of target company assets acquired by purchasing company is the same as if owned by target.<br><br>Tax attributes of target, including net operating losses, are transferred to purchasing company. Net operating losses may be limited. | Purchasing company has no gain or loss.<br><br>Assets acquired at fair market value by purchasing company. |

| | | | | |
|---|---|---|---|---|
| Target company | Target company is unaffected, except that net operating loss carryovers may be limited. | Target company is unaffected, unless Sec. 338 applies. Net operating losses may be limited. | Target company goes out of existence. No gain or loss is recognized. | Target company will recognize a gain or loss on the sale of its assets.<br><br>Tax attributes of target company are unaffected, unless target company liquidates, in which case they disappear. |
| Shareholders of purchasing company | Shareholders of purchasing company are unaffected. However, dilution of their control of purchasing company will result. | Generally, there is no dilution of control to shareholders of purchasing company. | Shareholders of purchasing company are unaffected. However, dilution of their control of purchasing company may result. | Generally, no dilution of control to shareholders of purchasing company. |

From a tax standpoint, a sale of many assets at once is similar to the sale of a single asset. Only the magnitude of the transaction and the need to allocate the purchase price among the assets differs. Also, non–income tax considerations related to transfer of title and transfer taxes enter into a bulk sale.

Whenever assets are purchased in a taxable transaction, their tax cost (the "basis") is the amount paid. Where something other than cash is paid, the basis is the fair market value of the assets transferred. A sale of assets by a corporation is taxable to that corporation. The same result occurs regardless of whether or not the sale is made by the corporation in contemplation of liquidation.

### Seller's Shareholders in a Taxable Acquisition

In any acquisition, the purchaser must be mindful of the seller's tax status. Because a taxable acquisition will likely result in a tax liability for the seller, its shareholders will frequently want a higher price in a taxable transaction in order to be made whole. Thus, tax cost will affect the acceptable purchase price.

For example, assume a sale of a going business is being negotiated. The purchaser wants a minimum cost. The selling stockholders own stock of a corporation that, in turn, owns land. (For purposes of this example, the selling corporation is assumed to own just one asset.)

The fair market value of the land is $200, and its cost was $20. Assuming that $200 is agreed on as the purchase price, the sale of corporate stock would clearly be preferable, as can be seen from this comparison:

|                                                      | Stock Sale | Asset Sale |
| ---------------------------------------------------- | ---------- | ---------- |
| 1. Gross proceeds                                    | $200       | $200       |
| 2. Corporate basis in land                           | –          | 20         |
| 3. Corporate-level gain                              | –          | 180        |
| 4. Corporate tax @ 34 percent                        | –          | 61         |
| 5. Proceeds to shareholder (item 1 – item 4)         | 200        | 139        |
| 6. Shareholder basis in stock                        | 20         | 20         |
| 7. Shareholder-level gain                            | 180        | 119        |
| 8. Shareholder tax @ 33 percent individual rate      | 60         | 40         |
| 9. Net proceeds to shareholder (item 5 – item 8)     | $140       | $ 99       |

In order for the seller's shareholder to net the same amount of cash ($140) from the land sale as from a stock sale, the price for the land would have to be $293.

| | Asset Sale |
|---|---|
| 1. Gross proceeds | $293 |
| 2. Corporate basis in land | 20 |
| 3. Corporate-level gain | 273 |
| 4. Corporate tax @ 34 percent | 93 |
| 5. Proceeds to shareholder (item 1 − item 4) | 200 |
| 6. Shareholder basis in stock | 20 |
| 7. Shareholder-level gain | 180 |
| 8. Shareholder tax @ 33 percent individual rate | 60 |
| 9. Net proceeds to shareholder (item 5 − item 8) | $140 |

In effect, this would transfer the cost of all tax burdens relating to the sale from the seller to the purchaser. The purchaser, in that case, would have a higher basis for the acquired assets, representing the amount paid. However, the benefit would at best result in future cash savings due to a lower capital gain at the time of resale, while the cost would be more cash paid now. Accordingly, it is hard to see how the parties would willingly agree to a sale of assets instead of stock unless, as noted above, the acquired corporation had tax attributes such as tax loss carryovers that could offset the corporate-level gain and that would become limited if the stock of the acquired company were sold.

An acquisition of the stock of an acquired company for cash or other property also results in a taxable gain or loss to the seller's shareholders. The purchaser's basis in the acquired stock equals the amount paid. However, the purchaser gets no other advantage until the stock is sold, because no depreciation is allowed on stock cost.

## When the Acquired Company Is a Subsidiary

When the acquired company is a subsidiary, its parent has a choice of selling the stock of the subsidiary or having the subsidiary sell its assets. Since either structure would involve the recognition of gain or loss, the parent might be tempted to base the decision on whether it has a higher tax basis in the subsidiary's stock or the sub-sidiary has a higher tax basis in its assets. However, this ignores the tax impact on the purchaser. A sale of stock might minimize the seller's tax, while preventing the purchaser from reflecting its ac-quisition costs in the depreciable basis of the acquired company's assets.

For example, assume the subsidiary being acquired has assets with a tax basis of $100, a fair market value of $1,000, and no liabilities, while the parent has a tax basis in its subsidiary's stock of $200. If the subsidiary sells its assets, it will have a taxable gain of $900, while a sale of the subsidiary's stock would limit the taxable gain to $800. However, the asset sale would give the purchaser a depreciable basis in the subsidiary's assets of $1,000. In contrast, the stock sale would leave the new owner of the subsidiary with an undepreciable basis of $1,000 in the subsidiary's stock while the subsidiary's depreciable basis in the assets remains at $100. As long as the present value of the tax savings from depreciating the additional $900 of acquisi-tion cost exceeds the seller's extra tax cost on the additional $100 of taxable gain ($900 on the assets vs. $800 on the stock), the trans-action should be cast as an asset sale. The parties can then negotiate how to divide their combined tax savings from this structuring and reflect the results in the acquisition price.

## When the Acquired Company Is an "S Corporation"

A special election in the Internal Revenue Code permits an unaf-filiated corporation owned by thirty-five or fewer individuals to be treated as a conduit. That is, no corporate-level tax is imposed and the shareholders take into account on a current basis their shares of the corporation's taxable income or loss. Generally, such an "S Corporation" can sell its assets to the acquirer and liquidate without incurring a double tax—a corporate-level tax and another share-holder-level tax.

### Section 33B Treatment

Under Section 33B of the Internal Revenue Code, a purchaser of stock may elect to treat the corporate assets acquired by stock pur-chase as if they were acquired directly. Where the acquired company is a subsidiary, a special election under Sec. 33B(h)(10) permits the parent to sell the stock of its subsidiary while treating the transaction as if its subsidiary had sold its assets instead. These elections generally achieve the same tax effect as a taxable asset transfer without such undesirable side effects as recording of deeds and exposure to state and local transfer taxes. However, in the case of an "S Corporation," such an election will not avoid the corporate-level tax, which, as discussed earlier, can be avoided if the "S Corporation" sells assets.

For the purchaser to elect Sec. 33B treatment with respect to an acquisition, many requirements must be met. Some of them are as follows:

- Acquisition of control
- Maximum twelve-month acquisition period
- Acquisition by purchase
- Possible adjustment for amount of deemed purchase price

A Sec. 33B election must be made within eight and a half months after the end of the month in which the acquisition occurs. In addition, the seller's tax attributes, such as net operating loss carryovers, capital loss carryovers, credit carryovers, earnings, and profits, as well as its accounting methods, disappear following a Sec. 33B election because such a transaction is treated as an asset sale.

## Allocation of Purchase Price as Tax Basis

A major factor in the purchase of a business is the price the purchaser is allowed to allocate for future tax purposes to each of the assets acquired. This allocation consideration applies either to a taxable asset purchase or to a purchase of stock followed by a Sec. 33B election. The 1986 Tax Reform Act placed strict limits on how such a purchase price can be allocated.

The specific mechanism of allocating the tax cost of a purchase is as follows: basis is allocated first to cash and cash items, then to marketable securities and like items, then to the various other assets acquired. If the total purchase price paid exceeds the total fair market value of the identified assets acquired, the excess is goodwill. No amortization of goodwill is permitted as a deduction in computing taxable income.

Neither goodwill nor "going concern" value are amortized for tax purposes; therefore, no tax benefits are derived from any portion of the purchase price allocated to these items until such time as the company is again sold. An allocation of purchase price to assets such as inventory, which is expensed as sold, allows the purchaser a deduction for tax purposes. Therefore, in valuing the seller's assets, a purchaser will want to find depreciable or amortizable intangible assets to which allocation of basis can be made, in order to maximize recovery of the acquisition cost through depreciation or amortization.

In this regard, the repeal of the special lower rate for capital gains by the Tax Reform Act of 1986 enhances the attractiveness of noncompete clauses. Allocations of purchaser price to such a provision results in ordinary taxable income to the seller, though the buyer can obtain a quick write-off over the period of the noncompetition. Prior to the Tax Reform Act, the interests of buyer and seller were adverse, since the seller would want to avoid an allocation to the noncompete provision in order to avoid ordinary income treatment while the buyer would want such an allocation to obtain a quick write-off. With the elimination of the special rate, the seller no longer cares about the allocation.

Many similarities exist between methodology used to value an acquired company's assets for tax purposes and for GAAP purposes. For example, the purchase price allocable to the assets is generally determined in the same manner for tax purposes as for GAAP; in both cases, it is the sum of cash and fair market value of any other assets paid plus liabilities assumed.

The rules differ in accounting for contingent liabilities. For book purposes, GAAP requires the recording of contingent liabilities based on both the probability of occurrence and the reasonable estimation of amount. However, tax rules do not permit contingent liability recognition until such liabilities are "fixed and determinable" with reasonable accuracy. Generally, GAAP definitions would result in the recognition of some liabilities that are not liabilities for tax purposes. On the other hand, the liability assumed by the purchaser for outstanding long-term debt may be higher under tax rules, which do not permit discounting such debt at current market rates, whereas such discounting is required for GAAP.

Valuation difficulties may arise when assets are acquired for stock and/or other noncash assets. In this case, the value of the assets acquired is the value paid. If stock given as consideration is traded on a recognized market, then the exchange quotes for the valuation date are generally the best evidence of fair market value. However, there are cases where market quotations are unavailable or may be considered an unreliable indication of value due to specific market conditions or stock characteristics. For example, if the stock is closely held, various factors are weighed for valuation purposes. These factors include the company's earning capacity, the industry's economic outlook, and the market price of similar stocks, and are similar to the guidelines for valuing closely held stock for estate-tax and gift-tax purposes.

## NONTAXABLE TRANSACTIONS (STOCK OR ASSET PURCHASES)

Like pooling-of-interest accounting, an acquisition can be treated as a nontaxable transaction (technically a tax-free reorganization) only if a variety of conditions are met. But while pooling-of-interest accounting will result where conditions set by the American Institute of Certified Public Accountants and the Securities and Exchange Commission are met, tax-free treatment requires that conditions set by the Internal Revenue Code, Income Tax Regulations, the Internal Revenue Service, and the courts be met.

In a tax-free acquisition, financial gain that otherwise would be realized in the transaction from the exchange of stock or assets is generally deferred. The historical basis of assets carries over. Also, the purchaser acquires the acquired company's tax history. Tax-free control of a target may be acquired either by acquisition of assets or stock.

A variety of conditions set by the courts must be met before an acquisition can receive tax-free reorganization treatment, including the following:

- Continuity of business enterprise
- Continuity of shareholder interest
- Business purpose to the reorganization

### Continuity of Business Enterprise

The continuity of business enterprise requirement is that the buyer either continue the acquired company's historic business or use a significant portion of the acquired company's historic business assets in a business. If the acquired company has more than one line of business, the first alternative is satisfied if the acquiring corporation continues a significant line of business of the acquired company. Where the acquired company is a holding company, the application of these rules will depend on an analysis of not only the acquired company itself but also its subsidiaries.

### Continuity of Shareholder Interest

All tax-free reorganizations require at least some of the acquired company's shareholders to receive an equity interest in the acquiring corporation or its parent. The rule is most liberal in a statutory merger, or "A" reorganization: any kind of stock may be used, common or preferred, voting or nonvoting, and as long as 50 percent of the acquired company's stock is exchanged for stock in the merged corporation, the continuity of shareholder interest requirement is satisfied, regardless of whether all shareholders receive stock and other consideration on a pro rata basis. (However, any shareholder receiving nonequity consideration will have to recognize any taxable gain to the extent of amount of cash and value of nonequity consideration.) In other types of reorganizations, such as acquisitions of target stock or target assets, much more stringent requirements are imposed: in a stock acquisition, only voting stock may be used and 80 percent control of the target must be achieved, while in an asset acquisition only voting stock may be used except under very limited conditions, and 90 percent of the fair market value of the net assets and 70 percent of the fair market value of the gross assets must be acquired.

## Business Purpose to the Reorganization

To receive tax-free treatment, a proposed reorganization must have a business (or nontax) purpose separate from its shareholders'. This requirement originated in the courts, but now is reflected in the Income Tax Regulations. Common business purposes include cost savings, economies of scale, and expansion into new markets.


## SURVIVAL OF TAX ATTRIBUTES

Over the life of a corporation, it will accumulate various items of tax history, referred to as tax attributes. These items fall into several categories:

- Accounting methods and like items
- Accumulated earnings and profits
- Carryovers of certain tax losses and benefits

Most of these items are transferred in tax-free acquisitions, but are eliminated in a taxable sale of assets or a Sec. 33B acquisition. Many of the items also survive a taxable acquisition of the acquired company's stock where no Sec. 33B election is made to treat the transaction as an asset acquisition. Even where tax attributes survive a transfer, the law limits the extent to which a purchaser may use carryovers of certain tax losses and credits.

One attribute commonly prized is the net operating loss (NOL). A NOL arises when permitted deductions exceed gross income subject to tax. In that case, the excess amount is allowed as a deduction in computing taxable income in the three years prior to the loss year and the fifteen years following the loss year.

The steps in determining how good a net operating loss deduction is following a tax-free reorganization or a taxable acquisition of stock without a Sec. 33B election are as follows:

**1.** *Assess the NOL:* Determine if income and deductions originally reported in the loss years were correct.

**2.** *Assess the business purpose:* Determine whether the principal purpose of the acquisition is a business (nontax) purpose.

**3.** *Assess consolidated return rules:* If the acquired company will survive the acquisition and be included in a consolidated return with the purchaser, the acquired company's loss carryovers will only be permitted to offset future taxable income of the acquired company. Sometimes this limitation can be avoided by liquidating the acquired company into the acquirer.

**4.** *Assess Sec. 382:* Where direct and indirect ownership of a corporation changes by over 50 percent within a three-year period, as would be true in most acquisition transactions, the annual amount of the acquired company's net operating loss carryovers that may be deducted will be limited to a "reasonable" return on the investment in the acquired company. "Reasonable" is defined as the long-term tax-exempt interest rate, currently about 8 percent. The investment in the acquired company is net of acquisition debt, whether or not the debt is pushed down to the acquired company. For example, if the company is acquired for $10,000 using $9,000 of acquisition debt, only $80 of the acquired company's net operating loss carryovers (8 percent of the difference between $10,000 and $9,000) may be deducted annually. However, this annual limitation can be increased to accommodate gain resulting from a Sec. 33B election with respect to the acquisition, and for the first five years it can be increased to accommodate certain gains that were accrued economically but not realized at the time of the acquisition.

**5.** *Assess Sec. 384:* Where either the acquired company or the acquiring corporation has net operating loss carryovers, generally the carryovers of the loss corporation cannot be used to offset the gains of the other corporation to the extent that they were accrued but not realized at the time of the acquisition.

## DISPOSITION OF UNWANTED ASSETS

Where stock of the acquired company is acquired and no Sec. 33B election is made to treat the stock acquisition as a purchase of assets, the acquired company's tax basis in its assets will not reflect the purchaser's acquisition costs. If the acquisition price represents a premium over the acquired company's net value for tax purposes, the acquired company most probably would have to recognize taxable gain on the sale of any of its assets that the purchaser does not want it to retain.

Prior to recent tax legislation, the acquiring corporation could form several subsidiaries that would "mirror" the groups of assets that the acquirer wasn't interested in and the residual group to be retained. The acquired company would then be liquidated into the mirror subsidiaries, with one receiving the assets to be retained and each of the others receiving a group of assets that would be sold as a separate package. In this way, the acquisition cost of the stock of each mirror subsidiary would equal the fair market value of the net assets it contained, even though the subsidiary itself would have the acquired company's old tax basis in its assets. The stock of each mirror subsidiary could then be sold immediately in a transaction that would produce little or no taxable gain, even though the mirror subsidiary might have had substantial taxable gain if it had sold its assets instead.

Recent legislation has blocked this technique and a variation of the technique. However, it is still possible to achieve the same tax result if the acquisition is structured properly. In addition, it may be possible for the acquirer and parties interested in the unwanted assets to achieve essentially the same economic consequences as a breakup of the target without actually breaking it up and incurring adverse tax consequences.

## MULTINATIONAL ACQUISITIONS

When the acquired company is a multinational corporation, many complications arise from a tax viewpoint. The most pressing problems usually stem from the acquisition debt. If a portion of the acquisition debt is not shoved down to the foreign subsidiaries of the acquired company, the interest expense may exceed the worldwide U.S. taxable income of the target (and, if the acquirer is a corporation that will file a consolidated return with the acquired company, consolidated U.S. taxable income). To the extent that interest expense does not exceed preinterest taxable income, the interest expense will be allocated in part to foreign-source U.S. taxable income. To the extent that such foreign-source taxable income has already borne foreign income taxes that exceed the U.S. tax on that income, the U.S. tax on that income will already have been offset by the foreign tax credits; in that event, no U.S. tax savings may be available for the interest expense allocated to that income. Even the portion of the interest expense allocated to U.S.-source taxable income may exceed such income; in such an event, there may be no U.S. tax benefit for the excess amount.

These problems can be solved or minimized by pushing acquisition debt down to the foreign subsidiaries of the acquired company. This can be accomplished in several ways, depending upon the countries in which the acquired company's foreign subsidiaries operate.

In addition, the opportunity to reflect the acquirer's acquisition cost in the tax basis of the assets of the foreign subsidiaries of the acquired company for foreign income tax purposes should not be overlooked. And the most tax-efficient way of repatriating excess cash from the acquired company's foreign subsidiaries should be reviewed.

## CONCLUSION

There are many ways in which the combined tax burdens of the acquirer, the seller, and the seller's shareholders can be minimized and deferred. The transaction should be structured to optimize the combined tax burden so that the parties will have a larger pie over which to negotiate.

# SECTION

# Integrating the Acquisition

## INTRODUCTION

The authors in this section all assert that the time to plan for post-acquisition integration of the people who come with the purchased company is before the transaction closes. Each chapter identifies different types of people issues and offers ideas for dealing with them.

Leading off the section is a chapter by a certified CEO, J. Tracy O'Rourke, who has an admirable record of acquisition successes. His breezy style and Irish wit make the considerable substance of his pragmatic advice a pleasure to read.

Larry Senn describes different management styles and corporate cultures in the second chapter of this section. Cultural fit frequently may be as important to the success of a transaction as strategic fit. But there are ways to meld two disparate cultures into relative harmony after the deal closes.

Many issues must be addressed in studying how the employee benefit plans of two merging corporations should be integrated. James E. Nelson and A. Lee Westervelt discuss the alternatives of merging into one plan or following other options in the third chapter of this section. Each alternative has different implications for the companies and for their respective employees.

The final chapter, by Gary Marsack, describes the problems that must be solved when the employees of the company being acquired are represented by a union. Most of the issues can be resolved more by business judgments than by legal requirements. Through thoughtful planning, the acquiring management has an opportunity to determine much of the future framework within which it will deal with its new employees.

# CHAPTER 15

# POSTMERGER INTEGRATION

## J. Tracy O'Rourke
**PRESIDENT, ALLEN-BRADLEY CO.**

If an acquisition came with an owner's manual—complete with a section on how to start it and operate it, a maintenance schedule, a guide to repairs, maybe even a warranty—then all a CEO would have to do is follow it, keep to the timetables, and fill in the blanks. The idea sounds farfetched, yet some theoreticians act as if postmerger integration were just that cut and dried. They try to prescribe what amount to formulas or recipes for corporations to follow after they buy a company.

Some try to help a company decide when to introduce its financial systems. Some tell how to replace the acquired company's inventory methods with those of the acquirer. Others discuss the importance of combining computer operations. Still others advise on how to impose a sales force onto another company's marketing network. As a bonus, some even tell how to run periodic checks to make sure everything negotiated in the deal is turning out the way it was planned.

If that is a formula for anything, it is a formula for failure—and failure is something that has plagued far too many U.S. corporate acquisitions.

There is no formula for postmerger integration. The reason is simple: no two acquisitions are alike, and no two acquirers are alike.

If there is any axiom at all to pulling off a successful acquisition, it is this: the acquisition must make sense for the acquirer from the beginning. The corollary is: follow the deal through at a carefully measured pace.

## WHAT MOTIVATED THE ACQUISITION?

Before a company can successfully integrate an acquisition, its leadership must stop and reflect on why it wanted to buy the company in the first place. Here are some of the usual motives for acquisitions, and the problems they can present after the deal is done:

• *Pure diversification:* Companies with cash or credit to spare realize the marketplace is beginning to eclipse them, so they buy a company in another industry to bolster their core industry's expected decline.

These are fairly rare. Almost any company that has been running well at all has been diversifying over time. If a company has been asleep, it is probably too late to save it with a diversification. And if a company is worth buying, it is going for a premium. So the acquirer needs not only money, but patient money, because it will have to wait a long while to get its money back. But if a company can afford the price of admission, and if it does not interfere too much in the company it buys, the acquisition can succeed.

• *Improved market position:* These can be tricky to pull off, particularly if the impetus for the acquisition originated with a small unit within the acquiring company. The unit may have convinced the CEO that it could boost its market share from, say, 3 percent to 30 percent if Company X were purchased. That is a dubious motive for an acquisition: if the division's management is that good, it should have more than a 3 percent market share to begin with.

Here is what often happens. Most CEOs of acquiring companies do not want to see their manager subjugated by the folks from the acquired company, even if they have a bigger market share. So "Old Joe" or "Old Joan" is put in charge of the combined company, even though he or she lacks the experience to run a company of that size.

Folks from the acquired company do not like that and leave. The little fish may have eaten the whale, but no one truly qualified to run the new company is still around.

• *Turnaround situations:* A company has gone bottom fishing, deciding to pick up a company that has good market position but is in trouble, which is why it is cheap. The top team thinks: "We're smart guys; we can manage this better."

Maybe so. But often those cheap companies are in real trouble and need a whole lot of managing. And if the acquirer is running lean, it probably cannot afford to cut loose some of its key people to play doctor.

What happens frequently in turnaround cases is that the acquirer fires everyone who got the acquired company in trouble, then goes out and quickly hires replacements. Often these people are unknown or untested, or worse still, as bad as the people who got the company in trouble in the first place.

• *Acquiring technology:* These can work out fairly well—*if* a company can make its corporate culture mesh with the other company's culture. But that is a huge *if.*

## THE TOUGHEST INTEGRATIONS

The most difficult company to assimilate into a large corporation is the engineer-entrepreneur company, precisely because the culture of the small company is so dramatically different from the acquirer's.

Conversely, the easiest type of company to assimilate into another is the public company that is willing to be sold. That is because its culture is likely to be much closer to the acquirer's. Management there is accustomed to being under scrutiny by analysts and the public. The company probably uses many of the same operating methods as the acquirer uses. More than likely, if the acquirer is buying a public company or a piece of a large corporation, it has a large database to look at and analyze in detail. If a fire-breathing dragon is hiding in there, more than likely it will show up in the data. Companies that end up surprised after they buy a big public company or corporate spinoff usually lacked the skill to analyze the available data.

But most successful small engineer-entrepreneur companies are run by mavericks, often with rogue operating systems that might be difficult to analyze. Most engineer-entrepreneurs are convinced their way is right, and they do not give a damn what the rest of the world thinks. That is why they are successful—and why they are so difficult to fit into a larger corporate structure.

I would estimate the odds of getting such a person to adapt to a larger company's culture are less than 1 in 100. And yet that is the person who started the company and grew it into the success that made another company want to buy it. The acquirer wants him or her around—for a while, at least.

But how should such a "loose cannon" be handled, particularly after he or she has become very rich?

Gingerly. Two rules:

- Do not be naive about the people you make rich.

- Take time. If naiveté is the worst enemy of deals like this, excessive speed is the second-worst enemy.

Large companies should not delude themselves that an entrepreneur is going to stick around and keep his or her company humming within a large organization just because that company has paid him or her a lot of money. More than likely, people like that will not stay long after the acquisition. After all, they did not start that company to be part of a large company—it is against their nature. They always wanted to be independent.

And if that arrogant entrepreneur leaves, those problems will not disappear. That maverick culture is deeply embedded in the company. If the folks at the new company are used to working in ripped T-shirts and shorts, they cannot be expected to go gladly into blue pinstripes. As many internal changes as possible should be deferred for as long as possible.

## THE NURTURING PLAN

How long does it take to assimilate a company after a merger or acquisition?

Again, there is no single answer, no timetable, no formula. Instead of following a formula, a company must have a plan, and have it in place going into the deal.

Years ago, when I worked at The Carborundum Co., my colleague Bill Wendel, the president, insisted that we develop what he called a "nurturing plan" before we actually acquired a company. It was part of the policy-statement checklist.

I learned a great deal from that exercise. It was an excellent way to force top executives to think the deal through.

Invariably, when we made presentations on acquisitions, Wendel would ask these questions:

- How are we going to merge the company?
- Are we going to crush it together right away with some other unit of our company, or let it run for a year or two and then slowly bring it together?
- Is the guy or gal running the company going to stay?
- Can we depend on his or her staying?
- Should he or she stay?

Most acquirers do not go through such a process. They simply do not give postmerger integration much thought. It is the conquest that gives them their thrills. They are like sharks in a feeding frenzy; once they land their prey they lose interest. I would guess that the senior management of most large corporations gets heavily involved in the decisions to acquire companies, but turns over the "do work," the dirty details of integrating the acquisition, to someone else.

That is irresponsible. After all, it takes a tremendous amount of time and effort to acquire a company. Unless a company is bailing another company out of trouble, it usually takes a year. In many ways, it is like having a baby. After having gone through all that effort, it does not make sense to walk away, to abandon it to someone else.

## KEEPING THE STAFF AT BAY

The early days—from a couple of months to as long as a year—are the most critical in integrating an acquisition. Acquiring the company was important enough to occupy a CEO's time for a year, so it stands to reason that the CEO must stay involved for a reasonable amount of time after the deal is closed if it is going to succeed.

And to that caveat I would add one other plea: keep staff people out of it as long as possible. One of the gravest sins in assimilating an acquisition is to allow staff people to go in willy-nilly and force change before it is necessary. That creates ill will and drives up costs.

I am not antistaff. When buying a company, a CEO must rely on staff for fact-finding. Experts must evaluate the target and look for things that can hurt the acquiring company later. That is what they do best. But once the acquisition has been made, senior management must take over and make the value judgments about what should be fixed and when.

The typical acquisition becomes an attractive nuisance. It is the new toy, and everyone wants to go see it and play with it—especially staff people, because they usually can find some free time. But well-meaning staff people can damage an acquisition faster than almost anything else. As outstanding as most staff people are, they are functional folks. They want excellence in a specialized area. And when they strive for excellence in their functional areas, they more often than not drive costs up rapidly.

They will often visit the acquired company and pester the people with lots of petty requests for information. They will bring in a stack of policy manuals ten feet high. And they will say, "Thou shalt, and within ninety days." Or worse, they will go tell those people that top management wants things done a certain way: "What do you mean, you don't have a personnel manager? Here's our organizational chart. See those blocks. Fill 'em in. And get a computer like our computer."

The CEO needs to make it clear to staff not to invoke his or her name in the interests of change. And the CEO must also be careful about what he or she says to the new company in those early days. Too much of what comes out of a CEO's mouth is interpreted as mandate.

When a nice, profitable little company is overburdened with rules and regulations, it sags. One morning the acquiring company's CEO will wake up and find that it is not making money anymore because some staff people are trying to organize it and staff it like a company ten times its size.

## INTRODUCING CORPORATE CULTURE

I'm always a bit amused to read that one thorny issue in assimilating new companies is introducing overhead allocations or transfer pricing to the new unit. As far as I'm concerned, that should be a nonissue. But too often it is not.

Engineer-entrepreneur companies do go into culture shock the first time they are told "You're going to be selling your product to another division. Your gross margin will no longer be 50 percent, but cost plus 20 percent. Now don't worry; it won't mean anything after the books are consolidated."

And try to explain that the company routinely charges all its businesses a certain percentage of assets employed for corporate services. That makes entrepreneurs wild. Faced with situations like this, I think it is best to leave them alone at first. Do not charge them anything for the first year. Then, slowly but surely, the company's standard transactional costs should be introduced. The new company should be given time to assimilate and understand these so-called charges. Although they are just memo journal entries, they are alien to anyone who has not come up through a large corporation's structure. They do not really mean anything except to the staff people, anyway.

## PERSONNEL PROBLEMS

A sticking point in many acquisitions occurs when personnel compensation is out of line with the acquirer's policies.

Frequently, the top three or four people in small companies are paid extremely well. Before the deal is closed it will have to be made clear that the acquirer does not pay $300,000 a year to someone running a $25-million business.

If it is important for the top managers to stay for a while, the acquirer might have to agree to that salary for a specific number of years. But this becomes part of the written deal. That can help soothe personnel problems later on. If someone asks what the new manager is being paid, he or she should be told the truth, and that the payments are being made for three years, or five, or whatever, so that the new manager—formerly the owner—will stay on for a transition period.

People problems are not limited to small, entrepreneurial companies. Although public companies or corporate spin-offs are usually the easiest to assimilate because of the similarity of corporate cultures, people problems are still going to occur. The key people in the acquired company probably did not want to be acquired. They often feel rejected.

## WINNERS AND LOSERS

The CEO's job is to work hard to prevent a feeling of we-they, winners-and-losers, first-class and second-class citizens from developing, in order not to lose good senior people. I do not have any specific advice for how to prevent that winners-and-losers mentality from developing, apart from keeping alert for signs of it and quashing it quickly.

But I am fairly certain a company will invite those problems if senior managers walk away after the acquisition is completed. The acquired company is certain to feel doubly rejected if it sees the acquirer's CEO all the time during the negotiating period but hardly ever after the acquisition is completed.

Although it is rare, occasionally one hears about a reverse situation in which the acquired company is exalted and the acquirer starts feeling like the loser. Sometimes, in such cases, the new company is given responsibilities it cannot handle. Sometimes its members are given special perks, or its methods are forced down the throats of old employees. All of this gives a terrible message to long-time employees, and they rebel, ending in a power struggle that erodes morale and productivity.

## WHY PEOPLE LEAVE

After almost every acquisition, people leave.

Some get fed up after finding themselves on the low end of a winner-and-loser situation. Some, like an engineer-entrepreneur made quite rich, would rather leave than adapt to the corporate culture. And some, unfortunately, end up being purely redundant. They are reassigned or given incentives to leave.

No one enjoys having to do that, but CEOs faced with having to cut some people loose must be open and candid about it. If there is going to be any kind of bad news, it should be made public quickly, rather than making people wait and fret.

CEOs courting a company should tell that company's management about potential major changes before the deal is closed and money is exchanged.

## THE WORST ENEMY

Change is the worst enemy in mergers and acquisitions because it erodes morale so badly. That is why I believe in delaying change as long as possible when buying a company.

And change costs money. If one or two operations are changed, it might not make much difference. But an acquirer's putting in its systems all at once can drive costs off the charts.

Sometimes, of course, it is not possible to delay change. Clearly, the speed at which an acquisition is integrated varies according to two factors:

- *The condition of the company:* In a turnaround situation, with a company that is in trouble, the acquirer must go in and do whatever is necessary, and quickly.

- *The price:* Sometimes the acquirer must get rid of unnecessary expenses—or staff—to justify the premium paid for the company.

But in the absence of those two conditions, acquirers should go as slowly as possible, nurturing the company even if the technology is known and the acquirer could do everything the target is doing better and cheaper. Acquirers should ask if the money saved would be worth the damage caused by yanking the target's initiatives.

The goal of a postmerger integration is a transformation, not a revolution.

The Allen-Bradley Co. acquired ten companies in 1985–87, and we were still nurturing some of them in 1988. We worked hard not to screw them up or overburden them with unnecessary changes. At the same time, we did not lower our standards or abandon our essential purpose.

For example, we are real sticklers for quality. We are convinced that we succeed in the marketplace because of our quality standards. But we have occasionally had trouble convincing an acquired company that we demand such a high level of quality, consistency, and reliability.

We have to convince them that we do not demand this level of quality because it is fun, but because we believe it is the reason that we have the largest U.S. market share in essentially every product category we have. We will not accept lower quality, and if we cannot get the other company to agree, then the deal is off. We tell them they have got to start instituting our quality system. It is going to take three to five years to get it fully in place, but they must start immediately.

Allen-Bradley itself was acquired by Rockwell International Corp. in 1985. Rockwell has pretty much left us alone, and we have been slow to talk about Rockwell around here. We did not use the Rockwell logo on our stationery for the first year. And we changed the signs at our airport hanger in 1988.

And Rockwell is in complete agreement with this go-slow approach. Allen-Bradley was a $1-billion, 80-year-old company with a strong heritage when Rockwell acquired it. It will take time to transform a company of this size and with that heritage, but it is beginning to happen.

Although change is the worst enemy in any merger, it is inevitable. Anyone who promises a company that it will remain the same after it is sold is either having delusions or lying.

## APPRAISING THE ACQUISITION

The mere fact that the company has been acquired changes it, but some people forget that. Then a year or two later, they cannot understand why the company is not performing the way it did before it was acquired.

That is just one reason I have such little use for those so-called postmerger audits or appraisals that some theoreticians recommend.

What use is an audit of an acquired company a year later or two years later? The acquirer ought to know how well it is doing from the monthly reports. And more than likely, its performance will not be what it was before it was acquired, since acquisition means change, and change means cost.

The better way to evaluate an acquisition is to decide ahead of time why the company is being bought and what constitutes a success for that particular company. If the company has been losing money, it is probably unreasonably optimistic to expect it to make money right away. Maybe one of the markers for success for that company will be that it simply reduces its losses.

Once what constitutes success for that company has been defined, and if those objectives are not achieved within a reasonable period of time, something must be done, even if that means divesting the company at a loss. That is rough, because it means recognizing that mistakes have been made. That is never easy, especially if a CEO has invested a lot of himself or herself as well as the company's money in the acquisition.

One of the worst things that can happen in business is a partial success. Clear failures are much easier to deal with. But partial successes can bleed a company to death slowly over a long period of time.

## SYNERGY

In the world of mergers and acquisitions, one of the most overworked —or at least misunderstood—words is *synergy*. Reduced to its simplest equation, the idea of synergy is $1 + 1 = 3$. It is saying that the new combination is greater than the sum of its parts.

I do not like that definition. It is too facile and too deceptive. In a poorly conceived merger and its aftermath, a corporation might borrow heavily to buy a company, slam it together with its existing business, and eliminate a lot of costs at the top. Everyone starts calling that synergy.

But it is not. Over the short term, the reductions in overhead might look good. But the surviving corporation by now has exhausted its profit-producing and credit capabilities; it has nothing left to invest in the combined company. Over time, it is going to look pretty bad. Bill Wendel of Carborundum used to say that if the only thing a company can bring to an acquisition is money, it is not going to work.

I define *synergy* as an acquirer's being able to use its significant strengths to improve the performance of the acquired company, or taking one of the acquired company's strengths to bolster a weakness of its own.

Two strengths or two weaknesses combined do not make synergy. Synergy is much more than just eliminating some duplication at the top. Synergy is taking a company that is selling $50 million a year in the United States, putting it through an acquirer's distribution system, and selling $100 million a year worldwide.

## NO PANACEA

If a company views acquisitions as the core of its strategy or as a panacea, it will probably end up disappointed, if recent history is any guide. Look at the conglomerates of the 1960s. Most deconglomerated in the seventies and are "restructuring" in the eighties. *Restructuring* is just a weasel word for "Let's write off all those mistakes we made in the last ten or twenty years." With a little help from the tax code, companies that "restructure" can make their earnings look better and push their stock price up. Some companies talk about "rebenefiting the core." That means getting back to basics by getting rid of bad acquisitions that do not help a company's primary industry.

Clearly, I am not anti-acquisition. I have supervised some acquisitions that did not do well, but most have done extremely well, and we will continue to acquire. The reason for our overall favorable record, I am convinced, is that acquisitions never have been the core of our strategy. Building a company through acquisitions alone is the equivalent of a pyramid scheme.

Except in rare circumstances, the rule of thumb should be to acquire new companies only to supplement or complement a company's basic industry. Finally, stay involved in the postmerger integration.

# CHAPTER 16

# CULTURE

**Larry Senn**
**SENN–DELANEY LEADERSHIP PROGRAMS, INC.**

Two companies merging based only on financial data is like two people marrying based only on height, weight, and vital statistics; both lead to a high divorce rate. And indeed, the *Los Angeles Times* noted that "only half of mergers end up on a happy note" (February 17, 1985).

While it is clear that successful mergers and acquisitions must be based primarily on strategic, financial, and other objective criteria, ignoring a potential clash of cultures can lead to financial failure or at least a substantial diminution of expected results. Far too often, personnel and organizational issues are assigned a low priority during the preacquisition evaluation process. Other times they are an afterthought. Increasing evidence suggests that cultural incompatibility is the single largest cause of failure to achieve projected performance, departure of key executives, and time-consuming conflicts in consolidation of businesses. "When companies combine, a clash of cultures can turn potentially good business alliances into financial disasters," noted *Psychology Today* ("The Merger Syndrome," October 1986).

Many acquisitions that looked very promising from a number of viewpoints fail or require major surgery and extensive subsequent hand holding because critical personnel and organizational issues were not adequately evaluated prior to closing. One of the most celebrated examples was Exxon's ill-fated journey into business products through acquisition of Vydec. Exxon's large-oil-company culture came into conflict with the sense of urgency and bias for action needed for decision making in the high technology electronic business products market. As a former manager told *Business Week* in 1985, "They were oilmen used to three-to-five-year planning cycles, but we were frequently required to make changes because of something that had happened at two that afternoon."

Successfully negotiated and integrated, mergers and acquisitions can play a major role in the growth and success of organizations. Unfortunately, statistics indicate that up to one-third of mergers fail within five years, and as many as 80 percent never live up to their full expectations. The majority of these shortfalls are due to human factors, not to quantitative analysis. (Incidentally, it is interesting to note the parallel in the merger and acquisition failure rate and the divorce rate in America, where the number of divorces each year is approximately 50 percent of the number of marriages.)

As one analyst told *Training* magazine, "You can run all your discounted cash flows and have the numbers come out perfectly, but it's the human resources side of the merger/acquisition that spells failure or success. . . . When the deal is inked and the financial wizards go home, that's when the trouble starts. You've got the numbers. Now, what are you going to do about the people?" ("The Forgotten Factor in Merger Mania," February 1987). Since the human factor in mergers and acquisitions is so critical, it is important to understand and address it in each phase of the process.

Over a period of time, organizations, like people, develop distinctive personalities. In recent times, this organizational personality has been referred to as "corporate culture." Like an individual's personality, a company's culture is made up of its collective values, customs, and the unwritten rules that govern behavior within the organization.

Popular management books like *In Search of Excellence, Creating Excellence,* and *Corporate Culture* have highlighted the role a healthy culture plays in the success of organizations and the implementation of their strategies. The term "cultural clash" has been coined to describe the conflict of two companies' philosophies, styles, values, and missions. This may, in fact, be the most dangerous factor when two companies decide to combine.

## CHALLENGING COMBINATIONS

A number of contrasting styles in organizations exist that can be a problem when combining two entities. For example, consider the following combination:

| Style A | Style B |
|---|---|
| Highly participative | Hierarchical |
| Nondirective | Directive |
| Informal | Formal |
| Centralized | Decentralized |

A merger that experienced difficulty because it tried to combine companies with such traits was the Fluor Corporation's acquisition of St. Joe Minerals Corporation. St. Joe was decentralized, lean of staff, frugal, informal, and run with a light hand. Fluor was highly centralized, with a large corporate staff, many reporting levels, and many controls on decision making. In contrast to St. Joe's frugality, Fluor had planes and helicopters for use by its large central staff. This cultural conflict was so great that none of the senior St. Joe managers who went to Fluor stayed on, and of the twenty-two senior officers in St. Joe at the time of acquisition, only a few remained two years later.

Some other classic conflicting cultural qualities are the following:

| | | |
|---|---|---|
| Seniority-based compensation and promotion | vs. | Performance-based compensation and promotion |
| Conservative, risk-averse | vs. | Innovative, risk-taking |
| Cost- and control-driven | vs. | Service- and quality-driven |
| Long-range planning and deliberate decision making | vs. | Opportunistic, rapid decision making |
| Analytical, cautious | vs. | Intuitive, daring |
| Autocratic | vs. | Participative |

Cross-industry mergers and acquisitions often yield conflicting cultures. Mobil's management of Montgomery Ward is a challenging one because of the differences between the long-term exploration mindset of Mobil and the short-term retailing perspective of Montgomery Ward.

It is easier to find strategic and cultural fits within industries, and when this happens the probability of success is dramatically improved. Nabisco and Standard Brands was a compatible marriage of complementary products and distribution. It provided for an orderly period of integrating two management groups. The two presidents did not talk just about undervalued assets and discounted cash flow. Instead, they discussed similar customers, business philosophy, and plans for teamwork and mutual support.

## SPECIFIC HUMAN PROBLEMS OF ACQUISITIONS

Two major human problems can occur in acquisitions:

- Loss of key people
- Loss of organizational effectiveness

Whenever acquiring an organization, top managers should remember that "the natives have the maps." Even if the ultimate goal is to trim some of the dead wood, if not handled properly the wrong people will leave and the venture can be jeopardized. A number of studies have documented the high exit rate from acquired companies. One survey, in the Summer 1982 issue of *Merger and Acquisition* magazine, indicated that only 42 percent of managers remained with the acquired company for as long as five years.

Uncertainty and insecurity are associated with almost all mergers or acquisitions. It is essential to identify those people critical to continuing success and to put in motion a plan to insure that these key people do not leave. As a merger is announced, fears and anxieties are fueled by uncertainty about what the changes will bring. There is typically a feeling of personal vulnerability and loss of control. People often spend time updating their resumes and begin to explore their options.

The uncertainty surrounding the change often causes employees to experience a loss of enthusiasm about their work and their organization, and a drop in morale and organizational pride following the merger. Countless hours are spent fueling the rumor mill and large numbers of people adopt a wait-and-see attitude.

The sooner some semblance of certainty about the future can be communicated, the sooner people will settle down. Once a new vision for the organization is created and new future targets are set, people can refocus their energy in a forward direction.

## CAUSES OF LOSS OF PEOPLE AND EFFECTIVENESS

There are two major causes of losses of people and effectiveness when an organization is undergoing change such as a merger or acquisition:

- *Insecurity:* The devil that is known and the devil that is not
- *Winners and losers:* A "we vs. they" attitude

In times of uncertainty it is virtually impossible to overcommunicate. Anything that can be communicated should be, since people better face the known than the unknown.

Harry Levinson, a psychologist and Harvard professor, stresses the psychological consequences of the merger experience. He states that even when a merger offers new opportunities, it still tends to be perceived as a threat to one's equilibrium. Whether a merger is for the better or worse, it throws out of balance relationships, norms, work behavior, and support systems. If these psychological losses are not addressed early on, they can lead to chronic problems in attitude and behavior.

One of the issues to address as early as possible is the new organizational structure. Failed mergers are characterized by a tendency to have unclear reporting relationships and frequent changes in the reporting structure. In the study reported in *Merger and Acquisition* magazine in the Summer 1982 issue, 81 percent of merger failures were found to be characterized by frequent changes in the reporting relationships after the merger, while successful acquisitions were characterized by clear reporting relationships established early and not changed.

When companies are acquired, people almost immediately focus on the differences in the companies. It is typical in an acquisition for the acquirer to see itself as the winner, and the acquired company the loser. Typically, the acquirer wants to impose changes and sees those in the acquired company as highly resistant to change. On the other hand, the most frequent complaint of companies that are acquired is that the new owners "do not appreciate us." People immediately keep score, tallying which side won or lost each issue.

During such times, it is critical for the acquirer to go out of its way to acknowledge as many positive aspects of the acquired company as possible. It is important to identify which cultural factors have historically made an organization great in order to avoid "throwing out the baby with the bath water."

For example, if a company has historically been successful based on its culture of service and quality, rapid and insensitive cost cutting could destroy what made that organization great. In a similar manner, the acquisition of a small, highly entrepreneurial company by a larger, more formalized one poses cultural challenges. Although it is often important to provide direction and additional structure, this must be done without killing the entrepreneurial goose that is laying the golden eggs.

One of the difficulties of meshing two organizations is that each group tends to see the world through its own biased cultural filters. This is often referred to as "familiarity blindness" or a "cultural trance." For example, if everyone in an organization is risk-averse, then it might appear to someone new to the organization as if the world is that way, and should be. When two organizations get together, they both look at the same events, decisions, and situations, but colored by their culture and past experiences, they legitimately see them from two different points of view. Learning mutual respect and being open to exploring different points of view is one of the keys to the human factor in any merger or acquisition.

## VARIATIONS IN THE NATURE OF
## MERGERS AND ACQUISITIONS

The list of steps necessary to deal with the human side of the merger or acquisition is greatly influenced by the basis for the merger as well as the culture of the acquired company. For example, in a merger where the acquirer is interested in only the physical and financial assets of the acquired company and expects to lay off most managers and employees, major efforts to manage culture are unnecessary. However, when a true marriage of two companies is the end goal, attention to the management of culture becomes critical and detailed planning is required to harvest the expected benefits of the transaction.

It is important for the management of the acquiring firm to communicate their expectations to the firm being acquired early in the process. This information should include:

- the goals and objectives of the merger,
- career opportunities within the combined companies, and
- the benefits and the latitude the acquired company will be given in such areas as capital, technology, and ability to make their own acquisitions.

Merger outcomes take three common forms:

**1.** *Autonomy or semiautonomy.* In the hands-off or near hands-off scenario, the goal is to create mutual support and synergy without necessarily changing the nature of the organizations. It is unrealistic to assume that the acquirer will not want some modifications. For example, it might want some shift in one or more qualities, such as innovation, bias for action, or level of expectations. However, when the basis for the acquisition is autonomy or semiautonomy, it is important to respect the reasons for the differences in culture and to proceed slowly in any transformational activities. The results of such a shift are shown in Figure 16-1.

**2.** *Absorption and assimilation.* If the primary goal is to completely absorb and assimilate the acquired company—as diagrammed in

**FIGURE 16-1  Merger outcome: Autonomy or semiautonomy**

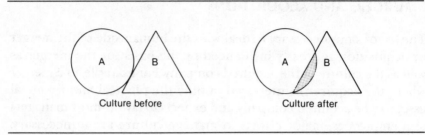

Culture before                    Culture after

**FIGURE 16-2  Merger outcome: Absorption and assimilation**

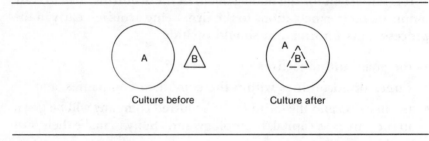

Culture before                    Culture after

Figure 16-2—then the primary need is to educate the acquired employees in terms of the new game rules in the combined organization. It should be remembered that they have been playing a different game under a different set of rules, both written and unwritten. Orientation to the new organization should include letting people know about the organization's vision and values, as has been determined during the preacquisition process.

**3.** *Cocreation of a new family.* A great amount of effort in cultural integration should take place in a true marriage of two companies, as diagrammed in Figure 16-3. In this case a joint integration team should decide on the organization's new vision and mission and should adopt a new set of shared values. In this way, neither of the old ways are made right or wrong, but instead all members are moving toward a new joint way to define the culture.

**FIGURE 16-3   Merger outcome: Cocreation of a new family**

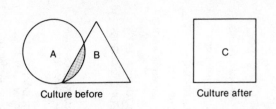

Culture before                                    Culture after

## PLANNING FOR THE MERGING OF CULTURES

A specific plan should be developed and implemented for merging culture as well as merging operations and finances. The process of merging can be broken down into three phases:

- Preacquisition
- Due diligence and negotiations
- Postacquisition

### The Preacquisition Phase

The guiding principle during preacquisition is "know thyself." This can be done through an instrument called a cultural profile. Both computerized and manual versions exist. One example of a straightforward manual version is shown in Figure 16-4.

To create the profile, a cross section of the management team is asked to rate the organization on a series of cultural strengths and weaknesses. In the example shown, the organization received good marks in terms of high standards and expectations, a healthy pace, and a sense of urgency. But cultural barriers exist in terms of too many excuses and blaming (lack of personal accountability), too much focus on "my area" (lack of teamwork), lack of clarity on goals and direction, and lack of a customer-oriented focus.

Some organizational characteristics are neither strengths nor weaknesses but simply differ from company to company. These characteristics can be evaluated in a manner similar to the corporate

**FIGURE 16-4  An example of a profile of cultural strengths and weaknesses**

| Strength | | Weakness |
|---|---|---|
| FOCUS ON RESULTS THROUGH PEOPLE | ——————x———————— | FOCUS ON TASKS |
| OPENNESS TO CHANGE | ——————x——————————— | RESISTANCE TO CHANGE |
| PERSONAL ACCOUNTABILITY/ SOLUTION ORIENTATION | ———————————x———— | EXCUSES/BLAMING OTHERS |
| TEAMWORK/MUTUAL SUPPORT/ INTERNAL COOPERATIVENESS | ——————————————x— | NARROW FOCUS/MY AREA |
| TRUST/OPENNESS | ——————x————————— | POLITICAL/CAUTIOUS |
| HIGH EXPECTATIONS | —x—————————————— | LOW EXPECTATIONS |
| TWO-WAY COMMUNICATIONS | ——————x————————— | TOP-DOWN COMMUNICATIONS ONLY |
| WILLINGNESS TO INNOVATE/RISK | —————————x——————— | DO WHAT IS TOLD/SAFETY |
| PRIDE/FEEL LIKE WINNERS | ——————————————x— | DON'T FEEL LIKE WINNERS |
| SENSE OF URGENCY | —x——————————————— | NOT DECISIVE |
| SELF-STARTERS | ———x———————————— | NEED DIRECTION |
| HIGH FEEDBACK/APPRECIATIVE | —————————————x— | LOW FEEDBACK/UNCERTAINTY ABOUT PERFORMANCE |
| SECURE | ——————x————————— | INSECURE |
| CLARITY OF GOALS AND DIRECTION (COMMON VISION) | ————————————————x | UNCLEAR ON GOALS AND DIRECTION |
| HEALTHY/HIGH PACE | —x——————————————— | OVERSTRESSED/BURNOUT |
| CUSTOMER-CENTERED | ——————————————x— | ACTIVITY-CENTERED (TASK) |

Senn-Delaney Leadership Programs Corporate Culture Profile, copyright 1987 culture profile. Figure 16-5 profiles two companies representing the extremes in the list of characteristics.

Once an organization has greater awareness of its own cultural strengths and weaknesses as well as organizational characteristics, it can use that information to begin to reshape a healthier culture to support acquisition and added internal success. And it can begin to create a profile of appropriate cultures for acquisition. These may be similar to the acquirer's culture or deliberately different to support new strategic directions. At this point, it is important for the CEO to be open and willing to identify those types of cultures that he or she would find difficult or impossible to support, or uncomfortable to manage or change.

## The Due Diligence Phase

The analysis of mergers and acquisitions during due diligence understandably focuses on financial information. But due diligence should also include analysis of human aspects. A number of things need to be done in this regard, such as the following:

- Develop a profile of the acquisition candidate's culture, and be aware of similarities and differences

**FIGURE 16-5   An example of a profile of organizational characteristics**

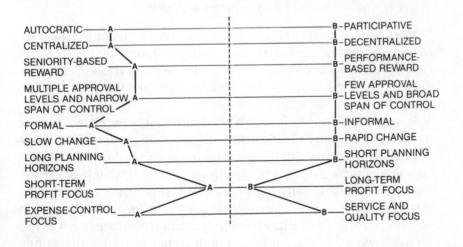

- Determine similarities and differences in the internal reinforcement system, including
  — compensation/benefit systems
  — performance review systems
  — performance criteria (written and unwritten)
  — hiring and firing criteria and practices
- Compare the philosophies of the dominant leaders, especially if they are both going to stay on
- Openly discuss not only financial considerations, but also the similarities and differences in culture and the proposed nature of the cultural integration

### The Postacquisition Phase

An integration team with members from both organizations should be established as soon as possible. In addition to all the financial and physical integration plans, a separate human resources and cultural integration plan should be developed, the key components of which should include the following:

- Communication plans and strategies
- Organizational structure and reporting relationships
- New vision, mission, and values development plan
- Personnel plan, including benefit packages, compensation packages, and policy and procedure packages

Most people understand that acquisitions take place for business reasons. It is important at the outset to communicate the benefits. People may not like the merger, but if they see that it has a legitimate purpose and the benefits are obvious, they are less likely to feel resentment and more likely to accept it.

When one company is acquiring another, it is important for the dominant company's leaders to communicate in person as much as possible. It is easier to be resentful toward an unknown, invisible ogre than a person one knows as being real, rational, and concerned. Successful mergers only happen when top managers make themselves visible and accessible to all employees affected by the merger and promote the benefits at all levels. As much information as can be made available should be communicated as frequently as possible in written form and in group meetings. This is a good way to minimize rumor and speculation, which can have a paralyzing effect on organizations.

During an acquisition, people need to be inspired to move toward new goals and visions. In the absence of a compelling purpose for a new organization, people tend to stay locked in the past and in speculation.

In a true merger designed to create a combined entity, the senior teams of each organization need to work together to clarify the new organizational mission and shared values. The relationships among vision, strategies, and values are shown in Figure 16-6.

Typically, this process is best handled with assistance by outside facilitators. It is useful to create a common, shared off-site experience for two teams to facilitate the consolidation process.

The greatest amount of speculation often surrounds the reporting relationships in organizational structure. The sooner they can be

**FIGURE 16-6  How vision, strategies, and values relate**

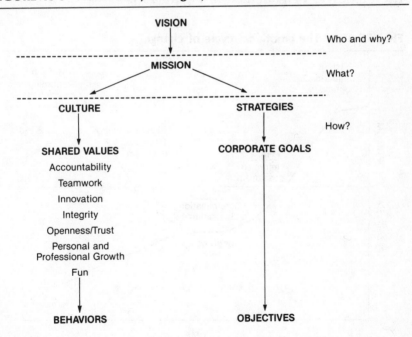

finalized and implemented, the sooner uncertainty and speculation can be ended. While this needs to be done quickly, it is important to do it with enough thought so that short-term revisions are held to a minimum.

One of the most sensitive issues is compensation. In the minds of individuals, compensation signals relative worth and perceived value, as well as overall status. The more autonomous the companies are to be, the less urgency exists in matching compensation packages. However, when companies are truly merged, nothing can create more resistance and resentment than differentials in pay and benefits.

## THE EMOTIONAL CYCLE OF CHANGE

The integration process should be entered into realistically, with full knowledge of the obstacles that can be encountered. Most acquisitions that are considered successful follow a pattern that has been described as the "emotional cycle of change." This cycle has five phases, as diagrammed in Figure 16-7.

**FIGURE 16-7   The emotional cycle of change**

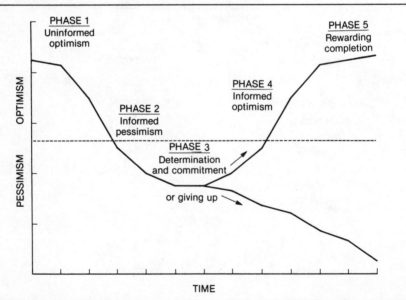

Phase 1 is uninformed optimism, when people are excited about the new venture and have not as yet faced the challenges and complications. Phase 2 is informed pessimism, when all of the issues, rumors, and disruptions are being faced. At phase 3, events can take one of two courses. Without a systematic plan in place, the pessimism can become reality and can be long lasting, leading to withdrawal of support for the change. On the other hand, with a plan in place and continued commitment, the tide turns and pessimism is replaced with hope. Hope builds to informed optimism and growing confidence in phase 4 and to completion and satisfaction in phase 5.

## THE BENEFITS

Using the ideas and tools described in this chapter to deal with the cultural aspects of mergers in a systematic way can dramatically increase the probability of success in any organizational integration and provide many benefits, including the following:

- Members know better how to effectively operate more quickly in their new or newly revised organization.
- A sense of community is present, since shared values link individuals to the organization and bind people together.
- The process of creating a vision, mission, and shared values creates excitement, inspiration, and commitment, with all people working for a new future goal, as opposed to living in the past.
- Fewer defections occur in the organization and the impact on morale is lessened.
- Productivity and profitability improve in a shorter period of time.

# CHAPTER 17

# EMPLOYEE COMPENSATION

## James E. Nelson and A. Lee Westervelt
**HEWITT ASSOCIATES**

Employee compensation and benefit plans are a key part of any acquisition strategy, and may actually dictate the form of the acquisition. In a few cases, the potential liabilities may even result in the transaction's being canceled.

The impact of employee compensation and benefit plans on acquisitions has increased significantly because of the labyrinth of legislation governing design, administration, expensing, and funding. The increased role of the Financial Accounting Standards Board (FASB) and the escalating cost of medical care benefits have reinforced this impact. The influence of legislation and the courts, particularly in the area of postretirement medical care, has also served to restrict an employer's freedom and potentially increase the financial liability for continuing coverage after employment ceases.

It is important to begin an analysis of compensation and benefit issues early in the acquisition process, possibly even before an acquisition candidate has been selected. Focusing attention on the desired compensation and benefit objectives may influence the selection of the entity to be acquired and may identify potential "deal breakers" early in the process. At the very least, a review of objectives and likely future directions allows the buyer to establish a desired approach before the hectic pace of negotiations begins.

## DECIDING HOW TO INTEGRATE PLANS

The treatment of the acquired organization's compensation and benefit plans following the acquisition varies, and depends a great deal on the buyer's philosophy and objectives. No one "best" procedure exists. A purchaser's objectives might best be met if (1) all employees are covered by the same plan, or if (2) the purchaser's plans and the acquired company's plans remain separate, or if (3) the purchaser's plans and the acquired company's plans are all dropped and replaced by a common new plan.

If the acquisition involves operations outside the United States, all of the same issues must be addressed within each country. It is generally not possible to have one plan that crosses national borders.

### One Plan for All Employees

All things being equal, most employers prefer one set of programs for all employees. Similar work forces usually expect similar compensation and benefit treatment. Work-force similarities can be production of the same or similar products, production in the same or similar geographic locations, or membership in the same union. Any one similarity tends to support the one-plan concept. Existence of two or more similarities only increases the logic for one plan.

Another supporting circumstance is the frequency of transfers. If employees are transferred between the purchaser and the acquired company, complications are reduced with one plan. A company's culture may also support the natural tendency for one plan. If a view exists that the entity is one organization and identification with and loyalty to the company is an objective, one plan reinforces this concept.

In addition, administration is easier with one plan. For example, plans need to be brought into compliance with a new law only once. Staffing needs can be minimized. Medical claims payers, pension actuaries, and others involved with administration need be familiar with only one plan, reducing the potential for errors. Also, limiting administration and communication costs to one plan is generally more cost-effective.

Finally, minor differences between the purchaser's and the acquired company's plans frequently are nuisances and irritants that go far beyond their financial worth. Elimination of unnecessary plan differences can obviate explanations about why employees are being treated differently.

### Different Plans for Different Groups

While many circumstances support the one-plan concept, situations exist where multiple plans may be more appropriate.

Work forces in dissimilar industries may be a sufficient reason to maintain separate programs. Each set of plans may be competitive within its respective industry, and a change to one plan may result in one of the work forces' being compensated inappropriately. Profit margins may support a rich compensation and benefit plan for one work force, but not another. Different geographic locations and concurrent costs of living may also provide a sufficient reason to maintain two sets of plans.

The acquirer's philosophy, or management style, may also influence the approach taken to compensation and benefits. A highly decentralized management style may be supported by a similar approach to compensation and benefits.

Decentralization of administration reduces some of the advantages of having only one plan, since each location maintains administrative support. More important, a decentralized management style typically holds the profit-center manager accountable only for the bottom line. It is inconsistent to preclude that manager's ability to control an expense—compensation and benefits—by mandating use of the "corporate plan." The use of multiple plans supports the objective of a decentralized management style better.

The long-term viability of the acquired company's operation also needs to be considered when deciding on one plan or many. An anticipated closing or resale of all or part of the business will generally support the maintenance of separate plans. Frequently, even uncertainty about the future of the acquired company may be sufficient reason to maintain separate plans, at least until the company's long-term viability becomes clearer.

## Modified Plans

Many times the purchaser's objectives are such that neither one plan nor multiple plans provides optimum support. In these cases, a modified approach may be a reasonable alternative.

For example, if a large number of transfers were anticipated, perhaps a common job evaluation system, pension plan, and incentive award opportunity could be maintained. The remaining compensation and benefit plans could vary depending on industry, geography, and profits. This strategy might best support an objective of facilitating management transfers while encouraging competitive industry and local health care, savings, life insurance, and vacation plans for the great majority of the employees who do not transfer.

Another approach might be to develop multiple levels of benefit plans: a "deluxe" plan, a "median" plan, and a "low-cost" plan. As acquired companies became part of the buyer's corporate family, they would receive one of the three benefit plans, depending on their industry, location, or profitability.

This strategy partially meets the objective of having plans that reflect the unique characteristics of the acquired company, yet minimizes the administrative burden of a plethora of plans. For companies making frequent acquisitions, this approach may be an attractive blend.

## A Totally New Plan

Sometimes an acquisition provides a window of opportunity to design and install a compensation and benefit plan totally different from that of either the acquirer or the acquired company, especially if the two companies are close to the same size.

This approach may be especially supportive of an objective to communicate that the new entity is a different organization from either of the two companies before the merger. It may be an especially effective way to reinforce the concept that neither of the initial companies is dominant after the merger.

Designing and installing a new compensation and benefit plan during this window of opportunity may allow a company to meet other objectives. Perhaps the new company needs to reposition itself competitively. Or certain health care cost-management features are required. In some cases, assigning responsibility for the redesign to be shared by representatives of both companies can help build postacquisition harmony.

But labor laws, primarily outside the United States, may restrict flexibility. The acquirer may be required to continue the working conditions, including the benefit plans, of an acquired company.

## Other Issues

The timing of any compensation and benefit changes is likely to be dictated by the circumstances surrounding the acquisition and the purchaser's objectives. Changes coincident with the acquisition may be made if the acquirer assumes liability problems, or to reinforce a management objective (such as getting everyone on the same team from day one) or to reinforce control by emphasizing who bought whom.

Delayed timing better meets some objectives. The process of finding and negotiating the acquisition may not always permit adequate analysis by compensation and benefit planners. A delay in implementing changes may result in a more appropriate plan for the organization and help reinforce the message that employees need not be concerned about rapid organizational change.

Delayed timing may also be appropriate if pending legislation affects compensation and benefit plan design. If the outcome of pending legislation is unclear, it may be prudent to delay any changes so they may be properly integrated with the requirements of the new law. Pending legislation also has an impact on the establishment of the objectives for benefit plan treatment.

## ANALYZING COMPENSATION AND BENEFIT PLAN VARIABLES

Each plan within the total compensation and benefit program of the potential acquisition needs to be reviewed to determine its impact, not only individually but when combined with other plans. The effects of acquisition-related changes on each plan vary significantly in complexity: effects of changes to salaries and wages are relatively straightforward, while changes to pensions have highly complex effects. The most seemingly insignificant points can have a staggering financial impact. For example, in an acquisition involving a multi-employer pension plan, the cost of withdrawing from that plan after an acquisition could be as high as $10,000 per employee.

A number of variables must be considered when analyzing compensation and benefit plans of a potential acquisition. Among them are the following:

*Compensation:*
- Salaries and wages
- Annual incentive awards
- Long-term incentive awards
- Employment contracts
- Perquisites

*Benefits*
- Retirement plans
- Health care plans
- Other welfare plans
- Labor agreements

### Salaries and Wages

The key comparison is between the potential acquisition's salaries and wages and those of the acquirer and other employers in the potential acquisition's industry and geographical location. While reviewing the salary for each position may not be practical, a comparison of the pay for benchmark jobs at the potential acquisition and at the purchaser and competitors normally provides a reliable indicator of relative cash compensation ranking.

In addition to analysis of the level of salaries and wages, an analysis of the potential acquisition's number of employees should be undertaken. Severance pay for reduction in force after the acquisition may be a hidden cost. Necessary staff additions may lower profit expectations.

### Annual Incentive Awards

A review of the potential acquisition's bonuses may indicate if they are consistent with the purchaser's philosophy, both in terms of award size and formula for payment. To the extent that either or both are not in accord with the purchaser's objectives, the purchaser needs to balance the potential of morale and turnover problems if a change is made against the need to conform to the purchaser's philosophy. In addition, any potential negative impact on productivity or financial results need to be considered.

### Long-Term Incentive Awards

Integration of long-term incentive awards can be more difficult to reconcile. For example, if the acquired company's stock is involved, how will the reward opportunities be continued if the acquired company's stock ceases to be in existence as a result of the acquisition?

In addition, the acquisition is apt to occur during one or more of the performance measurement periods. The procedure for measuring performance and providing for pro rata payments needs to be resolved.

### Employment Contracts

Executive contracts need to be reviewed, particularly if they take the form of a so-called golden parachute, which provides compensation under certain conditions resulting from an acquisition or merger. If the contract makes it easy for the executive to claim a diminished position, and if the size of the payments under the contract are significant, the purchaser may be faced with hiring an entirely new management team. The situation can be exacerbated if the contracts remain in place after the acquisition. In that case, not only is the acquirer faced with losing the management team, but it also must pay the cost of the contracts, which may be as high as three years' total compensation per executive.

### Perquisites

By any standards, perquisites are not as important an issue as most other compensation and benefit items. Perquisites in the United States tend to amount to about 3 to 5 percent of an executive's total compensation package. But the removal of perquisites can have an impact on morale disproportionate to their real economic value. Conversely, maintaining a rich perquisite package at the acquired company while the acquirer's executives have a significantly more modest package can be equally disruptive in the acquirer's organization.

Outside of the United States, perquisites may be much more significant. In many countries, for example, company cars may be provided to a large number of managers as a tax-effective way to deliver compensation value to the employee. Generally, countries with higher personal income tax rates will have a greater prevalence of perquisites.

### Retirement Plans

Determining the optimum treatment of retirement plans is likely to be the most complex of all compensation and benefit issues. The administration of qualified retirement plans is guided by many tax and labor laws, as well as numerous accounting guidelines, and large amounts of funds are typically involved. Not surprisingly, most of the time spent on acquisition-related compensation and benefit issues is often devoted to retirement plans.

There are two kinds of retirement plans: defined-benefit and defined-contribution. A defined-benefit plan is one where the ultimate amount to be received at retirement is defined—for example, 1 percent of final average pay multiplied by years of service—and the amount contributed to the plan by the employer is whatever it takes to fulfill the benefit promise. Defined-contribution plans fix the amount contributed to the plan by means of a formula—for example, 10 percent of net income or fifty cents for every dollar contributed by the employee—and the ultimate benefit varies depending on the amount contributed, the number of years over which contributions are made, and the earnings on all contributions.

**Defined-Benefit Plans**    If the potential acquisition maintains a defined-benefit plan, the purchaser needs to determine if the plan or the portion of the plan to be received by the purchaser is partially funded, fully funded, or even overfunded. Are the assets of the plan less than, equal to, or in excess of the present value of accrued retirement benefits? In most cases, an actuary can approximate whether the plan is an asset or a liability by using the latest actuarial report and asset statement.

Determining the financial status of a defined-benefit retirement plan can be one of the most difficult aspects of evaluating compensation and benefit plans in a potential acquisition. It is complicated because the retirement benefit promise not only is expressed in terms of years of service, but also is frequently based on pay at some future date of retirement, death, disability, or employment termination. Thus, the benefits earned by employees up to the date of acquisition, and possibly the employees' expectations of these benefits, will grow with future pay increases.

If the plan is continued unchanged after the acquisition, the buyer funds this growth. If the plan is terminated, the future pay changes do not affect the actual retirement benefits, but employees may expect some growth in benefits. The resulting position is that the buyer needs to determine the adequacy of assets in relation to the liabilities of the plan, both on a termination basis (to assure that no new money needs to be added if the plan is terminated) and on an ongoing basis (to reflect the impact of future pay changes). The buyer's anticipated action on terminating versus continuing the plan unchanged is likely to determine which measure of the plan's financial status deserves primary attention.

Defined-benefit plans may be significantly underfunded or overfunded. With this wide variance, the funding status can have a major impact on the purchase price of the business. Therefore, the adequacy of the defined-benefit plan's funding should be determined before the purchase price is fixed.

It is also important to realize that the plan's liabilities are the result of calculations made by the actuary based on assumptions regarding future interest rates, mortality rates, turnover rates, disability rates, retirement ages, and marital status, in addition to any assumptions regarding future increases in pay and Social Security benefits.

Some other factors the purchaser needs to consider so decisions can be made on adopting, modifying, merging, or terminating a defined-benefit plan before or after an acquisition are as follows:

- The plan needs to be in compliance with current legislation. If not, additional, unrecorded liabilities may exist. Further, any recent changes in the plan need to have been submitted for approval to the appropriate government agencies. Evidence of approval—an IRS qualification letter, current plan documents, and recent annual report filings—needs to be reviewed. Finally, any pending legal actions against the plan must be disclosed.

- The method of distribution of any excess assets needs to be identified if the plan is to be terminated. The plan usually states whether the excess assets are for the benefit of the participants or revert to the company. Or the plan may have a "pension parachute" clause that requires any excess assets to be used for the plan participants in the event of a takeover.

- The responsibility for continuing benefits for former employees needs to be addressed and funds divided accordingly.

- The nature of the plan's assets can change the "real" value of the fund. If the potential acquisition's stock is among the plan's assets, the disposition of shares and value may need to be determined. Unrealistic values for assets may currently be on the books, such as nonliquid insurance contracts, bonds carried at book value, or real estate owned by the potential acquisition.

- Commitments to continue the plan made in employee communications may create unexpected liabilities that have not been valued as a part of the normal actuarial process. All current communications related to the plan need to be reviewed.

In reviewing plans outside the United States, the same issues arise, although the specific approaches may be different. Funding requirements, for example, are very different from country to country. In Japan and Germany, there may be no outside assets to cover benefit liabilities. In Belgium and the Netherlands, insured deferred annuity contracts may not be adequate to meet accrued benefit liabilities by U.S. standards. In Italy and some South American countries, there may be no pension plan at all, but there are statutory severance indemnities payable upon any termination, including retirement. Such liabilities may be significant and not supported by outside assets. The prudent buyer needs to explore any situations where unfunded liabilities are potentially material.

**Defined-Contribution Plans** Savings, profit sharing, and other defined-contribution plans normally do not have the same potential liability problems as defined-benefit pension plans. The benefit derived from the defined-contribution plan is generally limited to the assets available, and therefore, no unfunded benefit promises or significant excess funds will result. However, other issues do need to be reviewed during the process of analyzing an acquisition candidate.

The plan's investments may require change, even if the buyer decides to retain the plan in its current form. For example, if the potential acquisition's stock is involved in the plan, that stock may not exist in the future. Also, some investments such as guaranteed investment contracts may not be transferable to a new buyer, particularly if the newly acquired operation is a division of a larger company.

**Other Benefits** Beyond considering factors relating to the defined-benefit plan and the defined-contribution plan individually, the buyer needs to review the total benefits provided by the retirement program. Many companies maintain both types of plans, with the pension plan providing the basic benefit and the defined-contribution plan serving as a supplement. The amount provided by the potential acquisition's plans may be inconsistent with the buyer's objectives. Also, the mix of defined benefit and defined contribution may be inconsistent with the buyer's ideal mix. It may also be that neither the buyer's nor the acquisition's plans meet the target retirement income level. An acquisition may provide a unique opportunity to rectify both programs with a new program for the newly combined corporation.

### Health Care Plans

One of the most often affected areas of employee benefits from the perspective of employees whose company has been acquired is health care. Health care plans are highly visible, and employees react strongly to any tampering with the benefit levels. More significantly, at many companies medical plans represent the largest single employee-benefit cost. Therefore, the basis for the potential acquisition's provision of health care becomes critical to the acquisition decision.

A comparison of the potential acquisition's medical plan with the purchaser's objectives in such basic areas as cost-sharing with employees (copayments, deductibles, and employee-paid contributions) and postretirement health coverage is appropriate. These are basic areas where most companies have established well-defined philosophies, and these philosophies may clash in an acquisition. In such cases, both the cultural and cost issues must be addressed and communicated.

While some variations may be permitted, the major features frequently must conform to a predetermined set of guidelines. In addition, preacquisition and postacquisition discrimination tests need to be applied to insure continued compliance with legislation.

A major area of potential liability is health care for retirees. For now, the cost is recognized on a pay-as-you-go basis. Expenses are escalating because of a higher level of inflation for medical costs and a concurrently diminishing role for Medicare. Further, several court cases in the mid-1980s raised questions surrounding possible legal obligations to continue these benefits, sometimes even in the face of bankruptcy. Therefore, any postretirement medical cost obligations need to be analyzed and recognized.

### Other Welfare Plans

Other welfare benefits requiring an analysis to determine if they conform to the buyer's objectives and a review to determine potential liabilities include life insurance and disability plans.

To a lesser extent, supplemental unemployment benefits, vacations, holidays, severance pay plans, educational reimbursement, and other more infrequent benefits like prepaid legal plans and child-care plans may also need attention. Although the cost of these benefits will generally be lower than the retirement and medical plans, the benefits themselves may be equally important to the potential acquisition's employees.

### Labor Agreements

Collectively bargained plans present a unique set of issues. Typically, the collective-bargaining agreement contains obligations of a defined-benefit plan, and in some cases, additional benefit promises. The additional promises may include full vesting or unreduced early retirement benefits in the event of a takeover or plant closing. Therefore, "successorship" of the plans may be determined by the buyer's successorship obligation to the union in general.

If the buyer is purchasing a company by acquiring stock, it assumes all the acquisition's obligations, including the collective-bargaining agreement. These obligations include the obligation to provide the agreed-upon benefits and the assumption of the plan's assets.

Of particular importance is a potential acquisition's participation in any multiemployer plan, sometimes called a Taft-Hartley plan. The potential liability of withdrawal from a multiemployer plan requires careful analysis prior to any decision that might lead to withdrawal at the time of or after the acquisition. When an employer ceases participation, the requirement for additional contributions depends on whether the employer is assessed any withdrawal liability under the plan. Withdrawal liability provisions vary widely between plans. However, even under those plans with no withdrawal liability provisions, the plan's board of trustees can change the benefit provision so that the liability for vested benefits exceeds the assets, which creates a withdrawal liability.

If the acquirer is purchasing assets, the multiemployer pension liabilities remain with the seller unless the acquirer voluntarily assumes them. Thus, the purchase of assets generally provides more freedom to negotiate appropriate treatment of defined-benefit plans than does stock purchase.

One note of caution needs to be added. Asset sales can trigger a withdrawal and result in a liability to the seller unless specific conditions are satisfied.

Chapter 18 has a fuller description of the effect of labor law on acquisitions.

## COMMUNICATING ABOUT COMPENSATION ISSUES

Almost invariably, a merger implies a threat to employees. It implies a change many employees view as working to their disadvantage. Most people dislike work disruption and uncertainty, and therefore resist major organizational change. Executives and rank-and-file employees alike become jittery and insecure. During the acquisition period, rumors and doubt infect employees' attitudes and can negatively affect company performance. It is a well-chronicled fact that many acquisitions have functionally "failed" because otherwise useful employees have lost their career motivation and able managers have felt forced to leave the merged company.

The major concerns facing employees as an acquisition approaches typically center on job security and career potential. The most serious of these concerns are:

- Will I still have a job here?
- Will I continue to serve in my present management role?
- How will the new owners view me and evaluate my performance?
- Will present top management continue to influence and control my career?

And of course the jackpot question:

- Will I be better or worse off?

These critical issues are often not openly articulated. Rather, they emerge in the relative privacy of individual and small-group interviews, and are anonymously written into survey responses. These issues are not raised in open discussion with management because employees feel that if they confess this insecurity and doubt, management will view them as negative or weak.

"Safer" questions about compensation and benefits tend to be raised as a way to mask the larger, overriding issues. It is therefore imperative that buyers work diligently to assure employees that transfer of their benefits from the acquired company to the new corporate entity will be both orderly and fair.

# STRATEGIES FOR DEALING WITH A LABOR UNION

## Gary A. Marsack
**LINDNER & MARSACK, S. C.**

The acquisition of a unionized company raises a wide range of legal and practical issues that can significantly affect the value of a contemplated purchase, especially where the company operates in a labor-intensive industry. These issues include the following:

- When a company is bought, is the union also "bought?"
- If the union is "bought," is the purchaser stuck with the seller's collective-bargaining agreement?
- Assuming there is flexibility and options exist, which course of action is best to take?

Labor law suggests that purchasers may avoid both bargaining and contractual obligations by properly structuring business transfers. The purpose of this chapter, therefore, is to introduce general legal principles and concepts regarding purchaser rights and obligations, and to provide some guidance in developing an appropriate purchase strategy.

These legal concepts are distilled from a long evolution of judicial and administrative decisions. As is always the case, facts in an individual instance will differ, and there is no substitute for competent legal counsel. The time to obtain this advice is well in advance, not after the purchase. A purchaser is in a unique position of creating, to a large extent, the very facts that will decide its legal rights and obligations. A detailed strategy developed early in the process may well be the key to success.

## BASICS OF SUCCESSORSHIP LAW

A discussion of a purchaser's rights and obligations necessitates use of a number of terms with very definite legal meanings. These terms are defined as follows:

- *Collective bargaining:* The process by which an employer and union agree, or disagree, as to the wages, hours, and working conditions of certain employees. A unionized employer has a legal obligation to bargain in "good faith." These obligations are defined under the National Labor Relations Act and National Labor Relations Board decisional law.

- *Bargaining unit:* Federal law recognizes that, for purposes of collective bargaining, certain groups or types of employees may be appropriately included together in one "bargaining unit." A typical example would be all full-time and regular part-time production and maintenance employees at a particular facility.

- *Union recognition:* Where a majority of employees appropriately included in a bargaining unit desire the representation of a particular union, the employer has the legal duty to "recognize" that union as the representative of all employees in that unit.

- *Predecessor* and *successor:* Within the context of the sale of a business, the seller is routinely referred to as the "predecessor" and the purchaser the "successor."

- *Legal successor:* For purposes of labor law, the purchaser who has a legal obligation to recognize and bargain with the incumbent union as the representative of certain of its employees is a "legal successor." A legal successor must bargain collectively with the union over the wages, hours, and other conditions of employment of its employees.

The question of when the purchaser of a business is required to recognize a union as the representative of its employees has brought to the courts and the NLRB a number of competing interests, all arguably protected by federal labor laws. A business transfer involves at least four different groups, all potentially adversely affected by the transaction:

- *Individual employees:* Individual employees often view the business transfer as a threat to job security and contractually achieved rights. Rights such as wages, seniority, vacations, and pensions are often viewed by employees as "vested," having only been obtained after years of struggle between management and the employees' representative. As such, an employee's perceived entitlement to a particular level of wages and benefits may be fiercely defended.

- *Employers:* If employers are to remain in business, they must have the right to transfer capital freely and to exercise their prerogative to rearrange their business as they see fit. When a business is transferred, the succeeding employer frequently must change corporate operating structures, labor forces, work locations, task assignments, and supervisors in order to operate profitably and to achieve the expected economic benefits of the acquisition. The Supreme Court has stressed that when the employer's right to make such changes is severely abridged, employers may be reluctant to take over failing businesses, with the result that the flow of capital in the free market may be inhibited.

- *Unions:* Unions possess an "institutional interest" in continuing to represent their perceived share of employees in the labor market. The loss of bargaining units as a result of an ownership transfer leads to a corresponding loss in total membership and a resulting effect on dues, thereby threatening the union's interest in self-preservation.

- *The public:* In order to accommodate the public interest in peaceful resolution of labor disputes, Congress enacted the National Labor Relations Act to form the framework for the resolution of the competing interests of parties embroiled in such disputes. The act is not, however, single-minded in the interests it is intended to further. On the one hand, a major goal of the act has been to achieve industrial peace by encouraging stability in labor relations. On the other hand, the fundamental policies of the act include recognition of the right to freedom of contract and encouragement of the transfer and flow of capital in a free market. Thus, the act creates tension between the goal of industrial stability and the survival of contractual rights in collective-bargaining agreements, and the goal of furthering deeply rooted traditions of freedom of contract and the free transfer of capital.

## SUCCESSORSHIP ISSUES

The Supreme Court has stated that the real question in any successorship case is: What are the legal obligations of the new employer to the employees of the former owner or to their representatives? When the issues are analyzed in this fashion, no single definition of *successor* is applicable in all legal contexts. Rather, successorship issues are decided under a case-by-case approach that addresses the unique circumstances of the matter at hand.

The two issues of particular concern in the business transfer context addressed by both the NLRB and the courts are the following:

- When is the successor employer required to recognize and bargain with the predecessor's union?
- To what extent should the successor employer be bound by the predecessor's collective-bargaining agreement?

From these issues flow numerous subsidiary issues.

On four occasions, the Supreme Court has addressed questions involving the legal obligations of a buyer of a business. Subsequent to each decision, the NLRB and lower federal courts have interpreted the decision, and expanded or contracted the holding. Through this process a balancing of competing interests has occurred, giving rise to a set of five generally followed principles:

- There is a distinction between asset transfers and stock transfers.

- The controlling factor in determining a buyer's obligation to bargain with a union is whether "substantial continuity" exists between work forces.
- Other factors can also affect a buyer's status as a "legal successor."
- Successors are not automatically legally bound to accept collective-bargaining agreements.
- The successorship doctrine overrides any successorship clauses in collective-bargaining agreements.

### The Asset/Stock Transfer Distinction

A crucial distinction has emerged in labor law between asset and stock transfers in terms of the buyer's flexibility. As a general rule, a mere change in stock ownership does not affect a company's obligation to recognize the union as the bargaining representative for company employees or the obligation to continue to live under the terms and conditions of an existing collective-bargaining agreement.

### Substantial Continuity Between Work Forces

Although the NLRB and the courts have historically looked to a number of factors in determining whether an asset purchaser should be deemed a "legal successor" and therefore obligated to recognize the union, a Supreme Court case established that the most important factor by far is the "substantial continuity" of the work force across the ownership change.

The emergence of this factor as controlling is well supported by traditional labor-law principles. An employer's obligation to recognize a union is rooted in that union's "majority status," which means that a majority of the employees desire the union. To encourage stability in labor relations once a union has established majority status, the law will presume that such status continues to exist in the absence of some affirmative action on the part of the unionized employees demonstrating that such is no longer the case. Thus, unionized employees are presumed to continue to desire union representation.

These principles have significant importance in the context of an asset transfer. Where the buyer hires a majority of its new work force from the ranks of the seller's unionized work force, the law will presume that a majority of the new work force continues to desire union representation. Conversely, if the new work force is substantially comprised of individuals whose union desires are unknown because they have had no prior affiliation with the seller, there is no basis in law by which to presume majority status and, accordingly, the buyer may refuse to recognize the union without running afoul of the National Labor Relations Act.

This general principle is subject to the premise that the failure or refusal to hire from the predecessor's work force was not motivated by a desire to discriminate based on the union support or activities of such employees. Thus, the refusal to hire the predecessor's employees must be based upon sound business reasons, not upon the predecessor's employees' union membership.

The numerical analysis is conducted from the perspective of the new, rather than the old, work force. In other words, the issue is not whether the purchaser hired a majority of the seller's employees, but rather whether the new work force is more than 50 percent comprised of members of the seller's work force.

A question can exist as to when the numerical analysis should take place. This is especially true where there is a time delay between purchase and obtaining a full complement of workers. If the purchaser initially hires a large portion of the seller's work force and later expands its employee ranks by hiring individuals from the general labor market, the timing of the analysis can be critical in determining the majority status of the union. The purchaser must implement a strategy that supports a preferred timing for the analysis. However, the purchaser's obligation, or lack thereof, to recognize a union must emerge as a consequence, rather than a predetermined goal, of its hiring strategy.

## Other Factors That Can Affect a Purchaser's Status

It is conceivable that a buyer could hire a majority of its workers from the seller's work force and still avoid the need to extend recognition to a union. To do this, a buyer would need to make a substantial change in the way the business is operated before and after purchase, with the result that the employees' required work experience is so dramatically different that it would be inappropriate to presume that such employees continue to desire a union given the changed circumstances. The changes in question would have to be extreme, such as dramatic and sweeping modifications to the production process resulting in different skill and ability requirements; changes in the way front-line and middle-level management make employee-related decisions; or other significant changes creating, in essence, a completely new employment experience for hourly workers.

## Acceptance of the Predecessor's Collective-Bargaining Agreement

The Supreme Court has ruled that where a purchaser hires a majority of its new employees from the ranks of the seller's work force, thereby creating a legal obligation to recognize the union, it nevertheless retains flexibility to decide whether to accept or reject the seller's collective-bargaining agreement with the union. A successor with a bargaining obligation is given the option of either assuming the seller's contract or establishing its own initial terms and conditions of employment unilaterally and then bargaining with the union toward a "first" contract from those initially established wages, hours, and working conditions.

A purchaser electing the latter course of action must exercise caution in assuring that its rejection of the seller's contract is clear and unequivocal, eliminating any potential argument by the union of an implied assumption of that agreement. An appropriately drafted purchase agreement unequivocally stating that the purchaser does not assume the labor agreement would satisfy this requirement.

## Control of Legal Obligations by the Successorship Doctrine

A purchaser is, from a legal standpoint, free to create its own recognition obligation through hiring decisions, or to reject a seller's collective-bargaining agreement even if that contract contains some form of successorship clause that purportedly binds a buyer to the contract terms. The NLRB and the courts have interpreted such clauses as putting the cart before the horse. This is not to say, however, that these clauses can be ignored. Although such contractual restrictions may not necessarily bind the buyer, their effects on the seller's rights and obligations must be considered in evaluating a contemplated business transfer.

## COLLECTIVE BARGAINING UNDER SUCCESSORSHIP LAW

Because under successorship law a successor employer may avoid its predecessor's recognition, bargaining, and contractual obligations through proper structuring of the business transfer, unions have adopted a new strategy. They now seek to accomplish indirectly through collective-bargaining agreements what they have failed to accomplish directly through judicial sanctions.

Within the collective-bargaining agreement, unions attempt to establish contractual remedies by negotiating for the inclusion of strong successorship language that may:

- require predecessors to notify unions of pending business transfers,
- require predecessors to notify successors of the predecessor's labor agreement,
- force predecessors to condition business transfers on the successor's assumption of the collective-bargaining agreement,
- provide a basis for enjoining and preventing business transfers, unless assumption of the labor contract by the purchaser is provided for in the purchase documents,
- impose significant liabilities on predecessors for breach of successor provisions by the predecessor or the successor, or
- impose personal liability on shareholders for breach of successor provisions.

A review of collective-bargaining agreements indicates that the various contractual obligations imposed on employers by successorship provisions may be broken down into essentially three categories:

- No contractual obligations
- Mild contractual obligations
- Strong contractual obligations

## No Contractual Obligations

According to a survey by the Bureau of National Affairs taken in the mid-1980s, 71 percent of collective-bargaining agreements reviewed contained no "successors and assigns" language. This statistic does not mean, however, that employers should take union proposals for successorship provisions lightly.

The study revealed an increasing prevalence of such provisions in contracts of four major employing industries: leather, utilities, transportation, and furniture. In these industries, successorship provisions were present in at least 50 percent of collective-bargaining agreements.

Furthermore, the NLRB considers proposals for successorship language to be a mandatory subject of bargaining. Employers should neither ignore nor willingly concede to union demands for successorship provisions. In fact, such provisions, with their inherent liability, may have a dramatic impact on the salability of a business, since it limits the universe of potential buyers to those who are willing to adopt the existing labor agreement.

Although it is true that collective-bargaining agreements impose no contractual obligations on predecessors to condition business transfers on the successor's assumption of the contract when the contract includes no successorship language, employers may still find themselves burdened with undesirable legal obligations if "boilerplate" successorship language of this nature is placed in the purchase agreement under which a business is transferred. The presence of such language in the purchase agreement may be interpreted as indicating that the successor has, in fact, assumed the predecessor's labor-relations obligations. The prospective successor who desires to function with its own work force and to rearrange the business operation should therefore scrutinize the purchase agreement for such successorship language and should insist on its elimination from the agreement.

## Mild Contractual Obligations

Collective-bargaining agreements that impose relatively mild contractual obligations in the case of business transfers may be of two types:

- Only a brief mention of "successors and assigns" may be made in the agreement's preamble.
- The agreement may contain "successors and assigns" language that only implies, rather than clearly imposes, contractual obligations on the predecessor employer. In the second type of agreement, the successorship provisions are separately placed within the body of the agreement.

As noted earlier, the mere existence of successorship language does not compel succeeding employers to bargain with or recognize the predecessor's union, or to adopt its labor obligations. The successor may structure the business transfer to avoid such obligations under successorship law. If the successor can accommodate its business needs to this structuring, it will not be obligated to bargain or arbitrate with the union despite any mild contractual obligation language.

However, the lack of clear obligatory successorship language does not relieve predecessors of all liability if the successor does not assume the collective-bargaining agreement. The predecessor's liability under these circumstances depends on the construction of the relevant contract language. The most crucial issue concerning agreements with mild successorship language is whether the language is strong enough to impose a contractual obligation on the predecessor to insist that the successor adopt the contract as a condition of the sale—that is, whether the seller is "contractually" bound to insist that such assumption take place even though the buyer is not "legally" obligated to assume the contract.

Despite the fact that the buyer may have no legal liability if it does not assume the contract, it would be a mistake for a potential purchaser to view the ramifications of mild contractual language as the seller's problem. In one case, the Supreme Court indicated that an injunctive remedy could lie under relatively mild successorship language in the predecessor's bargaining agreement.

Relying on this language, unions have successfully prevented business transfers based on contracts containing nothing more than "boilerplate" successor language. Unions have convinced courts that the failure to enjoin the transfer pending resolution of the issue of the effect of the successorship language could result in irreparable harm to the employees covered under the old contract.

These cases, when resolved, have yielded conflicting results. Some arbitrators' decisions have said successorship language has no force and effect and is only "boilerplate" that signifies at the most the parties' willingness to have the successor assume the agreement if it desires to. Arbitrators who view the language in this light have refused to impose an affirmative duty on the seller to insist on the purchaser's adoption of the collective-bargaining agreement.

Other decisions have imposed an obligation on the seller to insist on assumption of the contract by the buyer based solely on a mere reference to "successors" in the preamble of the collective-bargaining agreement. However, this view should not prevail because it conflicts with well-established principles of arbitration that prohibit arbitrators from adding new or different provisions to a collective-bargaining agreement. This view may also conflict with the grievance provision in the agreement, which may expressly bar the arbitrator from adding provisions to the agreement.

The problem is compounded because much depends on the forum and timing of the union's challenge to the business transfer. If the union selects the grievance/arbitration forum after the sale, the purchasing employer would have had adequate time to structure its operation to establish indications that it is not a legal successor. However, if the union tries to enjoin the sale before the transfer, then the potential purchaser and the predecessor may be unable to persuade a court that the contemplated structural and organizational plans would make the imposition of successor obligations inappropriate. Further, a court may be more impressed with the contractual language cited by the union than with the unsubstantiated claims of "no successorship" presented by the employer.

## Strong Contractual Obligations

Collective-bargaining agreements increasingly contain successorship provisions that impose certain duties on predecessors contemplating business transfers. Typically, these provisions mandate that the seller condition the sale on the purchaser's agreement to be bound to the collective-bargaining agreement.

Often these clauses impose legal liabilities on the seller for all damages to the union and the employees covered by the contract as a result of the purchaser's failure to assume the contract. Under such language, the seller's potential monetary liability in situations where the buyer either fails to hire a substantial number of the seller's employees and/or establishes a wage-and-benefit package substantially lower than that contained in the contract, could be astronomical.

Notwithstanding strong language, the succeeding employer who is a legal successor under case law incurs little risk by refusing to adopt the contracts containing such language, for reasons discussed earlier. If the succeeding employer is not a legal successor then, under some arbitral precedent, it may be required to remedy the predecessor's breach of contract. This could result, in effect, in adoption of the collective-bargaining agreement by the successor.

The predecessor's liability for violating strongly worded successorship provisions is clear. Such provisions have been interpreted as unequivocally requiring a sale or transfer to be conditioned on the adoption of the contract, regardless of whether or not the purchaser is legally a successor. It is highly unlikely that any sale or transfer of a business under such an agreement could be consummated unless it were conditioned on the adoption of the predecessor's contract.

Thus, strong successorship provisions essentially restrict business transfer only to those parties who will agree to adopt and ultimately comply with the union's collective-bargaining agreement. An analysis of the language and a review of the case law interpreting strongly worded successorship provisions indicates that predecessors who are hamstrung by these provisions have few options.

One possibility is to forego planned transfers until the contract terminates, but under these circumstances, the employer must ensure that the successorship clause does not survive the contract's termination, either by negotiating the language out of the contract or by unilaterally implementing a final offer eliminating the provisions after impasse has been reached in negotiation.

## PRACTICAL CONSIDERATIONS
## IN STRUCTURING THE TRANSFER

Because employees' rights to be unionized are protected under federal law, a purchaser's deliberate decision to hire less than a majority of the seller's employees for the sole purpose of avoiding any bargaining obligation would be unlawful and would open the door to potential back-pay and reinstatement rights for the seller's employees who were adversely affected by the buyer's decision. Thus, the purchaser's decision to hire less than a majority of its work force from the ranks of the seller's employees covered by the collective-bargaining agreement must be based on factors unrelated to the employees' desire, or lack thereof, to have a union.

A company's decision to staff its operation by hiring the "most qualified" applicants from a generalized pool of available individuals in the relevant labor market at the time of purchase would constitute lawful hiring, regardless of the ultimate impact of that policy on the unionized or nonunionized composition of the work force.

Circumstances may exist where it simply is not practical for a company to justify any act other than hiring a substantial part of the seller's work force in order to provide the operation with a pre-trained, skilled employee body familiar with the operation in question. This would be especially true where the nature of the business necessitated the employment of a highly skilled work force not generally available in that labor market.

The ultimate feasibility, therefore, of a company's ability to avoid the union may well turn on its own analysis of the need to keep existing personnel in order to ensure the company's continued efficient operation.

As noted earlier, even where a purchaser is the legal successor it is not bound by the seller's collective-bargaining agreement. There are obvious advantages to establishing unilateral conditions of employment, then bargaining a new "first" contract with the union.

The decision to avoid or not avoid a contract usually turns on two factors. One is the acceptability of the existing contract, both in terms of language restricting management flexibility and in terms of cost. The company's ability to withstand a labor disturbance at the time of purchase is a second relevant factor, because bargaining from unilaterally established wages, hours, and working conditions creates at least the potential risk of a strike. For example, the existence of a no-strike clause in a contract with two and a half years remaining may outweigh any other provisions in the contract the buyer would like to change.

The contract decisions will, of course, depend on the particular circumstances of the transfer in question.

The purchase of a struggling company, where employees have experienced great insecurity about their future job security, may afford the purchaser the ability to exact language and wage-and-benefit concessions from the union. On the other hand, the purchase of a thriving company that offers wage-and-benefit levels commensurate with those in the area for similarly skilled employees may effectively preclude the purchaser from maintaining a strong position on reductions without the necessity of going through a strike.

One relatively successful technique in the context of the acquisition of a struggling unionized company is the concept of prepurchase negotiation. Under this concept, the prospective buyer preconditions the purchase on the buyer's ability to secure from the union the desired level of relief from the existing contract.

If the union sees an advantage from the sale to a financially stronger corporate entity, it may be willing to enter into a significantly concessionary contract with the potential purchaser. Our experience demonstrates that under these circumstances, potential buyers have secured cost reductions and language restructuring that was previously unavailable to the seller.

Although this approach is subject to numerous legal constraints and involves certain risks, its appeal is apparent. Where the success or failure of a prospective purchase will be determined by a reduction in labor cost, the prospective buyer has the ability to walk away from a deal if the employees and union are unwilling to accede to the type or level of modifications deemed necessary. Moreover, the prospective buyer can capitalize on the insecurity of a work force that fears asset liquidation as an alternative option available to the seller, a factor that disappears upon the purchase of the company as an ongoing operation.

The important point to remember when considering dealing with unions in a business to be purchased is that the purchaser has options. Proper structuring of a business transfer and preacquisition planning with regard to labor relations are absolutely essential to reach the desired business objective.

# SECTION VI

# Acquisitions Outside the United States

## INTRODUCTION

Acquiring companies outside the United States takes the acquirer into unfamiliar territory in more ways than one. In addition to different languages and legal systems, a would-be acquirer must deal with differences in customs and practice.

Identifying potential candidates, obtaining adequate information about them, and gaining an introduction all are more difficult in Europe than in the United States, according to Laurance R. Newman. In the leadoff chapter of the section, Newman also describes the difficulties of coping with multiple legal systems, including the rules of the European Economic Community. Based on his experiences, the author suggests solutions to the unfamiliar problems a U.S. acquirer may encounter.

Canada and the United States have always enjoyed a special relationship, in commercial dealings as well as in politics. Although Canada is the country most like the United States, Fraser Mason and David Climie point out in the second chapter of this section, there are nevertheless some unique laws that must be complied with in making acquisitions there. The authors also describe some of the cultural differences and attitudes a U.S. company may encounter.

Japanese companies rarely acquire other Japanese companies, Steven B. Schlossstein reports in the final chapter of the book. (Observers have noted that many of those companies recently have overcome their prejudice, at least as it applies to acquisitions in this country.) Ultimately, the author asserts, the Japanese economy will become more open to foreign companies that wish to operate there. If not through outright acquisition, some other form of business combination may represent the most advantageous way for a U.S. company to gain access to that market.

# CHAPTER 19

# ACQUISITION IN EUROPE

**Laurance R. Newman**
SC JOHNSON WAX

Undertaking an acquisition in Europe can be exhilarating, frustrating, challenging, and rewarding—all at the same time.

Making an acquisition in Europe should not be a strategic goal of any organization, but the result of a well-studied program to identify various alternatives for achieving a company's European corporate mission and strategy. Too many companies plan to make an acquisition in Europe in a particular year, rather than properly defining the role of a European presence.

A European acquisition can bring a company a number of advantages, including the following:

- An identified ongoing European business with brand franchises, successful products, and known brand names
- New European distribution systems, especially in countries like France and Germany, where it is critical to have a complete infrastructure, including a sales force
- Manufacturing facilities in the European market, where a company must be effective in selling products across a series of national borders

- New customers, both in terms of national geography and product categories
- New technologies to enter or to serve identified European markets

## EUROPEAN ACQUISITION STRATEGY

A company should have a clear mission and mission statement that defines its objectives. For example, the mission statement for Europe might be to provide the European marketplace with value-oriented food specialty products based on the corporation's technology in the area of hybrid grains and aseptic packaging.

Acquisitions are, by nature, opportunistic, especially in Europe, but opportunistic purchases should and can only be made within a framework of agreed-to, well-thought-out business development strategies. Otherwise an acquisition is not opportunistic, but truly random. In the European market, acquisitions require a company to move quickly to develop and execute both a relationship and an ultimate purchase. Having an agreed-to, approved plan to approach and attack the market is critical to the effective and proper execution of an acquisition program.

The European acquisition model has a multidimensional matrix of countries, cultures, governments, markets, and even unions. The basic focus of the European acquisition discussion is making acquisitions of products, product lines, or companies, but the principles and methodology can be applied to licensing, joint ventures, and purchased technology.

The acquiring company's management should develop and approve a strategy for entering and/or expanding in the European market, either by segment, by country, or in total. Only by having a clear vision of objectives and strategies can a company orchestrate and execute the appropriate business development program.

In 1992 the European Economic Community will become completely pan-European, crossing all national borders. With 1992 rapidly approaching, a pan-European plan for an interested acquirer is both necessary and critical.

## GETTING STARTED

After a company has identified acquisition as a viable option in executing its European strategy, it is important to answer five questions with regard to any possible acquisition: Who? Where? What? Why? and How?

### Who Is Responsible?

An individual must be identified and charged with the responsibility for developing and executing a successful acquisition. No matter how the person charged with the program is shown on the corporate organizational chart, this is an entrepreneurial line function. That person must be located in Europe to provide continuing interaction with the target companies, finders, investment bankers, and the business community. Because of the dimensional complexity and cultural differences of Europe, this function usually cannot be performed as successfully by trans-Atlantic phone and ocean-hopping.

### Where Does the Company Want to Buy?

An American company in Europe must currently deal with not only the Common Market and non–Common Market countries, with Spain and Portugal in transition, but with dramatically different cultures. Strategy discussions need to identify target countries or areas of Europe. This is critical to ensure that appropriate search techniques are used to identify potential candidates. While single-country focus is important, it must be integrated with an understanding of the relationship of the business to be acquired and the Common Market—today and tomorrow.

### What Does the Company Want to Acquire?

Identification of the business or product line to acquire must be done in conjunction with identification of the target country or area. Consideration of volume levels, market position, technical competence, manufacturing characteristics, distribution and warehousing skills, and employee relations are all critical to the evaluation of a potential acquisition. An understanding of the "exportability" of the company's products or concepts throughout the Common Market is key to determining if a company can be made pan-European. Habits and cultures, even within Europe, are very different. Creation of a two- or three-dimensional matrix like the one shown in Figure 19-1 will aid in better identifying a logical acquisition. The negative side of 1992 must also be viewed, in terms of greater competition, different pricing, and so on.

### Why Acquire?

The question Why acquire? may seem redundant if a company has worked out a strategic plan. But the process of re-asking the question provides a double check on strategic direction. The answer must make business sense.

Why acquire a potato chip company in Austria? Answer: To provide a distribution system for store-delivered snacks, a technical strength of the purchasing company. On the other hand, the real question may be whether the company could expand into Germany or Switzerland.

Why acquire a pasta company in Italy without a factory? Answer: To provide additional volume opportunities for an underutilized manufacturing facility in France.

### How to Go About It

The "how" question also provides some structure and substance to an acquisition search. The answer to this question should define what and how a company is willing to spend.

- Does the company have a spending limit?
- What purchasing structure is appropriate? Will a company only pay cash, as many private companies do, or will it dilute equity by issuing new stock?
- Does the company want 100 percent ownership, or will it live with a minority position—not uncommon in Europe—with an option to gain future control?

**FIGURE 19-1   A matrix to assess potential acquisition candidates in terms of whether the business can be expanded to other countries**

| Countries | Potential Acquisition Candidates | | | | |
|---|---|---|---|---|---|
| | A | B | C | D | E |
| UK | yes | home country | home country | no | no |
| Germany | yes | yes | no | yes | no |
| France | yes | yes | yes | yes | home country |
| Spain | home country | yes | no | yes | yes |
| Italy | yes | yes | no | yes | yes |
| Switzerland | no | yes | no | home country | yes |

- Is the company willing to make an unfriendly takeover bid, which is almost unheard of in Europe and considered almost totally irresponsible in Japan?
- How can the European equity or private investment market help finance the program?
- How will the regulatory agencies react to the acquisition?

Answering these questions will be very important as a company begins to develop a list of key candidates and a marketing program to contact these companies.

## IDENTIFYING THE TARGET

Searching for the candidate that fits a company's acquisition criteria in Europe involves a three-pronged, simultaneous approach, using:

- the old-boy network,
- external contacts, and
- internal development.

## The Old-Boy Network

Getting entrenched in the old-boy network is an evolving process, and one that requires extreme skill in balancing the aggressive nature of a U.S. acquirer with the more urbane style and timing of European management structure.

Unlike in the United States, where many companies are managed by nonfamily professional managers, the European marketplace relies on interlocking or family ownerships or control. This is especially true in Germany, Spain, and France.

It is important to use friendships and contacts to establish dialogues with members of boards of directors of key companies within the target country. Patience is critical at this phase, because members of the boards of directors seem to have a much greater influence on potential acquisitions, spin-offs of operating divisions, or products than they do in the American marketplace. These contacts are very personal and very sensitive.

Contacts need to be made first on a personal level, possibly at a luncheon or dinner where a potential buyer is introduced to and meets with appropriate directors or key executives of the company whose products or product lines could match the acquisition strategy.

The "working relationship" is as key in a European acquisition as in a Japanese acquisition. However, the time frame between establishing a working relationship and actually beginning the acquisition is considerably shorter in Europe than in Japan.

Most European companies, especially those managed by families or controlled by historic, long-term management, see a frontal approach concerning acquisition as showing in many respects a lack of confidence in their ability to manage the enterprise. On the other hand, discussions concerning possible working relationships recognize the strength and vitality of their business; if they see an acquisition approach in this light they will likely consider it valid.

When an acquisition candidate is a small company or a family-owned company, the old-boy network is probably the most important vehicle for developing a relationship that can lead to an acquisition. A U.S. company acquiring in Europe should use all of its worldwide networking skills in identifying potential company directors or members with whom a relationship has already been built by a friend, colleague, or outside director.

## External Contacts

When dealing with companies managed by professionals, multi-nationals, or conglomerates, the use of traditional European investment bankers, merchant bankers, or finders is both an appropriate and necessary vehicle for any multipronged acquisition strategy. Contacts with local, well-connected bankers who understand the company and the country's culture are necessary.

European finders are, in reality, small, independent investment bankers without the normal financial resources and backing to help with the transaction execution. While they lack the resources to finance deals, they have their own old-boy networks and insights into companies.

Commercial and merchant banks play a much more important part in European acquisitions than in the United States. In many European countries, banks take equity positions in many of their clients and are more closely involved with a company's operation at the board level. They often have selected shareholder rights, options, or convertible stock.

The best way to approach these groups is by visiting Europe, meeting principals, and working the streets, calling on every possible bank that could be of service. In addition to potential acquisitions that have already been explored, these banks can develop other candidates that have not been considered. Especially key in this area of exploration is to take advantage of these banks' specific knowledge of their respective country markets.

In Europe most investment bankers, finders, and merchant bankers want to work on a fee basis, plus some sort of success override. In the United States, it is more traditional for the investment-banking community to work primarily on a success-fee basis. For an American, a first test as a negotiator is negotiating the relationship with a bank. While the so-called Lehman formula is used in many U.S. transactions, no set European formula exists for a relationship between a bank and its client. (The Lehman formula is a success fee based on the transaction price: 5 percent of the first $1 million, 4 percent of the second $1 million, 3 percent of the third $1 million, 2 percent of the fourth $1 million, and 1 percent of each successive $1 million.) In Europe, the final cost may be higher or lower than what it would be in the United States, depending on the company,

country, and effort of the finder. Having the right contact to set up
the right meeting and provide the right interaction throughout
negotiations is absolutely critical, and worth significant compensation.

In addition to the European banking community, the worldwide
investment banking community should not be forgotten. It is critical
to go to Europe, to go to the key countries where the banking community is active, and talk to bank management. But a purchaser
should not stop there. It should go to New York and spend a week
talking to every major multinational investment banking organization and Big Eight accounting firm.

Great patience is required to work through this process with the
banking world. Constantly following up on leads and keeping chan-
nels of communication open is imperative.

### Internal Development

Concurrent to the old-boy and external efforts, the internal business
development group should be generating information on both the
market and potential candidates. This internal homework allows the
buyer to be knowledgeable and results in a better candidate list and
more knowledgeable negotiations.

## NEGOTIATING STRATEGY

A few key points are important to keep in mind in negotiating any
transaction in Europe.

First and foremost, a negotiation is a recognition by the purchaser
that it does not need to make the purchase. If a company enters
into negotiations committed to the purchase, it is not negotiating,
but only agreeing to what the seller desires. Before sitting down with
a potential seller to discuss an acquisition, a company should have
already developed a fairly well-thought-out position evaluating the
property to be bought, specifying the desired structure for the transaction, and suggesting an integration strategy and plan that would
optimize the particular purchase.

In Europe, because of potential government and union involvement in transactions, structure and integration programs may be-

come part of the contract. For example, a scenario in which a company would use the acquisition as a stand-alone business is different from a scenario where the acquired company would be stripped and used only for its products and brand names. These two scenarios would have very different values to the acquiring companies. In addition, governments of many Western European countries would look differently upon these two acquisitions in the approval process.

## ACQUISITION STRUCTURE

Some key areas of concern in structuring or negotiating a transaction in a European market are the following:

- *Acquiring stock or assets:* If stock is acquired, the purchaser accedes to all the company's undisclosed liabilities and off-balance-sheet liabilities. A special concern, especially in many southern European companies, is unknown federal tax liabilities incurred because of the way a company may have been operated. An asset purchase may give the purchaser the ability to execute certain tax-deductible transactions to reduce the after-tax net present value of the transaction.

- *Seller tax problems:* It is very important to recognize the tax problems of the seller, especially in countries like Sweden, where there are very high taxes on any sale; or in Spain, where there is no capital gains tax. The seller's tax problems may allow the purchaser to more effectively execute a transaction. Many times in negotiating a transaction, a purchaser is dealing with an arbitrage rate that is the tax savings it may get by structuring a deal toward the buyer's benefit versus the negative effect of that structure to the seller. Again, the arbitrage rate can be negotiated to optimize both of the net after-tax present value gains/costs.

- *Multicountry asset ownership:* In many European transactions, actual ownership of the stock or assets of the company are spread among a number of countries through both blind and open companies and/or trusts. The purpose of these structures in many cases is to prevent government knowledge concerning ownership of the company, and to give the company an opportunity to avoid a particular country's currency transaction laws while moving money in and out of countries. It is very important for a purchaser to understand the laws of the country in which it is dealing, especially as they relate to currency transactions, so that the purchaser does not induce or participate in a violation of law. In many European countries, illegal currency transactions are a criminal act, not a civil matter.

• *The company books:* It is important to understand clearly the bookkeeping systems and methods of the company being evaluated. If necessary, books should be redone on a pro forma basis under the GAAP system that you are familiar with. Most European countries have both statutory and tax books, which are constructed much differently from U.S. books. Different tax rules exist regarding depreciation schedules, write-offs, reserves, and the handling of employee benefits, which can dramatically affect the company's perceived profitability.

    Tax avoidance is a much more sophisticated art in many European countries—especially those in southern Europe—than in the United States. It is critical, prior to closing, for a purchaser's financial advisors, usually an outside auditor, to carefully examine the tax returns and the statutory books to determine that the purchaser is really buying what it thinks it is buying.

As part of the negotiating strategy, it is also imporant to determine the method, vehicle, and structure to acquire the European company or companies.

If cash is paid, will the purchaser:

• form a new company in the country?
• borrow locally?
• bring new capital into the country?
• buy through a series of step transactions that may include having the proprietary rights bought by a separate company, the assets bought by a local company, and the distribution facilities bought by a third company?

In all of these cases, government approval may have to be obtained.

It is important for the tax and legal advisors to review the tax laws of each country involved to determine what structure best:

- optimizes the after-tax net present value of the transaction, and/or
- optimizes the earnings per share characteristics of a transaction to the company, and/or
- gives the company the optimum protection against the acquired company's unknown liabilities, and/or
- optimizes the purchaser's opportunities to bring dividends or service fees out of the country into the parent company.

These considerations, and combinations of them, are all important in structuring a European transaction. Changes in 1986 in the U.S. tax law related to the relationship between asset and stock transactions, investment tax credits, and foreign tax credits will all have a significant effect on how a company may structure a European transaction in the future. Current understanding of the new tax law and system of foreign tax credits is very important to the purchaser.

## THE ACQUISITION RECOMMENDATION DOCUMENT

Once either a letter of understanding, a nonbinding letter of intent or a "heads of agreement" document has been negotiated with the seller, it is important for the buyer to codify the transaction in a single concise, well-written acquisition recommendation document. The document should be reviewed and approved by the buyer's senior management and should contain the following areas of discussion:

- The recommendation
- Strategic objectives that led to the transaction
- The company to be acquired and its characteristics
- The strategic fit of the company to the strategic plan objectives
- Price/value, including return on investment, return on assets, profit margin, and earnings-per-share effect
- The integration plan

Since the integration plan in Europe must balance business objectives, cultural habits, and government policy, it is critical that it be well documented in terms of both actions and timing. It should specify:

- who will run the company,
- how the company will be run,
- how the company will be integrated,
- what functions or people probably are redundant to the company, and
- how the purchaser will deal with workers' councils, unions, and governments in the transition.

## DUE DILIGENCE

In any transaction of either a stock or asset nature, a thorough due diligence process should be conducted by business, legal, tax, personnel, and research and development professionals prior to closing. The following list details items critical in a European transaction. Each country in Europe is different. Nothing should be taken for granted.

Key areas to center due diligence efforts on are the following:

- *All financial statements:* Make sure they are true and accurate, and represent the company's condition.

- *Employees and unions:* What rights do they have? Can the workers' council veto a transaction? If workers are declared redundant, what is the cost of their redundancy? Or, as in some cases in France, can they not be made redundant? If workers are made redundant, how will it be done? Is there a plan?

- *Government permissions:* What permissions are required? As with Hart-Scott-Rodino in the United States, many European countries require government permissions for a transaction to be made, especially if that transaction requires foreign currency to be brought into the country. Can the government where the acquisition is being contemplated require a local company to bid against a multinational purchase?

- *Undisclosed liabilities:* These relate to liabilities both of an on- and off-balance-sheet nature. The selling company should be forced to disclose any known or threatened lawsuits, liabilities, business problems, unique changes in the market, problems with customers, problems with government agencies, or any activity that could affect the purchaser's ability to effectively manage and execute a business plan in that country. Don't forget the emerging area of environmental concerns that relate to both products and plant sites, as voiced by the Greens.

- *Other matters:* It is important for the seller to provide to the purchaser a proper review of all the company's activities, including legal relationships and problems, local permissions that must be obtained, currency laws and regulations, and historical tax situation.

Each country is very different. Local legal, tax, and business experts should be used to make sure that a purchaser understands and meets the requirements necessary to execute the transaction. A little bit of consulting help up front usually pays for itself tenfold in the future.

## NEGOTIATING THE CONTRACT

There is no such thing as a standard contract for a transaction, especially one concerning the purchase of a company's assets or stock. It is important for the seller to warrant and represent all those things it has shown and told the purchaser about the company. The purchaser should not be bound by prior knowledge, verbal disclosures, or its own investigation. It is critical that the seller represent the condition of the company through the papers and documents it gives the purchaser. The warranties and representations need to be clear and concise. Exhibits should be used to define exceptions to any complete warranty and representation. This will allow the buyer to properly investigate exceptions the seller wishes to make to its representations.

Some additional areas to consider in a purchase contract are:

- noncompetition clauses for the owners or companies in the business they are selling, especially within Common Market Treaty of Rome restrictions,

- employment contracts with key employees the purchaser wishes to retain, and
- transition help from the seller.

In many instances, the seller is unwilling to give the warranties and representations the purchaser wishes. In these cases, the purchaser must decide whether it is willing to take on the risks involved and continue the acquisition.

## THE INTEGRATION PLAN

The most important part of a European acquisition, as mentioned earlier, is the development of a sound, well-thought-out operation and integration plan. When the average acquisition is going for upward of twenty times earnings, a plan that cannot envision growth, structural changes, and substantial profitability of a long-term business enterprise will not make economic sense.

This is especially important in Europe, where companies deal with a multiphased matrix of companies, cultures, employees, and products. A number of issues must be thought through and planned for:

- How will employees in the factories be handled?
- How will the Common Market problems be handled?
- How will sales force integration problems be handled?
- How will the currency hedging activities between factories and countries be handled?
- Where is the best country to manufacture what type of product?
- How is the risk of freight versus the risk of currency going to affect inventory buildup and inventory location?
- Has the company worked with workers' councils before, and does it know how to operate with both workers' councils and unions?
- Who is going to run the company? What is that person's role? What is the role of the board of directors?
- Does the company management understand the traditional vacation policies in Europe? Often, no one is at work in August, which

may be the acquiring company's key month for corporate or strategic planning.

All of these things must be considered and thought through, and responses evolved via an integration plan.

## THE CLOSING

A tremendous amount of work usually goes into the closing day: the day when both parties meet at a long table to sign a myriad of papers relating to all the negotiations of the entire transaction, the transfer of trademarks and proprietary rights, the movement of people and factories, and people's futures.

A transaction should not be closed unless the purchaser believes it really knows what is happening, and believes that the promises that have been made and the information that has been given are truthful and honest. When all these conditions have been met, close and enjoy!

# CHAPTER 20

# CANADA

**Fraser Mason**
**David Climie**
**CLARKSON GORDON/WOODS GORDON**

Merger and acquisition activity in Canada has increased significantly through the 1980s. According to Canadian government statistics, the number of mergers and acquisitions in Canada exceeded one thousand for the first time in 1987, an increase of more than 150 percent from 1980. During the same period, the percentage of domestic transactions involving foreign-owned or foreign-controlled corporations acquiring Canadian companies directly or indirectly remained just below 60 percent.

Canada has historically been an attractive location for foreign investment because of its political and economic stability and its close proximity to the U.S. market. However, due to the nature of Canada's democratic parliamentary system, the economy is often subject to restrictive market policies as the government in power effects fiscal, monetary, and/or social policy. For example, concern about rising levels of foreign investment in Canada prompted the Canadian government in 1974 to create the Foreign Investment Review Agency (FIRA) to review those transactions having a possible negative impact on the Canadian economy. Shortly thereafter, the National Energy Policy was also introduced to regulate domestic oil pricing and foreign ownership of energy resource property in Canada.

Since that time, however, the Canadian government has dropped those regulatory policies in favor of less onerous legislation. To encourage greater foreign participation in Canada, federal review procedures have been greatly simplified under the Investment Canada Act. That act, proclaimed in 1985, essentially established an open-door policy regarding foreign investment in Canada. Officials estimate that approximately 90 percent of the cases requiring federal regulatory approval under previous legislation are now exempt. The federal industry minister, however, retains the option of reviewing transactions affecting Canada's cultural heritage and national identity where he considers it to be in the public interest.

Although the government's goal is to build an internationally competitive economy through less restrictive policy, Canada's economy remains small in comparison to the U.S. economy. The gross national product is about one-tenth that of the United States, in proportion to the ratio between the respective populations.

Canada has a high degree of corporate concentration. A 1986 study conducted by the Toronto Stock Exchange—the country's largest—showed that fewer than a dozen families in Canada own, directly or indirectly, nearly one-half of the shares traded on the TSE. Of the 1,208 companies listed on the exchange at the end of 1987, fewer than 30 reported a capitalization value in excess of C$1 billion ($1 billion Canadian). As a result, a limited number of large widely held corporations exist in Canada, and foreign companies may face significant barriers to entry in certain industries given this high degree of concentration.

To increase market efficiency, the Canadian government has revised its antitrust legislation. In 1986, a twelve-person competition tribunal was formed to review restrictive trade practices in Canada, and the Competition Act was proclaimed to replace the outdated Combines Investigation Act. A key element of the new act is that civil rather than criminal law is applied when examining mergers and anticompetitive activities. In a case where a merger is likely to unduly reduce competition, the tribunal may block a transaction or order the disposal of shares/assets where a merger has been completed.

Overall, the tone of legislation is to recognize the importance of foreign ownership in Canada and the role it plays in expanding Canadian participation in world markets.

In addition, the bilateral free trade agreement between the United States and Canada will reduce tariff and nontariff barriers between both countries, allowing for greater integration of commerce between the two trading partners. The agreement, which is to be introduced over a ten-year period ending in 1998, is expected to create an increase in cross-border transactions as U.S. and Canadian companies position themselves in each other's market. The agreement is also expected to create greater integration in securities regulation and taxation between the two countries over time.

## THE ACQUISITION PROCESS IN CANADA

In general, the environment for initiating and completing an acquisition in Canada differs little from that in the United States. Foreign ownership and Canadian taxation rules must be considered throughout the acquisition process, but similar cultural and financial environments between the two nations provide U.S. companies with an easy transition into the Canadian market.

An important feature of the Canadian economy, however, is that there are fewer noncontrolled public companies. This tends to restrict the availability of corporate product and market information, and results in potential acquirers needing to meet personally with Canadian owners and managers to determine directly their corporate interests.

For individuals and companies interested in purchasing Canadian operations, there are two acquisition processes that can be followed, depending on the degree of knowledge the acquirer has of the Canadian marketplace.

For those U.S. corporations that have a considerable degree of intelligence about Canada and have a well-defined acquisition program, a "rifle" approach can be taken to the market. This approach requires a company's corporate development team to produce an acquisition criteria list, to be followed by a survey of potential target companies within an industry. In broad terms, the acquisition criteria should include the following:

- Nature of the business to be acquired
- Preferable geographic location

- Size of company (revenue, assets, employees)
- Growth potential (historic vs. projected)
- Profitability (minimum stated return on capital employed)
- Financial condition (based on current balance sheet ratios)
- Investment capital requirements (expenditure programs)
- Management capability and retention
- Interest sought (100 percent control, minority)
- Potential for hidden value (synergies)
- Matching of acquirer's strengths and candidate's weaknesses

Once a U.S. company has identified a Canadian corporation or subsidiary as a candidate, acquisition professionals can be engaged to assist in the pricing, structuring, and completion of the deal.

For those corporations that have yet to develop comprehensive acquisition criteria, discreet inquiries in the financial community will often produce varied candidate lists. Because most acquisition professionals in Canada will conduct target searches for their clients, this "shotgun" approach will produce a broad spectrum of investment opportunities. Fees charged for such services will vary depending on the immediacy, depth, and duration of the work undertaken. A number of possible professionals will generate leads and provide full acquisition services for U.S. corporations.

- *Investment bankers:* There are fewer independent investment bankers in Canada than in the United States. However, many large commercial banks and financial holding companies have developed investment banking operations of their own since 1985. In addition, many of the large U.S. investment banking firms are expanding their operations into Canada following the recent move toward deregulation of the Canadian financial services industry.

- *Investment dealers:* Most large dealers have dedicated acquisition staff in their corporate finance departments. Potential deals vary in size from small private companies to large publicly owned corporations. Their regional contacts and aggressive sales teams produce assorted acquisition opportunities, usually with the focus of underwriting the transaction. In 1987, the four largest Canadian investment dealers were acquired by the four largest Canadian domestic banks.

- *Public accountants/management consultants:* Management consultants and chartered accountants have excellent exposure to a wide variety of businesses, and their role often leads into strategic planning for their clients. Their national networks assist in generating a large number of opportunities. These firms usually work on a per-diem fee basis rather than a contingent-fee basis like the dealers and bankers. A few of these firms have acquisition staff dedicated to acquisition activities.

- *Commercial banks:* Due to the close relationship that often exists between bankers and customers, a bank may have early knowledge of a customer's desire to divest or acquire. Major Canadian banks have national retail networks that feed information to their corporate banking departments.

  In many circumstances, especially when a potential buyer's financing is not in place, U.S. companies may approach large domestic chartered banks ("A" institutions) or foreign banks ("B" institutions) to assist them in both the acquisition process and the raising of funds required to complete the purchase. Unlike commercial banks in the United States, which are prohibited under the Glass-Steagall Act from actively investing in and underwriting potential acquisitions, A and B banks in Canada are allowed to participate in and underwrite such transactions for their clients. The availability of this commercial banking service increases competition in the Canadian market and provides acquirers with additional means to both search for and execute their deals. As noted earlier, the four largest Canadian investment dealers were acquired by the four largest domestic banks in Canada in 1987.

- *Business brokers/finders:* A business may engage a broker with the authority to sell it. The potential deals tend to be smaller and the broker is compensated on the basis of closing a deal. Finders, on the other hand, simply bring two parties together for a fixed fee. There are relatively few brokers and finders in the Canadian market.

## PROFILE OF THE CANADIAN MARKETPLACE

Canada is a confederation of ten provinces and two territories. Two-thirds of the Canadian population inhabit the central provinces of Ontario and Quebec, where the two largest urban centers are located: Toronto in Ontario and Montreal in Quebec.

Each province in Canada has its own legislature, which enacts laws relating to its jurisdictional affairs. In addition to the ten provincial legislatures, there is a federal legislature, which convenes in the Parliament Buildings in Ottawa.

The federal legislature is composed of the Senate, which is an appointed body, and the House of Commons, whose elected members are chosen at least every five years. Following the election, the political party with the greatest number of elected members in the House of Commons is called on to form the government. The leader of the winning party becomes prime minister, and a cabinet of elected members is formed to manage the government.

The federal government has the broadest jurisdictional powers in Canada, which include defense, criminal law, regulation of trade and commerce, fisheries, banking, currency, and unlimited taxation powers. The provinces, on the other hand, are given control over local works and have direct taxation powers to raise revenue for provincial purposes.

In a federal/provincial accord signed by the ten provinces and the Canadian government in 1987, Quebec was granted full constitutional status and the ten provinces given greater discretionary powers regarding spending on social services. However, the federal government's broad taxation and fiscal powers allow it the greatest impact on the Canadian economy, and the foreign investor must be aware of federal government incentive programs, regulatory changes, and tax reform.

In deciding on which jurisdiction (federal or provincial) to operate within, an investor must determine the nature and structure of the company and the rules of the jurisdiction being considered. Areas in which variations occur between jurisdictions of interest to a foreign investor are financial disclosure requirements, residency requirements for directors, and restrictions on loans to directors and shareholders. While it is possible to change jurisdictions once incorporated, it is wise to match the business requirements of the company carefully with the proposed jurisdiction's rules prior to incorporation.

Canada's legal system is based on British common law, except in Quebec, which operates under civil or Napoleonic code. Politically, a separatist movement thrived in Quebec through much of the 1970s, but it has been replaced by a provincial government emphasizing economic prosperity within the federalist structure.

Canada has two official languages, English and French. The predominance of Francophones are located in Quebec, where American investors may encounter some language and minor cultural problems. However, the majority of business people in Quebec are also well versed in English.

## CORPORATE STRUCTURE IN CANADA

When a foreign investor is considering an acquisition within Canadian borders, a number of corporate structures are available, each with certain legal and tax implications.

### Corporate Entity (Subsidiary)

The most common form of corporate structure used by foreign investors is a Canadian corporation. The legislation governing Canadian corporations is similar to that in the United States. The corporation provide shareholders limited liability and a consistent framework within which to operate.

Companies may be incorporated either federally under the Canada Business Corporations Act or provincially under any one of the ten provincial corporations acts. Corporations carrying on certain specialized activities, such as banking, are incorporated under special legislation rather than under general corporate legislation.

Since federal and provincial laws are similar, the decision as to which jurisdiction to operate under depends largely on the business and structure of the company and the rules of the jurisdiction being considered, rather than strictly legal considerations. For example, while federal private companies with assets in excess of C$5 million, or gross revenues in excess of C$10 million, are required to make their financial statements public, no such requirement exists for private companies incorporated in a province.

Furthermore, the Canada Business Corporations Act requires a majority of the directors of a federally incorporated company to be "resident Canadians," which includes landed immigrants. For holding companies earning less than 5 percent of their gross revenues from Canadian operations, only one-third of the directors must be resident Canadians. Most of the provinces have taken steps to align their laws with the federal act in this regard.

Canadian subsidiaries are taxable in Canada and subject to a withholding tax of 10 to 20 percent on repatriation of after-tax earnings to the foreign parent, depending on the nature of the payment and subject to the various tax treaties in place. Generally, under bilateral tax agreements, the withholding tax is 15 percent.

### Joint Venture

A joint venture is defined by the Canadian Institute of Chartered Accountants as an arrangement whereby two or more parties jointly control a specific business undertaking and contribute resources toward its accomplishment. The joint venture may be incorporated or unincorporated.

If the joint venture is incorporated, the legislation affecting it is consistent with that for corporate subsidiaries. If the joint venture is unincorporated and owned by non-Canadian investors, the foreign venturer/investor is responsible for its proportionate share of the venture's income, assets, and liabilities. The advantage of a joint venture arrangement, common in the resource industry, is that each participant may determine income from the venture separately from other participants. Thus, depreciation allowances, income recognition methods, and special elections can be chosen independently.

## REGULATIONS REGARDING INVESTMENT IN CANADA

Regarding mergers and acquisitions in Canada, management must be fully aware of the rules and regulations governing foreign investment, market competition, securities law, and corporate taxation.

## The Investment Canada Act

The Investment Canada Act, established in 1986, created an Investment Canada agency to replace the previous Foreign Investment Review Agency (FIRA). In a significant departure from prior legislation, the Investment Canada Act has as its mandate the promotion of investment in the country by both Canadians and non-Canadians. This is to be done through assistance in exploiting opportunities for technological advancement and research in the area of domestic and international investment.

The act differentiates between "Canadian" and "non-Canadian" investors, where the latter are entities unable to meet the tests of Canadian status. A Canadian investor is:

- a Canadian citizen or permanent resident within the meaning of the Immigration Act (except a permanent resident who has not taken out citizenship within one year of becoming eligible to do so,
- a Canadian government or its agency, or
- a Canadian-controlled corporation or joint venture, or one that is deemed to be Canadian-controlled as defined by the act.

Control by non-Canadians is considered to exist:

- where one non-Canadian or two or more non-Canadian members of a voting group own a majority of the voting interests in an entity, or
- where two people equally own the voting shares of a corporation and one of those people is a non-Canadian.

Except for investments in areas that may be viewed as related to Canada's cultural heritage or national identity, investments by non-Canadians in new business ventures are subject to a "notification only" review under the Investment Canada Act. The investor must notify Investment Canada of an investment either before it takes place or within thirty days thereafter. Only if the transaction is deemed to have cultural heritage or national identity implications is such an investment subject to detailed review and assessment.

"Notification only" is required when a non-Canadian investor acquires control of an existing Canadian business and either:

- the Canadian business is being acquired directly and the assets of the business are less than C$5 million, or

- the Canadian business is being acquired indirectly—for example, by the acquisition of a U.S. parent company of a Canadian subsidiary—and the Canadian assets have a value of less than C$50 million and represent no more than 50 percent of the total assets being acquired, or the Canadian assets represent more than 50 percent of the assets being acquired but have a value of less than C$5 million.

Indications are that such areas as book publishing and film production and distribution will be viewed as sensitive industries, but provisions for the federal cabinet to define such business activities through regulation are available.

With some defined exceptions, investments by non-Canadians to directly acquire control of an existing Canadian business with gross assets of more than C$5 million are "reviewable" for purposes of assessing net benefit to Canada, and a similar requirement applies to indirect acquisitions where Canadian assets exceed C$50 million or constitute more than 50 percent of the total assets involved in the transaction and have a value over C$5 million.

When an acquisition is subject to review for purposes of assessing benefit to Canada, the following factors are considered:

- The acquisition's effect on the level and nature of economic activity in Canada

- The degree and significance of participation in the business by Canadians

- The acquisition's effects on productivity, efficiency, technology, and product innovation and variety in Canada

- The acquisition's effects on competition within Canadian industries

- Compatibility with the industrial, economic, and cultural policies of the federal government and any provincial governments concerned

- The contribution of the investment to Canada's ability to compete in world markets

Of note in the Investment Canada Act is the requirement, relative to reviewable transactions, that only a showing of net benefit to Canada is required, rather than the significant benefit stipulation under the old act. The focus of the net benefit assessment is primarily on showing that no detriment to Canada will result from the transaction.

When an acquisition review is required, the investor must file a prescribed form with Investment Canada, which has fifteen days from its receipt to issue a notice of deficiencies or the application will be deemed complete. The industry minister then has forty-five days (with provisions for an extenstion of up to thirty days) to decide on the question of net benefit to Canada. If it is determined that a net benefit results from the transaction, the deal can proceed. However, if the transaction is shown to have an overall negative impact on economic activity in Canada, then it must be restructured and a re-application made.

## Other Federal Statutes Governing Foreign Investment

Certain Canadian statutes control the degree of foreign ownership of certain industries or limit the growth of foreign-controlled enterprises. Some of the most important restrictions are as follows:

- *Banking:* Although banks may be controlled by nonresidents, the Bank Act places restrictions on the number of branches and the size of banks controlled by nonresidents.
- *Broadcasting:* Nonresidents are limited to 20 percent of the voting stock and 60 percent of the total capital of broadcasting companies.
- *Uranium:* Unless exempted by legislation, nonresidents may not own more than one-third of the equity of uranium-producing companies. This limitation may be increased to 50 percent, however, if Canadian control is assured.

Similar types of restrictions apply in the newspaper, airlines, fishing, coastal shipping, sales finance, and consumer loan industries.

## Antitrust Legislation

In June 1986, Parliament passed amendments to existing antitrust legislation. These amendments were contained in Bill C-91, which introduced a Competition Tribunal Act and significantly revised the Combines Investigation Act, which was renamed the Competition Act.

The Competition Tribunal, consisting of four judges and eight other members, has the jurisdiction to hear and rule on restrictive trade practices in Canada, including consignment selling, exclusive dealing, refusing to deal, tied selling, market restrictions, and abuse of dominant position. In addition, the Competition Act gives the tribunal the power to regulate trade and commerce in respect to conspiracies and mergers affecting competition.

Under this legislation, antitrust investigators can no longer charge corporations under criminal statutes for being a party to an illegal merger. However, a merger or proposed merger can still be attacked on the basis that it prevents or lessens competition substantially. When reviewing a merger, the tribunal examines such factors as whether the target company is failing, the effect on foreign as well as domestic competition, barriers to entry, availability of substitutes, the likelihood that a vigorous and effective competitor would be removed, and the extent to which competition would continue if a merger took place.

Even if a merger is deemed to lessen competition, the tribunal must allow it to proceed if gains in efficiency from the transaction outweigh the possible effects of reduced competition. Yet, the tribunal is given extensive powers to deal with anticompetitive mergers. It can prevent a merger or allow it to proceed only on certain conditions, or if the transaction has already taken place, set it aside or order the divestiture of assets or shares.

While in the United States there is a test for mergers that substantially lessen marketplace competition, the civil merger review is an aid to the general antitrust law under which monopolization is a crime. U.S. merger review procedures will not serve as legal precedent in Canada, and businesses may face some uncertainties until a case-by-case history is developed.

In addition to the review process, the Competition Act also mandates prenotification for large acquisitions. The salient points of the legislation are that prior notice must be given if:

- the parties to the transaction and their affiliates have consolidated assets or gross revenues in Canada in excess of C$400 million, and
- the value of the shares or assets of the target company, or its gross revenue, exceeds C$35 million (in an amalgamation, the target threshold for the assets or the shares outstanding is doubled to C$70 million), and
- the transaction results in a holding of 20 percent—or 50 percent if a 20 percent interest is already held—where the shares are publicly traded; or the acquisition results in a holding of 35 percent—or 50 percent if a 35 percent position is already held—where the shares are not publicly traded.

If a transaction meets the requirements of prenotification, the parties must inform the government that the transaction is proposed and supply the following items:

- A description of the proposed transaction
- A statement of the business objectives to be achieved
- Copies of the legal documents
- Names and addresses of participants
- A list of affiliates
- A description of principal businesses undertaken by those involved, including their affiliates
- A statement of gross and net assets, and gross revenues for the most recent fiscal year
- Copies of documents such as proxy solicitation circulars, prospectuses, and other information filed with a securities commission, stock exchange, or other similar authority
- The financial statements, where available, of the acquiring party, the continuing corporation, and the combination, prepared on a pro forma basis as if the proposed transaction had already occurred

## Securities Regulation and Its Effect on Takeover Bids

In Canada, no all-encompassing general securities act exists. Regulation of the securities industry is primarily the responsibility of the provinces, except where the Canada Business Corporations Act (CBCA) may affect securities procedures for federally incorporated companies. In general, the Ontario Securities Act, which oversees the activities of the Toronto Stock Exchange and investment dealers in Ontario, contains the most stringent and widely applied securities regulations in Canada. To a large degree, the province of Ontario and the federal government have led the way in allowing greater foreign ownership of securities and investment dealers in Canada. Interprovincial cooperation in securities regulation, however, has allowed a common voice to be heard at the federal level, despite minor regulatory differences. Securities sold or offered for sale in each province must meet the requirements of the respective provincial securities act, which can differ slightly regarding registration and disclosure. Other securities exchanges in Canada are located in Montreal, Calgary, and Vancouver. A commodities exchange is located in Winnipeg.

The takeover of a publicly traded company in Canada can be executed by means of a circular under Canadian securities law or through the facilities of a stock exchange. Federal legislation under the CBCA applies to takeovers of companies incorporated under the act. The CBCA defines a takeover bid as an offer that, if combined with shares already beneficially owned or controlled by the offeror or an affiliate, exceeds 10 percent of any class of stock of a target corporation.

Depending on where in Canada the target company is incorporated, the threshold level may change. For federally incorporated companies, the cutoff point is 10 percent as previously described. Under most provincial securities laws, however, a takeover bid is not launched unless 20 percent of the shares of the target company are in the possession, directly or indirectly, of the offeror.

But takeover bids are exempt from federal securities regulation if the offer is made:

- to fewer than fifteen shareholders to purchase shares by separate agreement,
- to purchase shares through a stock exchange or in the over-the-counter market, or
- to purchase shares of a corporation that has fewer than fifteen shareholders, two or more joint holders being counted as one shareholder.

If an offer is neither exempt nor conducted through a securities exchange, the offeror must meet the circular requirements of the appropriate securities act governing the transaction. If an offeror tenders for less than all shares of the target and more shares are offered than it intended to buy, then it must take up the shares on a pro rata basis. If an offeror increases its offer price while the bid is still outstanding, all shareholders accepting the bid must receive the increased price even if the bid was accepted prior to the increase.

And under the Ontario Securities Act, if the value paid in consideration for a class of securities in a takeover bid exceeds the "market price" at the time of the agreement plus reasonable brokerage fees or commissions, the offeror must make a "follow-up offer" within 180 days after the initial date of the takeover bid to purchase all additional securities of the same class at a price at least equal in value to the greatest consideration paid under any such agreement. "Market price" defined under the Ontario Securities Act permits a 15 percent premium. So only if the amount paid exceeds the closing price plus a 15 percent premium, would a follow-up offer be required. A similar rule exists under the Quebec Securities Act whereby the offeror must offer the same price to all holders of a class of securities subject to a takeover bid.

As mentioned, however, an offer will be exempt from takeover regulations if the takeover bid is made in compliance with the laws, rules, and regulations of a Canadian stock exchange.

According to the governing rules of the Toronto Stock Exchange, a takeover bid is defined to be a purchase or an offer to purchase listed voting shares that, in aggregate, exceed 20 percent of the company's outstanding listed voting shares. If a company is incorporated under the CBCA, then the 10 percent threshold applies.

The key provision for making a takeover bid through the stock exchange, however, is that it must be made in cash only. Furthermore, the only conditions that can be attached to a bid conducted on the exchange are:

- the maximum number of shares to be taken up, and
- a withdrawal clause allowing for the possibility of a material change.

Regarding disclosure rules, if an insider—a person or company that beneficially owns directly or indirectly 10 percent of the voting securities of a company—buys or sells a publicly traded stock, the transaction must be reported each month to the provincial securities commission.

### Corporate Taxation in Canada

In broad general terms, determination of income tax in Canada is similar to that in the United States. However, before proceeding with a transaction, an acquirer should consult the federal and appropriate provincial income tax acts and/or a qualified tax professional.

Generally, an acquirer will prefer an asset purchase, and the seller a share sale. An acquirer's preference for an asset purchase is based on the following:

- Assets acquired will be recorded at market value, thereby maximizing deductibility of the purchase price.
- One-half of purchased goodwill qualifies as a deduction for tax, on a 10 percent per annum declining-balance basis.
- With purchase of shares, the full amount of the purchase price is allocated to the cost of the shares, thus providing no immediate tax deduction.

The seller will prefer a share sale for the following reasons:

- It allows maximization of capital gains, only one-half of which is taxed.
- It avoids realizing any recapture of capital cost allowance and inventory gains, both of which are taxed as ordinary income.
- It offers the possibility of deferring a portion of any capital gain if noncash consideration is involved.

Noncapital losses can be carried forward or passed up to a purchaser, but subject to several considerations including continuation of the business activities and availability or expectation of future income. Net capital losses expire on sale.

The Income Tax Act contains a "thin capitalization" rule that limits interest deductibility if certain debt/equity thresholds are exceeded where debt is supplied to the Canadian subsidiary by a foreign parent or affiliate.

Corporate residency will determine the source of the income that is subject to tax. Generally, the income of a corporation consists of income from a business or property and one-half of net gains realized on disposition of any capital assets. Business income is subject to federal tax, and to provincial tax in some provinces. The combined effect ranges between 35 and 46 percent. Certain incentives, including manufacturing and processing credits, foreign income tax credits, and investment tax credits, will reduce the effective rate.

## INCENTIVES

In the acquisition of Canadian-based businesses, both the federal and provincial governments offer a wide array of incentives for investment or expansion in accordance with their economic and social objectives. The federal government was expending C$1.3 billion per year on economic development programs in the mid-1980s.

The Canadian government provides grants, loans, loan guarantees, and insurance to promote economic development. Certain types of activity are also promoted, either through grants or other assistance. Provincial government incentives generally consist of loans, grants, and occasionally equity participation.

## REPATRIATION OF CANADIAN EARNINGS

There are no foreign exchange controls in Canada and no limit on the amount of earnings that can be repatriated. Canada and the United States ratified a new income tax treaty on August 16, 1984. The withholding tax rates under this treaty are as follows:

| | |
|---|---|
| Interest: | 15 percent |
| Dividends: | |
| general: | 15 percent |
| corporate shareholder owning 10 percent of voting stock | 10 percent |
| Rents: | |
| real property | 25 percent |
| tangible property | 10 percent |
| Royalties: | |
| general | 10 percent |
| resources | 25 percent |

# CHAPTER 21

# JAPAN

## Steven B. Schlossstein
SBS ASSOCIATES

Japan in the late 1980s is going through a very difficult transition period, from export-led GNP growth to a domestic-led economy. This period of transition, which is likely to last through the early 1990s, is as historic as the period over a century ago when Japan was forced to open up to the West. It is characterized by the following eight factors:

- A strong yen, which could make foreign imports much more competitive in the Japanese market, provided they are positioned aggressively

- A relatively open domestic market, with fewer bureaucratic obstacles to import penetration than in the past

- An aging society, which will generate the world's second largest pension fund market by 1990, as well as the second largest consumer market

- An increasingly deregulated and privatized domestic economy as the Japanese government sheds its ownership in state entities such as Nippon Telegraph and Telephone and the Japan National Railways, and stimulates domestic growth through deregulation or privatization rather than fiscal measures

- Growing corporate disloyalty, as Japan's top companies slim down in an era of slower growth, which will mean that foreign companies will be able both to recruit and pirate away first-class managerial talent

- Increasing affluence—Japan already represents 75 percent of the East Asian GNP—and high capital formation and domestic savings rates relative to other OECD countries, making Japan the world's primary capital exporter through the rest of the century

- An increasing trend toward convergence and interdependence between the U.S. and Japanese economies, as opposed to past insularity and vulnerability, further encouraging strategic partnerships

- The continuation of very aggressive domestic and international commercial policies; simply put, Japan will continue to be our most formidable commercial competitor

These factors mean that Japan—and by extension East Asia—represents the most important global corporate priority for U.S. companies for at least the next generation. The Japanese market may be tough, but it is getting incrementally easier to compete there. No major U.S. company can afford to ignore Japan's position in the hierarchy of global competitiveness.

The four newly industrializing countries (NICs) of East Asia—Korea, Taiwan, Hong Kong, and Singapore—plus China, represent another two billion potential consumers, as well as formidable staging bases from which to launch competitive strategies in Japan. Income is distributed widely. Entrepreneurial values and a vigorous business class are alive and well in the region. Private sector initiatives and economic development are not only recognized but encouraged.

These factors together represent tremendous opportunities for American companies interested in expanding their positions in Japan and East Asia via strategic alliances, providing American management takes a longer-term, strategic view toward the region rather than adopting the narrower financial concern characteristic of American companies, a concern that has contributed to their competitive downfall.

## DIFFERENCES BETWEEN AMERICAN AND JAPANESE OBJECTIVES

The fundamental objective underlying the execution of mergers and acquisitions in the United States is financial—maximizing shareholder value. In Japan and East Asia, however, the fundamental corporate objective is strategic—maximizing market share.

The American preoccupation with financial results per se stems from three primary factors:

- First, the expectations of our investment community have become increasingly short-term, so that examination of quarterly and even monthly performance results is now routine.

- Second, managers concentrate more on the enhancement of short-term profitability than on the development of long-term competitiveness.

- Finally, senior management of major American companies has come to be dominated by bankers and lawyers, so that by 1985 nearly one-half of American corporate presidents were people trained in the narrower skills of either finance or law. Fewer than one-third of American corporate presidents had technical backgrounds, and fewer than one-fifth were marketing specialists.

It was not surprising, therefore, to find in a poll of senior corporate management conducted in the early 1980s that the overwhelming majority believed their principal corporate purpose should be "to increase their short-term return on investment in order to maximize shareholder value." Consequently, domestic American acquisitions can be said to be driven principally by financial considerations—what the impact will be on the buyer's bottom line and what the extent of the payout will be for the seller.

But in Japan and East Asia, maximizing shareholder value is not a priority concern of companies or their managements. Purely financial concerns rank much lower on their lists of corporate objectives. In Japan, especially, maximizing market share ranks highest as a strategic goal. This means growth rather than increasing a financial return on investment—growth in revenues, growth in product, and particularly growth in market share.

A Japanese company cannot increase its market share in any given industry overnight; the goal takes years to achieve. In the 1950s and

1960s, major Japanese companies leveraged themselves heavily to achieve demonstrably faster rates of growth in revenues and market share in those industries they had targeted for long-term international competition: shipbuilding, steel, petrochemicals, consumer electronics, computers, automobiles, and capital goods. While their profitability was comparatively low, their growth rates were far higher than those of American companies. By the 1970s, as a result of their strategic focus on market share, their profitability had improved to the point where they were able to retire much of their debt and generate more of their own necessary financing internally.

In addition, the Japanese investment community and Japanese banks have supported the longer-term objectives of their major corporations. By virtue of there being no capital gains tax in Japan, Japanese investors prefer long-term capital gains, through a company's growth, to dividends, which are taxed at short-term ordinary income rates. And through their short-term lending facilities, the Japanese banks in effect extend long-term, evergreen loans to their corporate borrowers, to underwrite the longer-term objectives. These banks also take small equity positions in the companies, becoming one of their institutional shareholders.

Japanese companies, by and large, are run by industry specialists, not by bankers and lawyers, so their focus is more on the future, less on the present. Consequently, since maximizing market share and not shareholder value is the operative strategic factor in Japan, acquisitions in the domestic Japanese market—or in any other major East Asian market—are the exception rather than the rule.

Major or second-tier companies in Japan are simply not for sale. This is not because of any restrictions imposed by the Japanese government or law, but rather because of the unique nature of the Japanese company as compared to its American counterpart. Among these differences are the following:

- The principal assets of a Japanese company are its people, not its products or its plant and equipment. Its management and employees are regarded as a team, as de facto owners of the business. Therefore, the buying and selling of companies in Japan carries with it the moral connotation of buying and selling people, not assets. This is a social stigma and avoided whenever possible.

- The typical Japanese company, large or small, functions as a microcosm of Japanese society as a whole, with a unique hierarchy and internal factions. In any merger or acquisition, such as those between the Dai-Ichi and Nippon-Kangyo Banks in 1971, or the Ataka and C. Itoh trading companies in 1976, these internal factions or management cliques can limit the effectiveness of the combined "team" for years afterward because of conflicting loyalties and allegiances.

- Shares of public Japanese companies tend to be fully priced in the market. The average price/earnings multiple in Japan was more than four times its American counterpart in mid-1988 (around 60 for the Nikkei 225 as opposed to under 15 for the S & P 500) and has historically been at least double. This is due to the Japanese investor's preference for capital gains over dividends, and to the fact that a company's growth in revenues and product output tends to be reflected fully in its share price. Thus an acquisition cannot be carried out in Japan simply to maximize shareholder value; in most instances it is already being maximized by the market.

## OTHER OBSTACLES TO ACQUISITIONS IN JAPAN

Theoretically, and on superficial analysis, an American company may consider an acquisition in the Japanese market to be both advantageous and attractive as a market-entry or market-penetration strategy. In a domestic economy as competitive and as fractious as Japan's, dominated by the heated rivalries of so many world-class corporate competitors like Matsushita and Sony, NEC and Hitachi, Makino and Okuma, Makita and Murata, or Toyota and Honda, an acquisition would give the foreign company immediate strength in competing against these giants, compared to the more costly and time-consuming effort of building from scratch.

Start-up costs in Japan are among the highest in the world. Purchasing land and building a factory can often delay the timing of a market entry unreasonably, and finding first-class employees willing to work for a foreign company is not easy, given the limited availability of staff. Acquisition of a major Japanese competitor can short-circuit many if not all of these problems, giving the foreign acquirer land, fixed assets, trained people, a recognizable name, and, most important, instant market share in the target market.

Practically speaking, however, the acquisition path in Japan is lined with a number of very formidable obstacles:

- Japanese companies in general are just not available for purchase. While this is certainly true as a rule of thumb, and exceptions may be found that prove the rule, it is even more applicable in the case of highly competitive, visibly successful Japanese companies. Cultural pride as well as competitive strength dictates that any overt acquisition move on the part of a potential foreign acquirer will likely be thwarted at all costs.

- Any acquisitions that do take place in the Japanese market tend to be between companies that are already related by virtue of their existing *keiretsu,* or industrial group, relationships. The decision by Sanyo, one of Japan's leading consumer electronics companies, to acquire 100 percent of Tokyo Sanyo—previously 21 percent owned—in early 1986 is a case in point. Acquisitions by original equipment manufacturers (OEMs) of their parts and components suppliers, in which they already have a small, or not so small, equity participation, are another example.

- Many acquisitions in Japan are occasioned by near bankruptcies, or business failures, and as such there is a loser's stigma attached to transactions that fall into this category. C. Itoh's acquisition of Ataka & Co. in 1976 stemmed from Ataka's having overextended itself badly in foreign markets, especially in petroleum refining, in which it had little previous experience. However, consensus among the company's major bank (Sumitomo), the Japanese government (notably the Bank of Japan), and a probable acquirer (Itoh) was reached in order to avoid the negative ramifications of a major Japanese trading company going under. Kyocera's acquisition of Yashica was similarly motivated.

    So, since Japanese companies that might be available for acquisition will in all likelihood be significantly problem-ridden, potential foreign acquirers must be extremely cautious. Few things are worse than beginning a major market-penetration effort in a major Asian market with less than a full deck, let alone one that is stacked against you.

- Any intended acquisition in Japan by a foreign acquirer that is perceived to be against the best strategic interests of either the Japanese target or the country as a whole will be opposed from the outset by both the Japanese company and the government.

   In the late 1970s, a Hong Kong investor group tried to achieve control of Katakura Industries, an Osaka-based spinning and textile company with considerable latent assets in the form of underutilized land on its balance sheet. The move was opposed by the company, which put pressure on its investment bankers to prevent any further purchases of its shares in the open market, and by the Ministry of Finance, which subsequently placed Katakura on its list of restricted companies, off limits to foreign investors for reasons relating to national security.

   In late 1985, Trafalgar Holdings tried to gain control of Minibea, Japan's leading manufacturer of miniature bearings, by acquiring a substantial position in the company's convertible Eurobond issues and warrants. Minibea outmaneuvered the foreigners by issuing a new class of shares and by further intensifying its relationship with its main Japanese bank. No doubt significant discussions occurred at appropriate levels within the Japanese government as well.

- Hostile takeover bids are just not part of the corporate landscape of Japan. Postacquisition, buyer and seller must work closely together—harmoniously, as the Japanese would say—to achieve common corporate goals and objectives. This would be impossible in the aftermath of a hostile takeover attempt.

   Again, the Minibea case is illustrative. Minibea is a maverick Japanese company that has grown through acquisition over the years (it once acquired a small subsidiary of Sony), has made acquisitions in the United States (New England Ball Bearings), and continues to study further diversification moves by way of acquisition (Key Electronics), all through the process of consensus building. Any hostile attempts by a foreign company to take Minibea over would be rejected.

   And Kyocera, formerly Kyoto Ceramics, the world's leading manufacturer of IC lead frames, recently acquired Yashica, a Japanese camera company on the verge of bankruptcy. But this takeover, too, was far from hostile; had the two companies not been able, in advance, to agree on the structure and the terms of the acquisition—a process called *nemawashi*—the transaction would never have occurred.

With such cultural antagonism toward acquisitions on the one hand and a bias against the whole takeover process on the other, what reasonable alternatives remain for foreign companies eager to penetrate the Japanese market more aggressively?

## REALISTIC ALTERNATIVES FOR ACQUIRERS IN JAPAN

The primary concern for a foreign company contemplating a market-entry or market-penetration effort in Japan must be strategic. Providing the foreign company is willing and able to dispense with the customary emphasis on short-term profitability that no doubt characterizes its behavior in the home market, and further, providing the foreign company accepts the premise that maximizing market share rather than shareholder value is, or should be, its raison d'etre in Japan, the key method becomes one of forging appropriate strategic alliances.

Prior to about 1980, when Japan's Foreign Exchange Control law was amended, about the only way a foreign company could operate in Japan was by means of a 50-50 joint venture, and usually with its fiercest Japanese competitor. Asahi-Dow, Yokogawa–Hewlett Packard, Kanebo-Stevens, Kanebo-Gilco, and Kanebo-Cadbury all come to mind.

On a case-by-case basis, where the Japanese government permitted foreign companies to own 100 percent of their operations, such as Texas Instruments, significant competitive concessions in the form of technology sharing were extracted. Overall, neither the joint venture nor the wholly owned subsidiary developed strategically into the most advantageous way of entering the Japanese market, but the alternatives were strictly limited.

Now that Japanese regulations have been eased, and neither the past constraints imposed on joint ventures nor the limitations on wholly owned operations are in effect, the opportunities for a foreign company to compete more effectively in Japan are significantly improved. But since outright acquisitions in Japan are of limited value and effectiveness, the emphasis should be on strategic alliances: the acquisition of a significant minority position in the equity of a Japanese company, or the formation of a strategic joint venture with a Japanese target, which will work to the advantage of both sides instead of to their mutual disadvantage.

Some strategic alliances have already been forged in the Japanese market. Years ago, before the Japanese automakers achieved world-class status, Detroit's Big Three took sizable minority positions in Japan. GM acquired 34 percent of Isuzu, Ford took 24 percent of Mazda Motors (then Toyo Kogyo), and Chrysler bought 35 percent of Mitsubishi Motors. In GM's case, Isuzu had been a leading manufacturer of trucks and diesel engines, but had lost out competitively in the tough passenger car market. Its Bellet and Bellel models never caught on. Had it not permitted an infusion of GM capital, it may have had to suffer the ultimate indignity, as a "troubled company," of being acquired by or forcibly merged into one of its major competitors such as Nissan (Datsun).

Unfortunately, the strategic alliances among these automobile companies worked more to the advantage of the Japanese than the Americans. While the Americans used their Japanese partners as a principal source of supply for engines, components, and occasional technological innovations or improvements, the Japanese learned more about the U.S. market. Neither GM, Ford, nor Chrysler ever seriously used these tie-ups as a means of trying to compete more aggressively in Japan by developing products designed specifically for the Japanese market. Today, American market share of the Japanese automobile market, the world's fastest growing, is statistically insignificant.

Other strategic alliances have worked better in Japan over the years, and they should be used as examples of what can be done. The Caterpillar-Mitsubishi tie-up between Cat and Mitsubishi Heavy Industries achieved, and continues to achieve, a dual objective: to get Cat into Japan in a significant way and to enable MHI to compete more effectively with a major Japanese competitor, Komatsu. In this case, neither Caterpillar nor MHI were outright competitors from the beginning, a crucial factor in forging a successful strategic alliance in Japan.

Sumitomo-3M, a strategic tie-up between 3M, Sumitomo Electric, and NEC, gave 3M a powerful distribution network in the Japanese market, leveraging the contacts of two of Japan's most competitive industrial giants. Again, the operative factor in the alliance was the absence of direct product competition between the Japanese and American partners. And 3M retained management control of the joint venture with its dominant shareholding, 50 percent compared to 25 percent each for Sumitomo and NEC.

Finally, Nippon Merck Banyu, a strategic alliance between Merck Pharmaceuticals and Banyu, a second-tier Japanese drug company, gave Merck the start it needed to penetrate the Japanese drug market with newly developed products via Banyu's strong marketing and sales force. This tie-up enabled the two companies to get to know each other closely and well over a long period, paving the way for Merck's ultimate 50.01 percent acquisition of Banyu in 1983, the first case ever of a major Japanese company listed on the first section of the Tokyo Stock Exchange having a majority of its shares acquired by a foreign company.

The point in each of these examples is that a strategic alliance works best when the strengths of one partner (new drug products from Merck, for example, or the Sumitomo distribution network) can be leveraged against the weaknesses of the other (Banyu's low R&D expenditures or Cat's comparative inability to compete head-to-head with Komatsu in Japan). Pitting strength against strength (as in the earlier cases of Asahi-Dow or Yokogawa-HP) or weakness against weakness (Kanebo-Stevens or Kanebo-Gilco) dooms the alliance to ultimate failure. HP now owns 80 percent of the Yokogawa tie-up, and the other joint ventures have all since been disbanded.


## GETTING PROFESSIONAL ASSISTANCE

A company's strategic objectives in this highly competitive region are not attained easily. Professional accounting, legal, and investment banking assistance is needed at all phases to work out the complicated tax and accounting measures, to draw up the necessary documentation, and possibly to devise creative ways of financing them. Companies hoping to enter the Japanese market also need the services of a strategic advisor, someone with the requisite experience in the daunting Japanese and East Asian markets, to help pull the diverse players together, to help orchestrate and implement a successful strategy, and to avoid the many pitfalls of failure.

A competent strategic advisor should be capable of assisting the CEO in the following critical ways:

- Screening appropriate candidates for a strategic alliance to make sure the strategic business fit is proper and the corporate/product tie-up is appropriate
- Helping to formulate an effective strategy in the light of specific national and regional economic trends and developments
- Making the complex cultural factors involved work to the purchaser's advantage, rather than disadvantage, as is often the case
- Providing local introductions of both a personal and professional nature that will serve to pave the way toward a more harmonious realization of the overall strategy
- Working with tax, legal, and financial advisors to appropriately coordinate the company's comprehensive strategy

## IN SUMMARY

The opportunity for strategic alliances in East Asia has never been better. It is incumbent upon us as international competitors to take a new look at these strategic alliances to see how we can make them work better for us both in Japan and in the fast-growing economies of East Asia. We should consider capital participations, joint ventures, licensing agreements, and technical tie-ups that are strategically driven, rather than motivated simply by financial considerations. Such alliances will enable us to put more effective pressure on our Asian competitors and help us build stronger market share positions both throughout the region and at home, thus insuring our own corporate and industrial survival.

# INDEX